Nature's Super Foods

TOP 40 *medicinal foods, herbs and supplements*

NANCY BECKHAM

Lothian
B O O K S

Author's note

In this book I have mentioned names of a few people and products. None of these pay me, or give me special discounts. The information is supplied for the benefit and information of readers.

Thomas C. Lothian Pty Ltd
11 Munro Street, Port Melbourne, Victoria 3207

Copyright © Nancy Beckham 1998
First published 1998

National Library of Australia
Cataloguing-in-Publication data:

Beckham, Nancy.
    Nature's super foods: top 40 medicinal foods, herbs and supplements.

    Includes index.
    ISBN 0 85091 914 2.

    1. Herbs – Therapeutic use. 2. Naturopathy.
    3. Medicinal plants. I. Title. II. Title: Top forty medicinal foods, herbs and supplements.

615.535

Design by Rob Cowpe
Front cover photograph by Lynette Zeeng
Illustrations by Janet Wolf
Printed in Australia by McPherson's Printing Group

Foreword

Cancer and heart disease, the major killers in our society, are preventable diseases. More than 70 per cent of diseases are diet related, and such diseases are costing Australia over $5 billion annually. Yet, for the most part, our medical schools are placing most of the emphasis on the treatment of disease and very little on prevention.

Medical treatment of disease mostly involves high technology. This may include the magic bullet of the antibiotic, or high-tech radiotherapy, chemotherapy or surgery. We have the best technology to treat diseases, yet we are sicker as a society. The waiting lists of the public hospitals are getting longer and longer, and the increased pressure on the staff at the hospitals is affecting the quality of care. Yet the amount of money allocated to sickness care is at an all-time high. The pharmaceutical industry alone is worth $280 billion worldwide, and this figure is estimated to rise by almost another $100 billion in the next two years because of the ageing population and the demand for new drugs. Despite all this money being spent on sickness care (as distinct from health care), we are no closer to defeating cancer or heart disease.

As a doctor practising nutritional and herbal medicine for over twenty years, I have seen changes in the attitude of the Australian public over the years. Initially only a small proportion of the public was interested in 'alternative' medicine. Now over 50 per cent of the population regularly take some form of alternative medicine. The general profile of those attending an alternative practitioner is of people who are well educated (usually with a tertiary qualification), and from a higher socioeconomic level. They demand more, and are prepared to take more responsibility for their health. They want to know why a particular medicine is being prescribed, and if a change in lifestyle will help. This, for me, is an exciting and challenging way to practise medicine. Instead of prescribing a symptom-relieving drug, I can advise on a disease-modifying way of life that includes diet, exercise, relaxation, and the way one interacts with oneself and with those around. Patients feel empowered when they know that they can modify their disease just by changing their diet. So simple, so cheap, yet so powerful.

The incidence of cancer, heart disease and other health problems can be reduced, and Nancy Beckham shows us how.

Most people know that if we eat a wide variety of wholesome foods we can be healthy. Nancy, however, tells us what the powerful foods are, and how they can help us to prevent or even cure disease. She does not expect you to take her word for it, for she builds an impressive argument for her claims with references from respected scientific journals. She tells us how simple and commonly available herbs can help us improve our health. Even some culinary herbs such as ginger, garlic and turmeric have powerful health-promoting and disease-fighting effects.

The health-promoting foods and herbs are described with the evidence, and then she tells us how to use these in practical recipes. If you really like the foods or herbs, and wish to grow them in your garden, she also tells you how.

Nancy is well qualified to do this, as she is also a horticulturist.

There is abundant evidence to prove the value of nutrients in the prevention and treatment of disease, and a growing body of scientific evidence attesting to the efficacy of herbs in certain disease states. Anyone, be they lay person, doctor or academic, who says that there is no evidence for nutritional or herbal medicine needs to read this book.

Dr Iggy Soosay, MBBS, FACNEM
Camberwell Medical Centre
President, Australian College of Herbal Medicine
Chairman, Australasian College of Nutritional and
Environmental Medicine

Contents

Introduction

This book gives you practical advice about foods, herbs and supplements to improve your wellbeing and energy, prevent diseases, and help treat illnesses.

Variety is the key to healthy eating

Are you one of those people who buy exactly the same foods each week, and cook the same meals year after year? Do you say you don't have time to do anything differently? If so, you are missing out on many taste experiences and health enhancing foods. If you add one new healthy food, recipe or herb to your diet every week you will see a major improvement in your health over a year. A gradual approach such as this is easy on both your nervous system and your digestion.

In this book I focus on simple ways of adding the recommended foods and herbs into your meals, and provide relatively simple everyday recipes that I use myself. You may prefer to create your own versions of these, or to try some from other cookbooks.

Making sense of conflicting nutritional information

For each food and herb I cover in this book I have studied hundreds of research papers, and my recommendations are based on the bulk of the available evidence. I have included some of this scientific information and given references to them in the endnotes, for you to see why and how they will improve your wellbeing.

Even the experts do not agree. For instance, some people will tell you that tomatoes are harmful, and others will say that they are beneficial. How are you supposed to work out the truth? If you do a thorough computer search, as I have done, you will find hundreds of papers on tomatoes and their components. Only a very small percentage of the population is allergic to tomatoes, and such people should not eat them. Tomatoes are *not* particularly acidic compared with, say, citrus fruit. Acid foods are sour to the taste, and you can test this for yourself: all you have to do is swallow a dessertspoon of un-diluted lemon juice, followed by a dessertspoon of unsweetened tomato juice. Tomatoes contain many valuable nutrients, antioxidants and plant chemicals. However, they do contain tiny amounts of extremely toxic substances (solanine alkaloids); these are higher in green tomatoes, so my advice is to eat only ripe tomatoes.

There is no reason why you should give up healthy, edible foods because a few people are allergic to them or someone has a pet theory against them.

There is also no reason for you to give up a particular food or herb that has been consumed for centuries without harming anyone on the ground that it contains a toxic component.

Edible plants contain around 500 different components, including tiny quantities of toxins, but the wide range of antioxidants and beneficial compounds in edible plants clearly offset the few harmful components. If this were not true, I would not be writing this book and you would not be reading it, because only flesh-eating beings would have survived!

Is food your best medicine?

Some foods have medicinal properties that will help to restore the body and prevent disease:

> It has been repeatedly demonstrated that diets consisting of foods containing carbohydrates, proteins and fats but lacking fruits and vegetables, give a level of tissue damage higher than for diets including fruits and vegetables which are rich in natural antioxidants.[1]

Researchers now state that antioxidants and other natural compounds in plants act together within every cell in your body and are like the many musicians making up a symphony orchestra. They are *all* required to produce healthy cell activity. This makes sense, because it only takes a tiny fault in cell functioning to set off a harmful chain reaction.

Why do we need remedies?

Even in the most health-conscious communities and apparently healthy environments, people get sick or age prematurely.

There are many causes of health problems, and we often become unwell through no fault of our own. Everyone knows a few people who, despite smoking, drinking excessive alcohol and eating truly unhealthy foods for decades, seem to be relatively healthy. They are exceptional people, which is why they get media attention. All their friends and relatives who followed a similar lifestyle probably died long ago, and so cannot talk about their 'secret of longevity'.

People who have followed a healthy lifestyle sometimes end up with major illnesses. They are also exceptional cases. Life is not always

fair, but, for the overwhelming majority of us, if we wish to avoid premature ageing and disease we must actively participate in improving our own health.

Did you know that an Australian government body has estimated that diet-related diseases cost about $5190 million each year, and that the potential years of life lost might be more than 200 000 years annually. The Australian Institute of Health and Welfare estimates that 75 per cent of many common ailments such as hypertension, gallbladder and diverticular diseases may be attributable to poor eating habits.[2]

Do we need nutritional supplements and herbal remedies?

Sensible use of supplements and remedies gives added health protection. Based on my twenty years of prescribing these, I can assure you they are very helpful, especially if you start treating a problem in its early stages.

When I first started practising herbal medicine twenty years ago, medical opinion seemed to be that these remedies were unnecessary, and didn't work. A decade later, scientists tended to say that they were harmful. Now it is surprising how many doctors are beginning to recommend them. All medical schools in Germany now teach herbal medicine as a compulsory subject, and it is part of the medical prescribing system in a number of other European countries.

Common culinary herbs have attributes beyond flavouring foods and improving digestion. Their regular use provides a measure of disease prevention, and can be useful for treating some conditions.

The importance of the whole person

Pharmaceuticals (prescribed drugs) tend to replace or take over some of the body's functions, whereas natural therapies usually work by *helping* some function in the body.

Japanese researchers have asked the question 'Why are natural plant medicinal products effective in some patients and not in others with the same disease?'[3] They concluded that those people who easily break down herbal products in their digestive system have the best clinical results. Herbs must be in an absorbable form, foods have to be properly chewed, and the body needs enough stomach acid and digestive enzymes to efficiently digest both nutrients and natural remedies. Circulation is another important factor for the nutrients and beneficial compounds in foods and herbs must be carried to the body's tissues and cells.

The cause of any health problems or weaknesses must be considered for a good result with natural remedies.

Self-help versus professional help

Although I recommend that you do all you can to improve your own health, do seek professional help if you are unwell. For example, in my clinic I sometimes see people who are taking twenty or more supplements each day. When I ask about the therapeutic purpose of taking the pills, the patients' reasons are often vague or baseless. These people might be just as healthy using a combined multivitamin and mineral supplement — or spending their money on something else.

Others take, for example, ginkgo for mental fatigue. While this may do no harm, it will not help if the cause of the fatigue is anaemia or diabetes. Taking an iron supplement will not help if the cause of the fatigue is lack of sleep, stress or a serious disease. Excess iron not only reduces the absorption of other essential minerals but it tends to oxidise, and may be a factor in cardiovascular and other diseases.

Finding the cause of a health problem is not always easy. However, taking inappropriate natural remedies is a waste of money. A medical practitioner is generally the best health professional to make a diagnosis, or at least to establish whether you have a known 'medical disease'. Technologically advanced medical screenings are designed to detect diseases at

an early stage, rather than preventing health problems.

A qualified natural therapist is the best person to consult about herbs and other natural remedies, as well as about preventive therapies. Although professional natural therapy training is now a three- or four-year, full-time training course, unfortunately no official uniform standards or registration yet exist. In Australia only a few doctors have been fully trained in herbal medicine and natural therapies.

You may not want to know it, but your treatment could involve stopping something that you are doing, rather than taking something for your problem.

Basic warnings

- Always read labels so that you know how to store and prepare foods. One of my patients bought some soya grits. Thinking they looked like bread crumbs, she used them to coat veal schnitzels. The result was a culinary disaster, and her husband told her not to buy any more 'health foods'. Soya grits need cooking (they take about as long as rice to cook); and you can add them to casseroles and rice dishes without causing any family dramas.
- Always follow the instructions for the dosages of herbs, nutrients and other supplements provided by a health practitioner or the information given by the manufacturer on the label. Some remedies (such as hot chilli and Asian ginseng) are not suitable for children. If the label does not indicate a child's dosage, check with the person supplying the product.
- Although culinary herbs used as flavourings and medicinal herbs such as chamomile and echinacea are generally considered to be safe taken during pregnancy and breastfeeding, I recommend that you seek the advice of your health practitioner during these times before taking any remedies.
- Make sure you can definitely identify all the foods and herbs that you pick from your

garden, or in the wild, because some poisonous plants resemble edible ones.

- Your doctor or health practitioner is there to help you. You should always give details of other remedies or pharmaceuticals you are taking, in case any of them unfavourably interact with each other, and so that the results can be correctly assessed.
- For each plant or remedy that I describe, I also present some cautions. Even a common herb such as ginger is an allergen for some people; if you get an adverse reaction, then avoid that plant. However, people also get reactions to contaminated food, environmental toxins, viruses, and so on, so, unless you had an unusually severe side effect, try the suspected plant again at a later date rather than condemning it forever.
- Many of our popular snacks are dense — they are high in kilojoules, but not very filling. In other words, what seems like a snack is often relatively unsatisfying, low in health benefits, and fattening.

Limitations

Throughout this book I give lists of nutrients and components in various foods and herbs. Plants vary according to growing conditions, age and other factors, so the quantities of their components are somewhat variable. Any such list is an approximate guide.

Most natural remedies must be taken for some months before an effect is noticed, although this does not apply to remedies for acute infections such as influenza.

Edible foods are generally not restricted to specific durations, although for a particular ailment it is sometimes recommended that they be consumed daily at a specified level for a prescribed period.

Sometimes there is not a clear distinction between a food and a supplement. For example, some medical mushrooms are available in dried form only. As a general rule, I recommend that whenever there is a choice it is healthier to use the food in its whole, natural state.

Dosages for children

Foods

This varies markedly according to ages and what they will eat! For instance, under citrus I have suggested that an adult dosage could be one or more citrus fruits daily, and for children one-quarter to a half daily. However, you must use your own judgement because if a child refuses most fruits and vegetables but is fond of citrus then it is sensible to allow them more, as long as this does not cause diarrhoea or any other adverse reactions.

Herbal remedies and supplements

Some remedies are not suitable for infants and young children, such as garlic oil, hot chilli and Asian ginseng and, although you will appreciate this from your own experience, these have been noted throughout the book. In general, if a product label does not indicate a child's dosage, check with the person supplying the product.

It is not practical or necessary to work out specific percentages based on your child's weight, and the following is a guide:

Age of child	Fraction of adult dose
Babies (0–1)	$\frac{1}{8}$
2–5	$\frac{1}{4}$
6–9	$\frac{1}{3}$
10–13	$\frac{1}{2}$
14–16	$\frac{3}{4}$

With sensitive or small-build children, go down to the previous category. If you are using liquid remedies, I suggest you use drops. However, there are different sorts of droppers, so you need to use a medical measure and count how many of *your* drops equal 1 ml. For example, with the dropper I use there are 20 drops to the ml, therefore if an adult dose is, say, 5 ml, this equals 100 drops, making a dosage of 25 drops for a three-year-old. Over-the-counter remedies should specify the dosages for children.

Generally, herbal extracts and other supplements are best taken just before or with meals, perhaps with a little juice or honey.

Unless indicated otherwise, all the foods and remedies in this book could be used for children in quantities in line with the table.

Throughout the book I have given recommended dosages of remedies or quantities of foods. The remedies have specified dosages, and usually are not taken forever. The quantities of food are a guide only, and are not restricted to a length of time. For example, under **Rice** in chapter 2, I have suggested an intake of about 3–4 cups a week. If you are allergic to most grains and do not eat many other starchy foods, then it is obviously sensible to eat more rice. The same principle applies to children who are fussy eaters, as they may need to eat larger quantities of a few foods in order to sustain their energy levels. For all ages, when the diet is not varied I recommend a combined multivitamin and mineral supplement.

As far as possible, you and your health practitioner should try to find the cause of any health problems so that the most appropriate remedies can be used for a curative effect, rather than merely treating the symptoms.

Ointments and creams

An ointment is an external application with a base of lard, lanolin, beeswax, petroleum jelly or similar 'oily' substance in which a remedy is incorporated.

Traditional herbal ointments were generally thick, and adhered to the skin because of their 'sticky' bases. Today most herbalists prefer to use bases such as sorbolene, aqueous cream, vitamin E cream or seaweed gel because these are lighter, less suppressive on the skin's functioning, pleasanter to use, and probably healthier.

Although these definitions are not official, I call the heavy sticky-based products ointments, and the lighter ones creams.

Plant names

Most plants have an assortment of common names. Milk thistle, for example, is also called variegated thistle, St Mary's thistle, Marion thistle, lady's milk, and various other names in different countries. To be sure that everyone is referring to the same plant, professional people use the botanical (Latin) names.

Plants are classified in families. Milk thistle is in the Asteraceae (daisy) family, which contains many thousands of plants. The botanical name of milk thistle is *Silybum marianum*; *Silybum* is the genus part of the name and *marianum* the species. Think of the family as being the ancestral part of the name, the genus as the parents, and the species as the children.

An added complication is that plant names are undergoing changes because modern botanical scientists now consider that many plants were not appropriately classified and named in the past. The Asteraceae family used to be called Compositae, and the botanical name of milk thistle was *Carduus marianus*. These old names will eventually be phased out.

In this book I use the modern botanical name and what I judge to be the most common name in English-speaking countries, sometimes giving an alternative if I think this is helpful.

If you are harvesting plants from your garden or in the wild, be absolutely certain that you have properly identified the plant because common names are unreliable, and many plants look the same. When in doubt, find out from a botanist or horticulturist, or leave out!

Are you what you eat?

Hardly, but the evidence is that if you eat healthy food you are more likely to be healthy. There's more to life than endlessly worrying about food or eating meals without enjoying them. A rational lifestyle, non-destructive and non-fanatical behaviour, exercise, relaxation, laughter and developing inner peace, all contribute to a healthy and fulfilling life.

Nine super vegetable and fruit groups

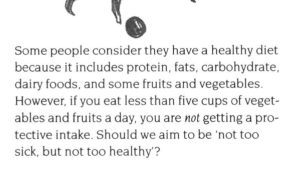

Background

If you look through food encyclopaedias you will find that well over 3000 edible plants exist, and that none of them are identical in the quantity and quality of their nutrients and other components. I chose the nine vegetable and fruit groups for their special health enhancing properties when eaten regularly. As examples they justify my recommendation that you should eat a wide range of plant foods in as natural a state as possible if you wish to reduce the risks of premature ageing and the degenerative diseases of 'civilisation'.

'Is moderation in everything' good advice?

Moderation means 'not too little, not too much' and many use the word to justify eating and drinking whatever they fancy. Can you eat too little junk food? Does a moderate amount of synthetic food additives make you feel better?

In our society truly active, dynamic elderly people are so rare that they are featured on TV!

Some people consider they have a healthy diet because it includes protein, fats, carbohydrate, dairy foods, and some fruits and vegetables. However, if you eat less than five cups of vegetables and fruits a day, you are *not* getting a protective intake. Should we aim to be 'not too sick, but not too healthy'?

Why are vegetables and fruits so important?

Degenerative diseases such as cancer and heart disease could be reduced by at least 50 per cent with appropriate, but non-fanatical, dietary and lifestyle changes. Evidence abounds that vegetables and fruits, in particular, contain many valuable disease-preventing components, as well as essential nutrients.

A report in a prestigious British medical journal stated that the rate of heart attacks and deaths was often higher in winter. Medical researchers now believe that increased vegetable and fruit consumption during winter would have a protective effect.[1]

Another medical review found that daily consumption of fresh fruit was associated with a 32 per cent reduction in death from stroke, 24 per cent reduction in death from heart disease, and a 21 per cent reduction in death from all causes.[2]

A survey in Crete comparing dietary changes since the 1960s revealed that a diet mainly of wholegrain bread, olives, olive oil, nuts, fruits and vegetables, together with small amounts of milk, cheese and meat, gave only a 0.7 per cent incidence of coronary heart disease.[3] In the following thirty-year period, when the consumption of meat and cheese increased, and that of olive oil, bread, fruits and potatoes decreased, and the level of physical activity decreased, the incidence rose to 9.5 per cent.

During a study of the risk of breast cancer vegetables, fruits and related nutrients were considered, and vegetables in particular appeared to decrease the risk. The researchers concluded that 'of the nutrients and food components examined, no single dietary factor explains the effect'.[4]

Sound evidence now indicates that a high consumption of foods rich in arachidonic acid, such as meat and butter, is associated with a high incidence of cancer, and the risk is even worse if there is an accompanying low consumption of leafy vegetables and whole grains. A group of American scientific researchers concluded that the total medical costs of meat consumption in the USA were somewhere between $US28–61 billion each year because of high blood pressure, heart disease, cancer, diabetes, gallbladder disease, obesity and food-borne illness.[5] A high consumption of meat, especially pork and processed meat, is also linked to breast cancer risk, whereas fish is a protective factor.[6]

Nitrogen fertilisers and pesticides are used increasingly in agriculture, and diseases like non-Hodgkin's lymphoma have increased dramatically, especially in rural areas. It is suggested that a high consumption of fruits and vegetables provides vitamin C and other compounds that will reduce the cancer-causing effects of nitrates[7] that are also used as taste enhancers and preservatives in some foods, notably processed meats.

Phytochemicals: the medicinal compounds in plants

In Asia a clear distinction has never existed between foods and medicine. Increasingly, nutritional scientists now acknowledge that many edible plants might indeed aid the body's natural healing process and help prevent disease. Stores in Japan already sell government-approved functional or pharma foods with specific health enhancing capacities.

Cabbage, for example, has long been used in alternative therapies, and scientists have confirmed it has antibacterial, anti-inflammatory, antirheumatic, immune regulating and anticancer properties. A component in cabbage, broccoli and related plants enhances an oestrogen biochemical pathway that might have an anticancer effect on breast tissue. Conversely, excess cabbage might depress the thyroid of sensitive people, so if they eat enormous quantities of cabbage this could diminish all its advantages.

Each plant is a unique blend of nutrients and literally hundreds of other compounds. If you eat a variety of foods, you should be able to avoid nutrient deficiencies or excesses. You will get a beneficial mix of various plant compounds, and so avoid a build-up of any particular naturally occurring toxin.

A plant may contain up to 500 known components, including one or two toxins that are usually part of the plant's own defence system. If you eat normal dietary quantities of a wide variety of edible foods, it is highly unlikely that you will experience a toxicity problem because of the benefits of the other hundreds of components in the food. Furthermore, your body has an enzyme system that can detoxify the tiny quantities of naturally occurring toxins that occur in edible foods. However, there are some very hazardous natural poisons in foods, such as the alkaloids in green potatoes, and ergot (a fungus that can occur in grains).

Plants supply you with the following:

- carbohydrates, necessary for the energy of every cell in your body
- amino acids, the raw material for protein and growth
- essential fatty acids that form cell walls and membranes in your body
- vitamins and minerals that function as co-enzymes, and regulate many of your biological processes
- antioxidants that reduce the side effects of harmful natural byproducts and environmental chemicals
- fibre for healthy intestinal functioning — vegetable fibre is linked to a 43 per cent reduced risk of colon cancer[8]
- numerous non-essential plant components, many of which have therapeutic effects, as you will see throughout this book
- fresh plants also contain enzymes that aid digestion, absorption and the functioning of the immune system — this is the case with *fresh* plants only.

Are designer foods the worst idea since sliced white bread?

The National Cancer Institute's Designer Food Programme in the USA reportedly had an initial budget of $US20 million. Its first recommendation was that everyone should be encouraged to eat at least five cups of fresh fruits and vegetables daily, as this would be a major step towards preventing cancer and other degenerative diseases. However, it was generally conceded that this was an unrealistic goal in the USA as the majority of American people would not eat anything like the recommended quantity.

Some scientists are now attempting to create 'designer foods' — that is, valuable plant chemicals would be collected from various foods and made into one technological food, probably about the size of a golf ball. People could continue to eat as they liked, and then take one of these — presumably expensive — designer foods with each meal.

In conclusion

I do not recommend that you eat enormous quantities of the foods described in this chapter, but rather that you should include them in your diet on a regular basis in normal-sized dietary servings (unless you are allergic or sensitive to any of them). In Australia we have an abundant and inexpensive supply of quality vegetables and fruits, so that it is not unreasonable to suggest you eat, say, two or three pieces of fruit throughout the day, a bowl of vegetable soup or a serving of salad with lunch, and cooked vegetables with dinner.

Fresh fruits and vegetables should form a major part of your diet because they have health enhancing and disease preventing benefits.

Antioxidant-rich foods

Background

Nineteenth-century chemists argued about whether parts of molecules acted independently in the human body. By the beginning of this century the term 'free radicals' and their existence were established. It has since been demonstrated that some of the body's own oxidation reactions and free radicals were harmful, and that these injurious effects could be offset by antioxidants.

The general types of damage offset by antioxidants are harmful fat breakdown in the body, damage to DNA leading to inappropriate cell growth, and damage to the body's protein and connective tissue.

What are antioxidants?

Antioxidants are nutrients and other beneficial compounds that reduce harmful reactions occurring as a consequence of the body's natural functioning, and from toxins such as cigarette smoking and pesticides. Although a well-nourished body makes some antioxidants, the majority come from food.

What are good food sources of antioxidants?

All vegetables and fruits, as well as whole grains, seeds and legumes, are good sources of antioxidants.

Antioxidants interact with each other and it has been demonstrated that beneficial interactions occur between different antioxidants when they are consumed in relatively low levels over long periods of time.[9] In other words, you get the best antioxidant effect from a varied wholefood diet, the bulk of which is comprised of plant foods. Although it may not be harmful to have an occasional day without consuming antioxidants, you will maintain your health status if you keep up an uninterrupted supply of them from childhood to old age.

Many nutrients indirectly function as antioxidants by acting as 'helpers'. For example, pantothenic acid (vitamin B5) increases the level of glutathione, one of the body's important natural antioxidants.[10]

Antioxidant culinary herbs

See the list on p. 129.

Medicinal herbs

All medicinal herbs contain antioxidants, although the quantities you would obtain from them are not as significant as that from foods.

However, some of these herbs, such as bilberry, ginkgo, hawthorn and milk thistle, contain antioxidant components, notably special types of flavonoids, that are known to have therapeutic benefits in medicinal doses.

Does a typical Australian diet contain a healthy amount of antioxidants?

If you take vitamin C as an indicator of antioxidant intake in Australia, almost 25 per cent of the population consume less than the recommended intake of 30–40 mg per day of this vitamin. This means that, although deficiency diseases are not widespread, millions of Australians are not getting a protective level of antioxidants.

Specific health benefits

The following is a small selection of the published scientific research on antioxidants.

Cancer

Most cancers are caused by environmental factors — what we eat, drink, breathe and absorb through our skin. Some are unavoidable, such as sunlight, which is harmful in excess but necessary for plant and human existence. Other factors are avoidable, such as cigarette smoking. What you eat may determine whether you develop cancer. A review of 172 studies confirmed that inadequate consumption of fruits and vegetables did relate to increased cancer incidence.[11]

Antioxidants reduce cancer by decreasing both DNA damage and cell division. Decreasing cell division means that there is a lower risk of developing cancer. Factors that cause cell division to increase include chronic inflammation or infections, and the metabolic activity of some hormones and chemicals.

Heart disease

A summary in 1996 (with 67 scientific references) concluded that 'antioxidants may be important beneficial factors or even preventers of heart disease'.[12]

Antioxidants may be able to reduce the development of atherosclerosis (clogged arteries) by preventing damage to the artery walls. Some researchers now recommend that antioxidant therapy should become part of the treatment programme for all those with heart or circulatory diseases, especially following heart attacks, surgery or angioplasty.[13]

Fertility and healthy children

Men with a low intake of vitamins C and E have increased levels of oxidative damage in the DNA of their sperm; this damage is worsened in smokers, who also have a lower sperm count.[14]

An antioxidant-poor diet (low in vegetables and fruits), combined with smoking, may increase the risk of birth defects and childhood cancer in their children. Antioxidant supplementation may lessen the adverse effects of smoking on the lungs, to a certain extent, but it is no substitute for both partners agreeing to stop smoking before and during a pregnancy.

The immune system

Blood cells involved in the immune system (the lymphocytes) are less prone to oxidative DNA damage when vitamins C and E, plus beta-carotene, are taken as supplements.[15]

The respiratory tract

The respiratory tract is your first line of defence against the environmental toxins that you breathe in every day from the outside air and inside your home. Vitamins A, C and E are the most important of the respiratory antioxidants.

Arthritis

People with inflammatory joint diseases, such as rheumatoid arthritis and lupus, tend to have low levels of selenium, beta-carotene, and vitamins E and A.[16]

As the inflammatory joint process is likely to result in oxidative damage, this is another reason for recommending an antioxidant-rich diet, as a preventive and as part of the treatment of conditions such as rheumatoid arthritis and lupus. High doses of vitamin E in animal studies reduced some inflammatory and sensitivity reactions (for humans I do not recommend that anyone self-treat with more than 1000 IU vitamin E a day).

Ageing and degenerative diseases

Free radical damage is linked to ageing and many degenerative diseases, but the damage can be offset by antioxidants. Every living thing ages and nothing can prevent this, but there is evidence to support the notion that antioxidants offset free radical damage and help reduce premature ageing and degenerative diseases.

The incidence of cataracts and other age-related eye diseases is linked to low levels of antioxidants.

Clinical trials are in progress in the United Kingdom, Italy and the USA to test the effects of antioxidants on over 100 000 people. You can be sure that the researchers would not be spending the time and money if there were no scientific support for antioxidants.

Strenuous exercise

Vigorous and sustained exercise causes high cellular activity, which also means high oxidation, and higher than normal free radical activity. Some detrimental immune responses also occur; for instance, long-distance runners have a high rate of upper respiratory infections, particularly following competition. High levels of physical activity result in a number of biochemical reactions, and therefore a higher need for antioxidants. Of course, if you don't exercise at all, you get different problems, such as obesity, diabetes, arthritis and heart problems.

The skin

The skin is vulnerable to damage from free radicals, mainly as a result of excess sun exposure. Antioxidants can protect the skin to a certain extent. Vitamins C and E applied to the skin before sun exposure can reduce sun damage, swelling and wrinkling. It may be beneficial to apply products containing these before using a sun block. As an internal supplement beta-carotene also gives some skin protection.[17]

General health benefits

The evidence clearly shows that a good supply of natural antioxidants will improve your well-being.

Cautions and adverse effects

- Large doses of vitamin A supplementation can be harmful, so be guided by the doses given on the product labels.
- When you consider that each plant contains hundreds of known components, it is obvious that no antioxidant pill in the world could be as beneficial as a healthy diet.

Known therapeutic components

Edible plants contain a wide range of nutrients and phytochemicals that function as antioxidants in the body.

Antioxidant supplements

The evidence to date, and simple observation of all the ill and tired people around us, suggest that antioxidants from food may not be enough for those at risk. I recommend at least modest antioxidant supplementation for the following:
- those with a high intake of fats, or who have a poor diet and poor lifestyle habits

- smokers, the elderly, and those with a serious disease or poor digestion
- people exposed to excess sunlight, radiation or chemicals (perhaps we all have too much chemical exposure)
- those suffering chronic infections or inflammatory conditions
- people with low cholesterol, especially if they are taking pharmaceuticals
- athletes and those who participate in sustained and vigorous exercise (a lot of activity results in high levels of oxidant reactions).

Suggested intake

At least five cups vegetables and fruits daily, proportionately less for children.

No one supplement contains all the valuable antioxidant components present in a range of foods. My advice is to choose a broad-spectrum supplement that contains at least vitamins C and E, as well as flavonoids and carotenoids.

Summary

Remember that the antioxidants your body produces are also aided by various nutrients — in their natural state all plant foods (particularly vegetables and fruits) contain antioxidants. Eat a variety of these foods every day to offset harmful oxidation.

The bilberry, and other berries

Bilberry (*Vaccinium myrtillus*) is the most beneficial berry according to the research so far. However, all edible coloured berries, such as the blackberry (*Rubus fruticosus*), mulberry (*Morus nigra*), black currant (*Ribes nigrum*) and blueberry

(*Vaccinium corymbosum* and *V. angustifolium*) are highly recommended, mainly because of the health benefits of their flavonoids (anthocyanosides). Some red berries, such as the cranberry (*Vaccinium cacrocarpon*), have specific health advantages, such as preventing urinary tract infections.

Background

Bilberry plants are native to northern USA and Europe, and their nutritional properties have been appreciated since the twelfth century. The fruits were said to promote menstruation, and were used to treat coughs. Later, the berries were eaten as a treatment for scurvy (vitamin C deficiency), rheumatic problems, gout, and some infections. The leaves were used for lowering blood sugar levels, for diarrhoea, bleeding, and various inflammatory and urinary disorders.

Specific health benefits

In France bilberry is one of the herbs medical specialists now prescribe when treating problems such as varicose veins. It actually inhibits enzymes, such as elastase, which break down collagen and other types of connective tissue. (Connective tissue includes the linings of blood vessels, the eyes and the digestive tract, as well as joint tissue, skin and bone.)

During World War II pilots reportedly ate bilberry jam to improve their night vision. Bilberry has long been used in folk medicine for eye health, and scientists have now confirmed in animal studies that bilberry does reduce capillary permeability in eye tissue — the tiny blood vessels in the eye are not as 'leaky', so more blood is circulated in the area; consequently more oxygen and nutrients are carried with it, resulting in better nourishment for the eyes. At least four scientific studies have confirmed that bilberry can improve the night vision of air-traffic controllers, pilots, car and truck drivers.

Animal studies show that bilberry stimulates the gastric defence mechanism, and therefore it has some antiulcer activity. No doubt it has some general protective capacity for the digestive tract.

Human studies confirm that bilberry can be helpful for the following:

- improved circulation in cases of diabetes, arteriosclerosis and hypertension
- treatment of visual disorders caused by impaired light-sensitivity or poor circulation to the retina; bilberry may reduce diabetic retinopathy and help prevent cataracts, simple glaucoma, myopia (nearsightedness), and retina and pupil insufficiencies
- poor circulation and discoloured skin of postoperative patients
- fluid retention, heaviness, burning, itching or tingling in the legs
- nose bleeds, bruises, haemorrhoids, and periodontal disease
- Raynaud's syndrome (a circulatory disorder related to impeded arterial blood flow)
- rheumatoid arthritis
- damage caused by cortisone therapy to tiny blood vessels in asthmatic and chronic bronchitis patients
- period pain and associated menstrual problems, such as breast swelling, headache, nausea, and heaviness in the legs
- blood thinning without affecting blood coagulation
- prolonged exercise, which can cause stress on the cardiovascular system — bilberry flavonoids activate enzymes that help to offset this stress
- a useful adjunct in treating some cases of high cholesterol and triglycerides.

Laboratory studies also confirm that bilberry (and similar berries) have anticarcinogenic potential.[18]

General health benefits

Bilberry flavonoids have antioxidant properties. Natural therapists have always maintained that flavonoid-rich foods are useful in treating many circulatory disorders because these foods help to strengthen the walls of blood vessels.

A study in mice showed that bilberry protected capillary circulation (tiny blood vessels) against the effects of injury.[19] This explains why it is recommended that patients take bilberry remedies before and after surgery to help in the healing process and to prevent fluid retention.

Bilberry should be useful as an adjunct in the treatment of diabetes because it is helpful for two of the complications of that disease, that is, circulation and eye problems. If your blood vessel walls are strong, this helps to protect your body and brain from being swamped with pollutants, and to cope with excess fluid and natural degradation processes.

Bilberry also has some anti-inflammatory activity.

Both the leaves and the fruit have been used externally to heal wounds, but it discolours the skin, which makes it difficult to monitor the effect, and people don't like the stain.

Cautions and adverse effects

- My clinical experience is that some people are allergic to berries; other therapists find that high doses cause diarrhoea. If you are allergic to a food, discontinue its use. It is equally unwise to eat foods that cause loose bowel motions, because this means that you are losing valuable minerals and other nutrients, and also irritating your intestines. Some people may need to use a lower dose, while those who are constipated might benefit from a somewhat higher dose.
- Very high doses in animal experiments did not produce adverse effects, except for darkening of urine and bowel motions.
- In all the human clinical scientific trials no serious side effects were detected, and only a few gastric or skin reactions occurred.

Known therapeutic components

At least fifteen different anthocyanosides (a category of flavonoids) have been identified in bil-

berry,[20] and they show a particular affinity for kidney tissue and skin. In general, they help stabilise collagen (part of bones, eye tissue, joints, and blood vessel walls), as well as linings of the digestive and urinary tracts and organs — this explains why bilberry is helpful for a variety of illnesses.

- These flavonoids have four antioxidant effects. They can scavenge superoxide anions, reduce lipid peroxidation, inhibit free radical damage to red blood cells, and lessen cell reactions caused by various oxidants, thereby reducing some of the harmful processes that lead to degenerative diseases. Black grapes, black currants and all blue-black berries contain these anthocyanosides.
- Bilberry contains vitamin C and beta-carotene, as well as other flavonoids such as quercetin, so it is clearly a valuable source of antioxidant nutrients.
- Bilberries, and berries in general, contain lignans, which are converted in the human intestines to hormone-like substances that lower the risk of oestrogen-dependent cancers.[21] In berries, high lignans generally occur in conjunction with flavonoids. More information on lignans is given in chapter 2 under **Linseed.**

Bilberry supplements

As fresh or frozen bilberries are not readily available, I recommend you take tablets and liquid extracts.

Growing your own bilberries

If you live in a cool climate, you could grow your own bilberries. Many blue-black berries only bear fruit in a cool climate, although some varieties of blueberry will produce quite well in warmer areas.

Consult your local nursery for advice about which species are available and suitable for your area.

How to use

Berry crumble (Serves 6)

400 g fresh or frozen berries
1 tablespoon water
1–2 tablespoons concentrated pear or apple juice
2 tablespoons desiccated coconut (optional)
2 tablespoons honey or rice syrup
2 tablespoons tahini or cashew paste
3 heaped tablespoons barley flakes
3 heaped tablespoons millet flakes
3 heaped tablespoons cornmeal
1 cup low-fat yoghurt (or 1 cup coconut cream and
    2 tablespoons whey powder)

1 Preheat the oven to 200°C.
2 Place the berries, water and juice in a baking
   dish with a capacity of about 1½ litres.
3 Sprinkle the coconut on top.
4 Place the honey and tahini in a saucepan, and
   heat gently (do not boil).
5 Add the barley, millet and cornmeal, and stir to
   combine.
6 Spread the mixture over the top of the berries.
7 Bake for 30 minutes until golden brown on top.

Serve with low-fat yoghurt, or coconut cream
blended with whey powder.

Suggested intake and duration of use

Many of the scientific trials I refer to use guaranteed potency products of bilberry at about 300 mg daily; the trials lasted between one and two months.

Concentrated bilberry extracts are available in Australia, and the maximum dose recommended is 2 ml, three times daily. Tablets of varying strengths are also available; take the label dosages.

For therapeutic purposes the suggested daily quantity of fresh or frozen berries is between 60 and 100 g. This seemingly high dose is because the whole berries contain fewer anthocyanosides than do the concentrated remedies; how-ever, the berries also contain other beneficial nutrients. All berries are suitable for children, in proportionately lower doses (see pp. 4–5).

Bilberry can be used indefinitely.

Summary

Bilberry has a potential to strengthen blood vessels and stabilise collagen. Because of these effects, together with the antioxidant activity, herbalists prescribe it for a wide range of problems relating to the eyes, the joints, and the respiratory and digestion systems. Berries should be a regular part of your diet.

Other berries

Cranberry

Cranberry can relieve cystitis, and helps to prevent relapse because it reduces the build-up of harmful bacteria in the digestive tract and in the bladder.[22]

Cranberry may reduce the recurrence of those kidney stones that tend to form in alkaline urine, reduce urine odour, and produce a healthier urinary flow.[23] My experience is that cranberry juice is more effective if it does not contain sugar or at least is not excessively sweetened, and it is often better as a preventive than as a treatment during a bladder infection because the urine might already be too acidic. Some patients report that it reduces nocturia (getting up during the night to urinate).

Blueberry

Blueberry juice is also helpful for preventing and treating urinary tract infections.

Black grapes, beetroot, black cherries, black currants

These other purple-coloured foods are highly recommended because of their flavonoid content. Other potential cancer preventing compounds in berries are caffeic acid, p-coumaric acid, ferulic acid, p-hydroxybenzoic acid, gallic acid and ellagic acid.[24]

The cabbage family

This plant family used to be called Cruciferae, but its new botanical name is Brassicacae.

The common edible plants in this family are:

Broccoli	Horseradish	Radish
Brussels sprouts	Kale	Swedes
Cabbage	Kohlrabi	Turnip
Cauliflower	Mustard	Watercress
Collard		

There are many varieties of these vegetables. Medicinal plants include shepherd's purse (used mainly for urinary tract problems), and horseradish (commonly recommended for sinusitis and colds).

Background

Cabbage has been cultivated for about 4000 years. Some types originated in Asia and the Mediterranean area. The ancient Romans reportedly did without doctors for six hundred years because they used cabbage externally and internally for various illnesses and wounds. Captain James Cook sailed in all climates on a three-year voyage without losing a single seaman to scurvy (vitamin C deficiency), a common cause of death during lengthy sea voyages before the nineteenth century. He attributed his good fortune to cabbage and to the cleanliness of his ship.

In 1975 Dr J. Valnet wrote a lengthy and fascinating commentary on the history and curative value of cabbage in his book *Heal Yourself with Vegetables, Fruits and Grains* (Cornerstone Library, New York, 1975). During the nineteenth century French doctors used cabbage for treating numerous ailments, and Dr Valnet gives details of cabbage therapy for more than eighty different internal and external problems. These days no one would dream of treating a life-threatening injury with a cabbage dressing or poultice — had these simple remedies cured every case there would have been no incentive to develop antibiotics and other pharmaceuticals.

Another point worth considering is that in 'the old days' only the strong survived, and this could explain why natural therapies seemed to be very effective. However, there is no doubt that cabbage has some therapeutic value. If natural therapies are used for minor conditions, they may prevent the development of more serious infections, thereby avoiding the necessity for antibiotics.

In traditional healing, cabbage has been used externally for wounds, ulcers, acne, inflamed joints and mastitis (sore, swollen breasts). It has also been used internally for gastric ulcers, inflamed and irritated intestines, bronchitis, and aches and pains.

Specific health benefits

A high dietary intake of vegetables in the cabbage family is linked to a low cancer risk.[25]

A study on broccoli showed that it activated a specific liver detoxification enzyme. Broccoli also increased oestrogen 2-hydroxylation — oestrogen was eliminated more quickly, so that, indirectly, this may decrease the risk of oestrogen-dependent cancers.[26]

In another study daily consumption of broccoli caused a notable rise in salivary enzymes considered to be detoxifying and disease preventing.[27] Many fruits and vegetables contain components that stimulate detoxifying enzymes, so it is not necessary to eat broccoli every day; however, you should certainly eat it on a regular basis.

Cabbage, in particular, has been found to have antibacterial, anti-inflammatory, antirheumatic and immune enhancing properties.[28] Of course, this does not mean that a daily serving of cabbage will cure a major bacterial infection or a serious disease, but rather that it is of therapeutic benefit.

In a small group of people given a diet free of plants in the cabbage family, some of them ate 300 g cooked Brussels sprouts for three weeks, and their urine was tested for oxidative damage. Those who consumed the Brussels sprouts had significantly less cell damage,[29] confirming that Brussels sprouts are an effective antioxidant.

General health benefits

Cabbage and all of the cabbage family are low in kilojoules, and are a good source of antioxidants such as beta-carotene. These plants are also rich in potassium, calcium, vitamin C, niacin and other B-group vitamins.

Cautions and adverse effects

- Some people are allergic or sensitive to all plants in the cabbage family, especially when they are served raw. I find it impossible to digest raw cauliflower and broccoli (which some people put in salads) — I recommend that you lightly cook and cool these vegetables for this purpose.
- If you want to try cabbage juice as an internal remedy, be mindful that there is a very faint possibility that your thyroid activity could be lowered, in which case you should discontinue the therapy. Early signs of low thyroid activity are fatigue, weight gain, constipation, cold intolerance and mental confusion; a blood test is the best way of assessing this, because many people have these symptoms. Otherwise, you could take cabbage juice long term; however, if you do this for more than one month, take a four-day break in each month's treatment. It is unlikely that

your thyroid activity would be affected by three or four normal-sized servings a week of plants in the cabbage family.

Known therapeutic components

Over 220 different constituents have been identified in cabbage. They include a wide range of nutrients, antioxidants and phytochemicals:

- Phenethyl isothiocyanate is found in cabbage and other plants in the family. It protects mice against some types of lung tumour, such as tobacco-specific nitrosamine.[30] A number of animal studies demonstrate that this plant component has the capacity to inhibit the oxidative activation of chemical carcinogens (substances in the body that can trigger cancer). It also protects cells from DNA breakdown, which can lead to cell mutation, and possibly cancer.
- Fresh broccoli sprouts contain a very high concentration of glucoraphanin, which the body converts to sulforaphane. This component stimulates the production of an anticancer enzyme — animal studies show that broccoli sprouts may even reduce breast tumours.[31]

  It has been estimated that you would have to eat about 1 kg broccoli each week to reduce the risk of colon cancer by 50 per cent, but broccoli sprouts have such a concentrated level of anticancer activity that you need to eat only about 35 g each week. Sprouts have many nutritional and other advantages; see the chapter on them in my book, *Menopause: A Positive Approach Using Natural Therapies.*[32]
- Indole-3-carbinol is an important anticancer compound found in the cabbage family. It creates a favourable oestrogen pattern that is protective against breast cancer, and it also helps clear toxins from the body. Indole glucosinolates in general have anticarcinogenic properties, which increase when cabbage is finely chopped. Coleslaw, including a healthy dressing, is therefore highly recommended.

Growing the cabbage family

Plants in the cabbage family grow in various climatic conditions. Your local nursery or a gardening book will provide details of the plants best suited for different seasons and localities.

How to use

Raw cabbage is commonly used in salads. As it is difficult to digest, I recommend you chop it finely and sprinkle a little lemon juice or vinegar over it, and leave it stand about an hour before serving. I like to mix it with grated raw beetroot and celeriac, other salad vegetables, rocket and various herbs. See p. 140 for healthy salad-dressing recipes, and pp. 30–1 for homemade herbal vinegars.

Baked cabbage (Serves 2)

2 teaspoons olive oil
2 cups bite-sized cabbage segments
1 onion, very finely chopped
1 cup chopped tomato
1 tablespoon fresh chives or other herbs (or
    1 teaspoon dried mixed herbs)
2 teaspoons salt-reduced tamari
1 cup milk (or soya milk, or coconut cream)
2 eggs
2 tablespoons grated soya or dairy cheese

1 Preheat oven to 180°C.
2 Grease a baking dish with the olive oil.
3 Combine all the ingredients (except the milk, eggs and cheese), and place in the baking dish.
4 Lightly beat the eggs into the milk, and pour this over the vegetables.
5 Sprinkle the cheese on top.
6 Bake for about 30 minutes.

Kale, collard and outer cabbage leaves

Although these vegetables are very rich in nutrients and beneficial phytochemicals, they are somewhat leathery and unpalatable. I use them very finely shredded in stir-fries, rissoles and soya burgers, or as a thickening agent in casseroles.

Try cooking potatoes and the greens separately, then mashing them together with herbs and yoghurt.

Unfortunately green vegetables, in particular, are heavily sprayed, and some pesticides are systemic and penetrate into plant tissue; however, washing the vegetables before using them will remove some types of sprays. Green vegetables are easy to grow, and you don't have to wait until they are fully mature — very young greens are tastier, and can be grown in small trays of soil.

I sometimes sprout mustard and radish seeds, but they are quite spicy and should be mixed with other vegetables.

Special note: All commercial seeds are treated with chemicals, so make sure you buy those that are left untreated specifically for sprouting.

Cabbage juice

Taken internally as a therapeutic agent cabbage juice has a long history of use for healing and strengthening the gastrointestinal tract, and could be taken as part of the treatment for gastric ulcers, colitis and inflammatory intestinal conditions. Start with a tablespoon dose, and gradually build up the dose to 1 cup daily – if you can tolerate it. Mix it with carrot juice if you wish to make it more palatable.

Cabbage juice can be used externally as a gargle for sore throats, or applied to pimples, sores and inflamed skin conditions.

Cabbage leaves

Cabbage leaves are often successful in relieving the swollen breasts of pregnant and breastfeeding women. They can also be used on bruises, injuries that have not healed properly, sore muscles and joints. Ideally, use the outer leaves of organically grown cabbage.

1   Wash the leaves, and cut out the hard main
    stems. For sensitive wounds dip the cabbage
    leaves into boiling water to soften them,
    then apply them when they have cooled to
    tepid heat.
2   Dry the leaves with a clean cloth.
3   Roll each leaf with a clean bottle or rolling
    pin until the leaves are softened, and the
    juice starts to ooze.
4   Place the leaves over the affected area in two
    to three layers.
5   Keep the leaves in place with a firm, not
    tight, bandage for up to four hours.
    The first time you try this, check after one hour
to make sure that the area of skin being treated
has not become hot. If it has, prepare new leaves,
and change them every hour or so. This is more
important when treating injuries or boils.

Serious infections and injuries should always
be treated by qualified health practitioners.

Suggested intake and duration of use

I always recommend that the same foods should
not be eaten every day, so include cabbage
plants every second day in normal servings.

Use 1 cup cabbage juice therapy daily for a
maximum of three months, with four-day breaks
at the end of each month. Then continue twice
weekly as a preventive.

Cabbage juice as an internal remedy is not
appropriate for children, but they should be
encouraged to eat plants in this family in normal dietary servings.

Summary

Edible foods in the cabbage family are low in
kilojoules, and are a good source of protective
nutrients and phytochemicals.

Recommended reading

Michnovicz, J. J. *How to Reduce Your Risk of Breast
Cancer*. Warner Books, New York, 1995.

The carrot family
(Apiaceae, formerly Umbelliferae)

The plants in this family are:

Vegetables	Culinary herbs	Medicinal herbs
Carrots	Angelica	Bupleurum
Celery	Aniseed	Celery seed
Different types of celery are available: perennial celery is somewhat like Italian parsley, and the leaves are used; celeriac produces a rough, roundish root that can be cooked or grated into a salad; the common stalk form is the most popular.	Caraway	Dong quai
	Chervil	Gotu kola
	Coriander	Wild carrot
	Cumin	
	Dill	
	Fennel	
	Lovage	
	Parsley	
Parsnips		

Background

Wild carrots are small and stringy, and probably
originated in Afghanistan.

Celery is mentioned in Homer's *Odyssey*. The
cultivated type was well established in Europe
by the fourteenth century. Its wild form was
used in Europe as a medicine, mainly for fluid
retention, and the cultivated stalk form was
used as a food in the seventeenth century.

Specific health benefits

A Chinese survey found that frequent consumption of carrots was the only dietary factor that
protected against lung cancer.[33] A review of the
scientific literature on foods and cancer risk
showed that raw vegetables generally, and

specifically the onion family and carrots, gave the most protection against non-reproductive system cancers.[34] Carrots, celery and parsley are invariably included in any list of foods that contain plant substances known to reduce the likelihood of cancer.

An Italian study concluded that carrots, tomatoes, fresh fruit, and the beta-carotene in foods, have the potential to protect against psoriasis.[35]

The pectin in carrots binds bile acids, and also helps to lower cholesterol.[36] When rats were fed celery, their cholesterol levels were lowered.

Although celery is a healthy vegetable, it is not particularly therapeutic. For medicinal purposes celery seed products are prescribed for rheumatoid and other types of arthritis, for fluid retention, and as an adjunct treatment for hypertension. Celery juice is an old folk remedy for laryngitis.

General health benefits

Celery and its vegetable relatives are generally low in kilojoules, and high in fibre and potassium. Herbs in the carrot family are an aid to digestion, as well as flavourings — they reduce the need for less-healthy taste enhancers.

Raw carrots make you feel fuller than do cooked carrots. If you are trying to lose weight, eat a large serving of raw, grated carrot in a salad at the beginning of the meal, or snack on raw carrots between meals. Chewing raw carrot also stimulates the salivary glands, and may therefore promote a healthier environment in your mouth.

Cautions and adverse effects

Some asthmatics, in particular, may be allergic to some plants in the carrot family.

Known therapeutic components

- Fennel, aniseed, parsley and other herbs in this family contain beneficial phyto-oestrogens that are helpful for menopausal symptoms.
- Carrots are one of the best plant sources of beta-carotene.
- Parsley is also rich in vitamin C and carotenoids.
- All the plants in the carrot family contain useful antioxidants, and some are medicinal herbs with various therapeutic effects.
- Cancer-preventive compounds in this family of plants include carotenoids, coumarins, terpenes, phenolic acids, phthalides and polyacetylenes.

Growing the carrot family

Vegetables and herbs in the carrot family grow in diverse climatic conditions. Your local nursery or a gardening book will give guidelines about which plants can be grown in your area in different seasons.

How to use

Celery seed products are helpful for some cases of arthritis and fluid retention. The seed contains a concentration of components. The plant itself is a good vegetable, but not specifically therapeutic.

Celeriac is available from some stores. This large, roughly rounded root is delicious grated raw into a salad, mixed with grated raw beetroot or carrot and other finely chopped salad vegetables and herbs.

Suggested intake

Eat the vegetables regularly in normal serving sizes.

Use the culinary herbs generously as flavourings.

Take those medicinal herbs as prescribed for specific health problems. In general, the medicinal plants in this family are not appropriate for children, although the vegetables and culinary herbs are recommended.

Summary

The plants in this family have wide-ranging nutritional and health benefits.

Citrus fruits

Calamondin
Grapefruit
Lemon
Lime
Kumquat
Mandarine
Orange
Tangelo

Tangerine
other varieties

The botanical names can be somewhat confusing because some plants are 'crossed' with others. They all begin with *Citrus*, and there are many variations of each type. For example, although the full name of the smaller thin-skinned lemon is *Citrus limon* 'Meyer', most retail nurseries sell lemons by their common name (Meyer, Lisbon, Eureka, etc.).

Background

Oranges probably originated in China, and the early types of most citrus species were first cultivated in Asia.

Specific health benefits

A number of dietary surveys in different countries suggest that citrus fruits are generally part of the diets of people who have a lower cancer risk. Laboratory studies of many citrus compounds show an inhibitory effect against various types of cancer cells, and some of the citrus flavonoids inhibit mutagens (substances that cause cancer).[37] Citrus intake is also linked to an increased survival time of patients with some types of cancer.[38] Experimentally, citrus flavonoids are an effective inhibitor of cell proliferation in human breast cancer, especially when paired with the flavonoid quercetin.[39]

Hesperidin, the most common citrus flavonoid, was shown to lower blood pressure and act as a diuretic in animals.[40] A few human case studies have confirmed that grapefruit juice, in particular, can have this effect. Regular use of citrus in the diet is recommended as an adjunct to the prevention and treatment of fluid retention and hypertension.

A comparison of people in Belfast and Toulouse showed that those in Toulouse have a much lower incidence of heart disease. Beta-cryptoxanthin, a carotenoid found in citrus, was one of the factors linked to the better cardiovascular health of people in Toulouse.[41]

Dietary surveys show that citrus fruits help lower the risk of cataracts.[42]

Lemon odour has antidepressant effects. The easiest way to benefit from this effect is to use lemon oil either as a perfume or in an aromatherapy burner. Lemon oil is also excellent as an inhalation for colds and sore throats.

General health benefits

One study showed that orange (and apple) juice increased the uptake of calcium.

Citrus are a good source of vitamin C and flavonoids.

Cautions and adverse effects

- Excess orange juice can cause urine to become too acidic, and lead to a higher level of calcium and oxalate excretion — even compared to ascorbic acid supplements.[43] This means that the risk of some types of kidney stones might be increased by excessive consumption of orange juice.

- My clinical experience is that various types of orange juice are drunk excessively by many people, and seem to cause sensitivity or allergic reactions, even burning urine and urinary frequency. The same people can usually tolerate small quantities of lemon juice and one whole orange. The whole fruit has more health benefits, as it includes the fibre and more of the potential anticancer components.

  No one has yet set a safe level of consumption of orange juice. Manufacturers recommend it wholeheartedly, and it is useful for people who refuse to eat fresh fruit, or as a substitute for large quantities of cola drinks, soft drinks and alcohol. However, I suggest that, if you must drink juices, it is healthier to dilute them in water or make them into ice cubes to add to water. If I had to set a limit, I would suggest you have a maximum of two glasses of orange juice daily.

- A few studies using grapefruit juice have shown that it can affect the absorption of some pharmaceuticals: it reduces absorption of quinidine sulphate, increases uptake of the oestrogen contraceptive, and increases the activity of Norvasc and Teldane.
- The combination of acids and fruit sugars is relatively concentrated in citrus juices, and this can detrimentally affect tooth enamel. As far as practicable, clean your teeth immediately after drinking these juices.

Known theraupeutic components

- Citrus fruits contain vitamin C and many different flavonoids that protect vitamin C in the body and have other beneficial effects. The main flavonoids in citrus are naringin, kaempferol, apigenin, quercetin and hesperidin.
- Hesperidin, a prominent flavonoid in oranges, can lower triglycerides and blood pressure (according to animal studies), and is active against the growth of breast cancer cells.
- The grapefruit flavonoid naringenin also inhibits human breast cancer cells. Four flavonoids — nobiletin, tangeretin, naringin, hesperidin — protect against some cancer-causing compounds.[44]
- The pectin in grapefruit (when used alone) can lower LDL cholesterol by 10 per cent.[45] This means that grapefruit in your diet may have a small beneficial effect on the 'bad' cholesterol.

Growing your own citrus fruits

Consult your local nursery on the varieties that grow best in your area. Some varieties grow successfully in large pots.

How to use

I prefer to eat citrus fruits before my meals because their acid improves digestion.

A grapefruit cut in half, then into bite-size segments, makes a good appetiser. To sweeten, add a little concentrated apple or pear juice.

Oranges cut into segments and chilled are very thirst quenching and cleansing to the palate — and perhaps one way of getting children interested in fruit as snacks.

Instead of drinking orange juice, make orange-juice ice blocks, and add them to water.

Use lemon juice as a salt substitute on many dishes, as it adds a tangy taste.

Lemon oil in an inhalation is excellent for colds and throat infections: add about 6 drops oil to 1 cup hot water.

Note: Whole fruits contain fibre and many valuable components that are discarded when juices are made. Juices are less filling, and contain more kilojoules than whole fruit.

Suggested intake

Eat one citrus fruit a day, or more if you are not eating other fruits and a wide range of vegetables. If you do not eat whole fruit, use the juice.

Children should be encouraged to eat at least a quarter or a half of an orange or mandarine daily. A lifelong citrus-eating habit is recommended.

Summary

Citrus fruits contain useful nutrients and phytochemicals that have a wide variety of general health benefits. At almost every stage of the cancer process, plant components such as those in the citrus family can have a favourable effect.

Coloured foods: carotenoids and flavonoids

Carotenoids

Background

Early this century two scientists discovered that a fat-soluble substance — vitamin A — stimulated the growth of rats that were fed a deficient diet. In 1930 another scientist confirmed that coloured plant extracts had similar effects, and that plant carotenoids are converted to vitamin A in humans.

By 1970 it was known that beta-carotene had antioxidant properties, although the significance of this for human health was not recognised. Research was stimulated by the observation that people who ate dark-green and deep-yellow vegetables had a decreased cancer risk.

For many years the focus remained on beta-carotene; the study of other carotenoids is quite recent.

What are carotenoids?

Carotenoids occur in nature as colours in plants, and over 500 types of carotenoid have been identified. The major ones found in human blood and body tissues that result from the consumption of foods are alpha-carotene, beta-carotene, lutein, zeaxanthin, lycopene and cryptoxanthin.

Carotenoids have diverse effects in the body:
- producing vitamin A
- antioxidant activity
- protecting the skin, eyes and cardiovascular system
- enhancing the immune system
- reducing the spread of cancer cells.

Carotenoids and vitamins C and E work together more effectively as a group — another reason I recommend a varied, whole-food diet that includes a variety of vegetables and fruits.

Light cooking generally improves the body's ability to absorb carotenoids. Lycopene in tomatoes is markedly better absorbed if they are cooked and served with oils — as in a typical Italian meal.

Seemingly similar foods can contain markedly different compounds. Ordinary grapefruit, for example, does not contain lycopene; compared to green capsicum, red capsicum has higher levels of some important carotenoids; green leafy vegetables contain high levels of lutein and zeaxanthin, which are particularly helpful for some eye problems.

It is highly probable that future researchers will discover that even tiny amounts of some of the other carotenoids have specific health enhancing benefits. Therefore, eating a variety of coloured and green vegetables and fruits is likely to protect your body from different types of damage and disease.

Does a typical Australian diet contain a therapeutic amount?

Based on clinical observation, a typical diet prevents obvious deficiency diseases. However, if you aim to offset cell damage by free radicals and to be optimally healthy, ask yourself how many elderly people you know who represent a model of good health?

Although Australian figures are not available, a typical American gets about 1.5 mg beta-carotene daily. The Alliance for Aging Research in the USA suggests that 10–30 mg beta-carotene are required to maintain the health and independence of older people.

If your daily fruit and vegetable intake consists of, say, corn, green beans, white potato, an apple and a pear, you would get about five cups of vegetables and fruits a day. This would provide about 1 mg beta-carotene, 2 mg of alpha-

Examples of carotenoid-rich foods[46] *(mcg/100 g)*

Food	Beta-carotene	Alpha-carotene	Lutein and zeaxanthin	Lycopene	Cryptoxanthin
Apple	26	–	45	–	–
Asparagus	449	9	640	–	–
Carrot	7 900	3 600	260	–	–
Broccoli	1 300	1	1 800	–	–
Capsicum, green	230	11	700	–	–
Capsicum, red	2 200	60	6 800	–	–
Celery	710	–	3 600	–	–
Chicory leaf	3 430	–	10 300	–	–
Grapefruit, pink	1 310	–	–	3 362	–
Greens, collard	5 400	–	16 300	–	–
Guava	812	70	–	5 400	–
Kale	4 700	–	21 900	–	–
Lettuce	1 200	1	1 800	–	–
Mango	1 300	–	–	–	54
Nectarine	103	–	15	–	43
Orange	39	20	14	–	149
Pawpaw	99	–	–	–	470
Potato, sweet	8 800	–	–	–	–
Potato, white	–	–	–	–	–
Pumpkin	3 100	3 800	1 500	–	–
Spinach	5 500	–	12 600	–	–
Tomato	520	–	100	3 100	–

carotene, lutein and zeaxanthin, but no lycopene or cryptoxanthin. On the other hand, if you ate pink grapefruit, broccoli, carrots, tomato juice and watermelon, you would get about 11 mg beta-carotene and over 20 mg of the other important carotenoids.

Of course, it is unreasonable to expect people to carry food composition charts of the forty-five or so essential nutrients, plus all the beneficial phytochemicals, so that they can meticulously plan to get them all. What you can do is to buy smaller quantities, and aim to eat about twenty different fruits and vegetables each week, and have about five cups of fruits and vegetables each day. Each week buy and eat one type of fresh food that is unusual for you.

Specific health benefits

Cancer

People with the highest intakes of fruits and vegetables rich in carotenoids have the lowest risk for most cancers, including some of the less common types. For example, one survey found that dark-green and orange vegetables, and the cabbage family, offered the greatest protection against kidney cancer.[47]

- Beta-carotene seems to lower the risk of breast and endometrial cancer.
- A carotenoid-rich diet is linked with an improved prognosis (outcome) after the diagnosis of breast cancer.[48]
- Tomatoes contain lycopene, a carotenoid

linked to a lower risk of prostate cancer and cancer of the digestive tract. In a large-scale survey of doctors, men with a low level of beta-carotene who received a supplement had a 36 per cent reduced risk of contracting prostate cancer, compared with men with low beta-carotene who did not take the supplement.

Heart disease

Population studies confirm that the risk of death from heart disease is significantly lower in those people with the highest intake of carotenoids. In one trial of beta-carotene supplementation the benefit did not occur until the second year of the programme.[49]

Cataracts and age-related macular degeneration

A number of population surveys show that people with higher levels of carotenoids and other antioxidants tend to have a lower incidence of these two eye problems. Zeaxanthin and lutein were the carotenoids most strongly linked to a decreased risk of age-related macular degeneration.[50]

Immunity

A long-term, controlled trial of a supplement of 50 mg beta-carotene on alternate days showed that this enhanced natural killer cell activity in elderly men. The same supplementation did not make a significant difference for middle-aged men.[51] This beneficial effect in elderly people is likely to help their immune system combat viruses and tumours.

The skin

Beta-carotene supplements taken orally are likely to prevent sun damage to the skin more effectively than will application of sunscreen alone.[52]

General health benefits

A carotenoid-rich diet promotes cell health, and therefore provides a wide range of benefits.

Are carotenoids useful for preventing and treating degenerative diseases?

In general, carotenoids are best considered as long-term preventives. Oxidative damage to cells, the eyes, the heart and other body tissues usually occurs within cells over a long period of time, and you are unaware of it.

- A study on elderly nuns concluded that those with high lycopene levels lived longer.[53]
- A trial on cystic fibrosis patients showed that beta-carotene supplementation 'may eventually prove to be a useful adjunct for the management of the disease' due to the effect of lowering lipid oxidation (the breakdown of harmful fat).[54]
- Lycopene has been researched extensively in the USA and Israel, and is said to be 'very close to fulfilling all requirements for use as a standard anticarcinogenic agent in humans' and 'the most potent nutritional antioxidant'. Supplements that include this valuable plant carotenoid will no doubt be available very soon.[55]

A diet rich in carotenoids is one of the factors that reduce the cumulative damage that occurs within our bodies every day. I imagine that if we got a little purple cross on our skin every time our body was short of antioxidants we would be queuing up to buy our daily intake of fruits and vegetables. Instead of people munching on chips, chocolate and confectionery there would be a demand for little snack packs of fruits and vegetables. Our lunches would include vegetable soups and salads, our liquids would include pink grapefruit and tomato juices, and we would be growing chicory, chard and collard greens, together with other vegetables, to include in our evening meal. Our weekly shopping list would include at least twenty different fruits and vegetables, and we would not buy the same things week after week. Perhaps the greatest preventive strategy that governments could make would be to subsidise the cost of growing organic fresh fruits and vegetables.

Carotenoids are unlikely to cure the problem if you are already ill, but there is a chance that a good diet and lifestyle will help slow down most degenerative diseases. You are never too old, or too young, to begin protecting your cells!

Cautions and adverse effects

- Healthy foods sometimes cause allergic or sensitivity reactions. If they are irritating to you, you should avoid them. Alternatively, you could get professional help to either desensitise yourself to the food or use the food in a different way.
- Carotenoids are fat soluble, which means that they are absorbed better with some type of fat in the diet. Since most foods contain at least some fats or oils, taking carotenoid supplements with a meal is the best strategy.
- A supplement of 30 mg beta-carotene daily, or excess carrot juice, may cause yellowing of the skin; this is harmless, and disappears when you lower the intake. I do not recommend synthetic beta-carotene as a supplement.
- Do not take more than 30 mg beta-carotene daily as a supplement, as some researchers suggest that beta-carotene may interfere with lutein — an important carotenoid for eye health. To avoid this, take your beta-carotene in one daily dose.
- Heavy smokers who drink alcohol and take high levels of *synthetic* beta-carotene may actually increase their risk of cancer.[56] It is not known how alcohol, tobacco and beta-carotene interact.

Carotenoid supplements

Trials of *synthetic beta-carotene* have resulted in the people's health becoming worse or no better. Trials of specific *natural carotenoids* or mixtures of carotenoids have given good results. In one study blood levels of lipid peroxidation activity (undesirable oxidation) were much higher in those who received synthetic beta-carotene compared to those who took beta-carotene and other carotenoids from natural sources.[57]

My research shows that all unsuccessful trials used synthetic beta-carotene, which does not have the same antioxidant ability and is chemically different to the natural form. All foods linked to cancer prevention contain only natural beta-carotene. There is no data showing that natural beta-carotene increases cancer risks, but there is good data showing that it can reverse precancerous cells.

Natural carotenoid supplements are useful for people who do not eat a wide variety of fruits and vegetables, and they are probably better absorbed than that in foods. Therefore, they may be especially useful for people

- with poor digestion or absorption disorders
- who are at risk from excess radiation from the sun
- who are exposed to stress, pollutants, pesticides and other chemicals.

If you are taking antioxidant supplements or making major improvements in your diet, do not expect a miracle, because it may take a few years to reduce your risk factors. At the time of writing, reliable and standard blood tests are not routinely available for checking carotenoid levels and biochemical evidence of general oxidative cell damage.

Growing your own carotenoids

Consult your local nursery or a gardening book for suitable varieties and information on ways to grow these plants. Try growing some hydroponically or in containers: I grow cherry tomatoes in large hanging baskets; lettuce is suited to hydroponics; and baby carrots grow well in a container.

Dosage and suggested intake

Carotenoid supplements are available as tablets, but avoid synthetic products. Be guided by the label dosages; use proportionately less for children according to age (see pp. 4–5).

Summary

Eat a variety of foods rich in carotenoids to help prevent diseases and reduce cumulative damage.

Flavonoids

Background

In the 1930s it was discovered that flavonoids helped support vitamin C in the body. Initially they were called vitamin P, but it was later decided that they did not fulfil the scientific criteria for vitamins and could not be classed as essential nutrients. In other words, you won't die without them, but you may not feel great either.

What are flavonoids?

Over 20 000 flavonoids are now listed in chemical abstracts. They are found in plants, and many of them make up the colours of flowers, fruits and vegetables, although a few are colourless. Synthetic flavonoids are also used as pharmaceuticals. In the body, some flavonoids work as a team with vitamin C.

Does a typical Australian diet contain a therapeutic amount?

I cannot say there is such a thing as flavonoid deficiency because flavonoids do not have the status of essential nutrients. However, based on dietary surveys, it can be assumed that at least a few million Australians are not getting a flavonoid intake that is high enough to be disease preventive.

Specific health benefits

Cancer

A large Dutch survey found that half an onion a day protects against stomach cancer. Onions are particularly rich in the flavonoid quercetin, and this flavonoid has a number of properties, including antioxidant, anti-inflammatory and antiviral.[58] This survey also found that those with the highest flavonoid intake had a 73 per cent decreased risk of stroke compared with those with the lowest intake.

Laboratory studies show that isolated flavonoids (such as genistein, quercetin, naringenin, biochanin A, rutin and kaempferol) also inhibit the growth of colon cancer cells. In addition, other studies show that at least six different flavonoids (galangin, genistein, quercetin, baicalein, hesperedin, naringenin) suppress the growth of breast cancer cells.[59]

Heart disease

The ten-year Zutphen Elderly Study confirmed that those who had the highest dietary intake of quercetin (mainly from black tea, onions and apples) had a 53 per cent decreased risk of heart disease compared with those with the lowest levels.[60]

General health benefits

A number of flavonoids are important therapeutic components in medicinal herbs. In general they have antioxidant and anti-inflammatory effects, and have a particular affinity in the human body to the walls of blood vessels and to connective tissue. Some flavonoids help immune functioning, while others, such as isoflavones, are a special category that have beneficial hormone-balancing effects. This hormonal effect is explained in detail in chapter 3.

Cautions and adverse effects

Extremely high doses may cause gastric upsets.

Flavonoid supplements

If you are not eating a wide variety of fruits and vegetables, take one of the supplements containing one or more of the bioflavonoids.

Growing your own flavonoids

Most of the flavonoid foods mentioned in this chapter can be grown in a wide variety of localities and climatic conditions, so consult your local nursery or a gardening book to see which varieties best suit your needs.

Dosage and suggested intake

Flavonoids supplements are available as tablets. Be guided by label dosages; use proportionately less for children according to age (see pp. 4–5).

Summary

Scientific investigation and dietary studies repeatedly confirm that known edible flavonoid foods are indeed health enhancing.

Medicinal mushrooms

Common mushrooms are one among 100 000 different types of fungus. Some fungi are beneficial as foods and medicines, but others are hallucinogens and poisons. Collecting in the wild for your personal use can be hazardous, so although only about 5 per cent of mushrooms are outright poisons, it is sensible to be cautious and eat only those mushrooms you know are safe.

A number of medicinal mushrooms are an acquired taste, and at first you may find the texture and taste somewhat unusual.

Background

Ancient Egyptian physicians purportedly stuffed mouldy bread into wounds. The notion that fungi have therapeutic activity was given scientific support by the discovery in the early part of this century that penicillin possessed antibacterial effects.

In Japan and China some mushrooms belong to the highest class of medicines. They have been used for centuries as tonics and antiageing remedies, and as a treatment for a wide range of health problems. Over 2500 years ago a Chinese emperor was said to have ordered explorers to search for 'the mushroom of immortality', and it is thought that the mushroom they were seeking was reishi. Fifteenth-century warrior priests ate shitake mushrooms to increase their strength. More than 200 varieties of mushroom are used in traditional Chinese medicine.

Reishi *(Ganoderma lucidum)*

Background

My basic computer search lists over 350 scientific papers on reishi, and these lend support for its use as both a preventive and a treatment for a number of diseases and health problems.

Specific health benefits

A study on mice demonstrated that reishi protects the spleen and assists the recovery of cellular immunity following gamma irradiation, suggesting that this medicinal mushroom may be useful for human cancer patients undergoing radiation treatment.[61]

The antitumour properties of the polysaccharides in reishi have been recognised for many years. Dr David Chu says that reishi can neutralise toxins secreted from cancer tissue, and strengthen white blood cells, making it useful in offsetting the side effects of radiation and chemotherapy.[62]

Reishi is used in Japan as part of cancer treatment where increased activity of the immune system is required, and is prescribed for the out-of-control immune disorder myasthenia gravis; this supports reishi's reputation as an adaptogen and immune balancer. (Adaptogens are natural remedies that can be used in ailments caused by excesses or weaknesses; see under **Ginseng** in chapter 3.)

In China over 2000 cases of asthma and bronchitis have been treated successfully with a syrup extract of reishi. The extract can be used to treat colds and influenza because of its antibacterial and antiviral effects. It also fights infections by activating cells such as macrophages and natural killer cells that form part of the body's defence system against harmful organisms. Research so far indicates reishi may assist chronic fatigue syndrome, candidiasis and possibly AIDS. In one study, for example, reishi reduced the incidence of the recurring eye infections common in AIDS patients, reduced night sweats, and improved immune function (based on T cell counts).[63]

In China fifty-four people whose blood pressure remained high, despite pharmaceutical therapy, were given 55 mg reishi extract or a placebo, three times daily for four weeks, together with their medical drugs. Those taking the reishi had significant reductions in both systolic and diastolic blood pressure, while those on the placebo did not.[64]

Reishi also has the capacity to reduce blood stickiness. You should not take reishi mushroom in addition to hypertensive and blood-thinning pharmaceuticals unless you are being monitored by a health practitioner, because the overall effect may be too strong.

Reishi has been used in China as a traditional treatment for liver and kidney diseases, arthritis, bronchitis, asthma, gastric ulcers, and as a heart tonic. It may also be helpful for altitude sickness, arrhythmia (irregular heartbeat), coughs, dizziness, insomnia and nervousness.

In a study on rats reishi offset the toxic liver damage caused by carbon tetrachloride, and gave strong antioxidant activity against two particularly injurious oxidants (superoxide and hydroxyl radical).[65] Another rat experiment showed that a polysaccharide in reishi protected liver tissue in cirrhosis.[66]

General health benefits

Reishi acts as a general tonic and an immune modulator by reducing inflammatory and allergic reactions, and stimulates the white blood cells that are necessary for the body's defence system — it tones down one aspect of the immune system while stimulating the other.

Cautions and adverse effects

- People who are truly allergic to mushrooms are unlikely to be able to tolerate reishi.
- I have not seen any adverse effects in patients attending my clinic, but there are reports of a few people with skin reactions related to the toxic elimination process; these reactions reportedly disappear as they continue taking the remedy. I usually stop people taking any remedy that causes any adverse reaction, then wait a few days and try it again at a lower dose. In the majority of cases it is not the natural remedy causing the reaction, and I suspect there is often extensive mild, and unreported, food poisoning.

Known therapeutic components

Over 150 different components have been identified in reishi. The most important are:
- polysaccharides, notably beta-glucan — this group of compounds has antitumour, anti-

hypertensive, immune modulating and blood glucose lowering properties
- ganoderic acids that reduce cholesterol and histamine (a cause of redness, swelling and allergic reactions)
- lanostanoid, a steroid-like compound that acts against liver toxins
- organic germanium, which increases the oxygen absorbed by the blood and prevents tissue degeneration
- other compounds with antiallergy, anti-inflammatory and mild heart tonic actions.

Reishi supplements

Reishi is available as a tablet, a powder, a liquid extract, a syrup or dried whole mushrooms.

Growing your own reishi

Reishi grows in the forests of China and Japan. Due to demand and reishi's relative rareness in the wild, it is now being cultivated in Asia. Only a few countries sell it fresh. As far as I know starter kits for reishi are not available in Australia.

How to use

To use in cooked dishes, soak the dried reishi in a little hot water for about twenty minutes, then drain and slice finely. Always also use the water in which the reishi have been soaked.

Christopher Hobbs's energy soup
(2 cups per serve)

10 cups water
1 or 2 reishi mushrooms
1 cup adzuki or black beans, presoaked or slightly sprouted
1 cup whole barley
1 cup chopped presoaked shitake mushrooms
2½ cups fresh, chopped vegetables (carrots, onions, celery, broccoli, etc.)
miso, ginger, garlic, herbs (to taste)

1 Combine the first four ingredients in a large pot and bring to the boil; simmer for 40 minutes.
2 Add the shitake and vegetables, and simmer until tender.
3 Add the miso, ginger, garlic and herbs, and serve hot.

To increase your energy, eat one to two bowls of this soup twice a week. For serious degenerative conditions, eat at least one bowl a day.

Suggested intake and duration of use

Be guided by the label dosage on products, because there is a variety of qualities and strengths.

Use reishi as an occasional tonic, or for a few weeks to treat mild infections. Serious diseases would need at least three months' treatment.

As a general preventive remedy, use a few small handfuls of dried reishi weekly in your cooking.

Children can be given reishi in proportionately lower quantities according to age (see pp. 4–5).

Summary

Reishi is one of the best remedies for preventing and treating illnesses related to immune functioning.

Recommended reading

Hobbs C. *Medicinal Mushrooms*. 2nd edn. Botanica Press, Santa Cruz, California, 1995 (877 references).

Shitake (*Lentinan* (or *Lentinula*) *edodes*)

Background

Shitake is one of the most commonly eaten varieties of mushrooms in Japan, and is deservedly in the category of a medicinal food.

In Japan it is classed as a general tonic, a restorative and a preventive, and is used medicinally for all diseases involving low immune function, including cancer and AIDS, environmental allergies, common fungal infections, bronchitis, colds and influenza, as well as for reducing high cholesterol levels and for regulating urinary incontinence.

Specific health benefits

Seventeen animal and human studies show that lentinan (the main isolated therapeutic component) increases survival time for various types of cancer patients, the best results being for cancers in the gastrointestinal tract.[67] However, it is not only the isolated component that has therapeutic activity; the consumption of shitake mushroom produces antitumour effects.[68] Compounds that block the formation of cancer-causing compounds (from nitrites) are produced in shitake mushrooms when the mushrooms are dried or heated.

An American doctor found that his patients did not lose their hair or get as sick if they also took shitake when having radiation or chemotherapy treatments.

In Japan the isolated component is approved by the government as a drug that prolongs survival time of cancer patients. The isolated component has also resulted in reduction of symptoms in AIDS patients, and in people suffering from chronic fatigue and low natural killer cell activity. In Japan a condition known as LNKS (low natural killer cell syndrome) has been treated successfully with lentinan. This condition corresponds to what we call chronic fatigue syndrome.

Shitake has the capacity to lower cholesterol, to lower blood pressure, and to protect the liver. Liver function improved in seventeen out of twenty-one long-term hepatitis B patients when they were given 3 g shitake powder daily.[69] Shitake provided liver protection to rats given liver-damaging chemicals.

General health benefits

Many studies confirm that lentinan assists immune function in a number of ways, including boosting natural killer cell activity, activating macrophages, and enhancing T cells. There is also evidence of some antiviral and antimicrobial activity.[70]

Although the whole mushroom gives these effects, it is obviously weaker than lentinan in pharmaceutical form. However, there is some evidence that the whole mushroom increases resistance to bacterial, viral, fungal and parasitic infections.

Cautions and adverse effects

- Allergic reactions, mild dermatitis and mild diarrhoea may occur from the use of shitake extracts, although these symptoms usually disappear once the body has adjusted. I have not heard of any Asian people with problems resulting from the consumption of normal dietary quantities of shitake mushrooms.

Known therapeutic components

- Lentinan has demonstrable antitumour and immune-stimulating properties. In some countries lentinan is available as an isolated, pharmaceutical remedy; it has been found helpful in treating hepatitis B, chronic fatigue and various viral diseases. It also has antiviral, antimicrobial and cholesterol-lowering effects. In Japanese hospitals this isolated compound has increased survival time and disease-free time of patients with gastric, colon and breast cancer. It does not destroy cancer cells but works via the immune system.
- In animal experiments lentinan limited the relapse of tuberculosis, increased resistance to bacterial infections and parasites, and improved liver function in animals with toxic hepatitis.

- Other components in shitake impart anti-tumour, antiviral and cardiovascular benefits.

Shitake supplements

Shitake is available as tablets, powder, liquid extracts and whole dried mushrooms from Asian food stores. The dried mushrooms are flavoursome and aromatic, but somewhat rubbery in texture.

Growing your own shitake

Large quantities of shitake are cultivated in Japan, and produced without synthetic fertilisers and chemicals. As far as I know, these mushrooms are not grown in Australia, and I could not find any starter kits.

How to use

The simplest way to cook shitake is to soak the dried mushrooms in hot water for about 20 minutes, then slice them very thinly for use in stir-fries or soups.

Shitake soup (Serves 4)

8 dried shitake mushrooms
6 cups water
1 cup wild rice
2 carrots, sliced into pieces (about 2 cm x 1 cm)
4 teaspoons miso
1 tablespoon finely chopped fresh coriander or parsley (or 1 teaspoon dried)

1 Soak the shitake in 1 cup water.
2 Bring the rice to the boil in 5 cups water, and simmer for 20 minutes.
3 Cut each shitake into three or more slices, and add to the rice, together with the soaking water; simmer for a further 20 minutes.
4 Add the carrots, and simmer for a further 5 minutes.
5 Turn off the heat, and stir in the miso.

Serve with finely chopped coriander or parsley.

For vegetarians, in particular, I suggest a vegetable and tempeh stir-fry to follow as the main course to complement the protein and vitamin B12 intake.

Shitake tea (Serves 2)

1 dessertspoon finely chopped shitake (for shitake in powder form, halve the quantities)
1 dessertspoon finely chopped ginger root
2 cups of water

1 Combine all the ingredients, and bring to the boil.
2 Simmer for 10 minutes.
3 Strain, and drink hot or cold.

Add any leftover tea to soups or casseroles.

Suggested intake and duration of use

This is basically the same as for reishi. However, do not double up with the two separate mushroom remedies — when you combine remedies, the total dosage becomes the same as a single remedy, so use only a few handfuls of either single or mixed dried medicinal mushrooms each week.

The traditional medicinal dose is between 5 and 15 g dried mushrooms daily.

For serious health problems I usually prescribe a concentrated liquid or dried extract dose of between 2 and 6 g daily, and some products have a guaranteed level of lentinan. Of course, if you have a serious disease, you should consult a health practitioner for specific advice on remedies and diet.

Children can be given shitake in proportionately lower quantities according to age (see pp. 4–5).

Summary

A tonic and balancing food that has antitumour, antiviral, and immune enhancing properties.

Recommended reading

Charalambous, G. (ed.). *Spices, Herbs and Edible Fungi.* Elsevier, New York, 1994 (the chapter on shitake and other edible mushrooms has 127 scientific references).

Other medicinal mushrooms

These are sold in Asian stores or from herbalists, and some are becoming generally more available in the form of dried or liquid remedies. I occasionally see oyster and other unusual mushrooms in fruit and vegetable shops. Below are summaries of nine other medicinal mushrooms: coriolus, hakumokuji, hericium, maitake, poria, straw mushrooms, tochukaso, turkey tail and umbellatus.

Coriolus (*Coriolus versicolor*) Coriolus is immune enhancing, antiviral and an antioxidant.

Hakumokuji (*Tremella fuciformis*) The main traditional use of hakumokuji (also known as snow fungus) is for coughs, respiratory problems and fevers. It stimulates both red and white cell activity, and studies have confirmed that it assists immune function and lowers cholesterol.

Hericium (*Hericium erinaceus*) This is used as a general tonic and to strengthen the digestive system.

Maitake (*Grifola frondosa*) This mushroom contains beta-glucan, which has been identified by research and clinical studies as being a potent enhancer of the immune system. Studies show that it can lower blood pressure and protect the liver from toxins, and that it has anticancer properties. Maitake mushroom has antidiabetic effects in animals.[71] It may be worth trying for the early stage of noninsulin dependent diabetes — with the permission of the treating doctor.

Poria (*Wolfporia cocos*) This has anticancer properties.

Straw mushrooms (*Volvariella volvacea*) These contain beta-glucan polysaccharides, which lower cholesterol.[72]

Tochukaso (*Cordyceps sinensis*) Scientists confirm that tochukaso is an immune regulator, and it has a traditional history as a general tonic and remedy to prevent disease, especially for older people. Some Chinese athletes have claimed that tochukaso has helped them in recent world-breaking athletic achievements. This mushroom is also helpful for regenerating the kidneys and liver, and to prevent blood stickiness.

Turkey tail (*Trametes versicolor*) Useful for inflammation and internal infections.

Umbellatus (*Grifola umbellatus*) Umbellatus is immune enhancing, a diuretic, and an anticancer agent.

Other Asian mushrooms that lower cholesterol include tree ear (*Auricularia auricula*), and oyster mushrooms (*Pleurotus ostreatus*).

A combination of five mushrooms (hakumokuji, maitake, reishi, shitake, tochukaso) was shown to be more effective at increasing natural killer cell activity and activated T cells to stimulate the immune response, than did individual mushroom extracts.

Various combinations of these medicinal mushrooms are now becoming available, and they have been described as 'immune umbrellas for the 21st century'.

Common mushrooms

These include button, closed cup, open cup and flat mushrooms.

The figures in the table are from the Australian Mushroom Growers' Association, *The Mushroom Lovers' Cookbook* (Custom Book Company, Beecroft, NSW, n.d.).

Key nutrients in raw mushrooms (per 100 g)	
Protein	3.6 g
Fat	0.3 g
Cholesterol	–
Carbohydrate	1.5 g
Fibre	2.5 g
Potassium	305.0 mg
Sodium	7.0 mg
Iron	0.2 mg
Thiamine	0.03 mg
Riboflavin	0.41 mg
Niacin	4.1 mg
Vitamin B12	0.26 mcg
Vitamin C	1.0 mg

Cautions and adverse effects

- Although mushrooms are low in kilojoules and a good source of nutrients, and one of the few plant sources of vitamin B12, they contain hydrazines. Experimentally, in common with many other foods and environmental substances, hydrazines cause cancer. The Australian Mushroom Growers' Association advised me that:

  > The risk of increasing tumour from the mushroom hydrazine dose is reported as many-fold less than that from a daily can of beer or a glass of wine. Further, there would be other environmental considerations that present humans with more significant risks … The suggested daily consumption rate of mushrooms is 15 g daily or around 5. 5 kg a year which is considerably more than the Australian average.

- Mushrooms are common allergens, and some people cannot tolerate them.
- A few researchers suggest that all edible fungi may be the cause of health problems. However, I am not convinced that eating one type of fungi (mushrooms) will increase another type of fungi (Candida albicans) in the body, and a number of medicinal mush-

rooms are actually effective at treating fungal diseases.

Because of these cautions I now recommend restricting mushrooms to one or two generous servings a week, and using medicinal mushrooms only when required for therapeutic purposes.

The potato family
(Nightshade (Solanaceae) family)

Everyone is familiar with the common edible plants in this family. I include it in this chapter mainly to illustrate that it is not only exotic foods such as medicinal mushrooms that have health advantages beyond those of their essential nutrients.

Vegetables

Capsicum
Chilli
Common potato
Eggplant

Fruit

Tamarillo (tree tomato)
Tomato (botanically tomatoes are a fruit, although usually eaten with vegetables)

Medicinal herbs

Bittersweet (*Solanum dulcamarra*)
Withania (*Withania somnifera*)

Poisonous plants

Belladonna (*Atropa belladonna*)
Deadly nightshade (*Solanum nigrum*)
Thorn apple (*Datura stromonium*)

Nearly all plant families contain poisonous plants. Anything that is not a known edible plant should be considered toxic.

Petunias and tobacco are also in the potato family

Background

The common potato is in a different family from sweet potatoes and yams. It originated in South America, where many varieties were grown traditionally. Sir Francis Drake is said to have brought the potato to England in the sixteenth century, and subsequently it became an important food crop.

By the eighteenth century a French scientist (Antoine Parmentier) had bred the types of potato that we eat today. However, people in France were initially very suspicious about potatoes, so Parmentier decided to make a show of stationing soldiers around his potato fields in the suburbs of Paris in the hope of enticing people into thinking that the crops were precious. It worked – people began pilfering the crops!

When the potato blight disease attacked the crop in Ireland in the nineteenth century, many people died of starvation, another reason why we should not be reliant on one food. This crop failure led to the massive Irish emigration to America and Australia.

Tomatoes, too, originated in South America. When they were first introduced into Europe they were considered by some to be poisonous, while others thought they had aphrodisiac properties — the French and Italians initially called them 'apples of love'.

Specific health benefits

Hot chilli

From a therapeutic point of view hot chilli is the most useful plant in this family. In some countries hot chilli is incorrectly called cayenne.

As long as it can be tolerated as an internal remedy, hot chilli is a wonderful digestive and circulatory tonic. It is a powerful antioxidant, and increases immune activity via macrophages.

Animal studies show that hot chilli can lower triglyceride and cholesterol levels.[73]

In traditional herbal medicine a little chilli has commonly been recommended for gastric ulcers. In a laboratory it can kill Helicobacter pylori (the 'bug' that causes most ulcers), but unfortunately many people with this problem cannot tolerate hot spices. Chilli increases the flow of mucus that protects the stomach lining from damage.[74] Various ingredients in some hot sauces may aggravate the stomach lining.

In winter I add concentrated chilli extract to most herbal formulas for coughs, colds and flu, *except those for children*. Hot chillies increase mucus flow and perspiration, so the body cools down and toxins are eliminated.

A number of external remedies are now available for pain relief; ask at your pharmacy or health food store. I have found hot chilli especially helpful for nerve pain such as sciatica, for arthritis, and for nerve and scar pain following surgery (once the inflammation has subsided).

Potatoes

In folk medicine potatoes have a number of uses; for example, ½ cup raw potato juice (with added carrot juice and 1 dessertspoon Manuka honey) was recommended three to four times daily for gastric ulcers.

For swollen eyes, bruises and cysts raw grated potatoes were placed on top of gauze (or fine cotton material) over the affected area. (If you use this remedy, you will notice that the potato absorbs the heat — at which point it should be removed, and another poultice added, if required.) Lie down for at least ten minutes while the potato is working.

As a poultice for coughs, a towel was placed on the chest, and then hot baked mashed potatoes were wrapped in a tea towel and put on top (care must be taken that the poultice is not so hot that it burns the skin).

Tomatoes

The most important component in tomatoes is considered to be lycopene (see under **Carotenoids** in this chapter).

Tomatoes have a reputation as natural deodorants. One suggestion for dealing with smelly cats is to bathe them in tomato juice, then in clean water. (My cat wouldn't let me try it!)

Fresh tomato juice applied externally is an old acne remedy.

General health benefits

Foods in the potato family are a good source of essential nutrients. For example, a 100 g edible portion of potato contains 2.3 g protein, 21 mg vitamin C, 430 mg potassium, with only 0. 2 g fat and 2 mg sodium.

Tomatoes are extremely low in kilojoules because they are about 95 per cent water. They contain valuable antioxidants in the form of vitamin C, carotenoids and flavonoids, as well as being a good source of potassium, and have minimal sodium. Capsicum is also a good source of antioxidants.

Cautions and adverse effects

- All the plants in the potato family are known to cause allergic reactions in a small percentage of the population. However, do not give up eating healthy foods because of someone else's pet theory. Tomatoes are not especially acidic, but some people report they worsen arthritis symptoms. In twenty years of practice I have taken many people off this family of plants for two months to test whether it helps their arthritis, but it seems to be a problem in only about 2 per cent of those with rheumatoid arthritis.

- *Never* eat green potatoes, because they contain a high level of poisonous alkaloids. The green is actually chlorophyll, which indicates that the potatoes have been exposed to light, and is a 'signal' that the alkaloid level is high. Cutting off the chlorophyll does not necessarily reduce the alkaloids to a safe level. At least thirty people are known to have died from eating green potatoes, and thousands have experienced adverse toxic symptoms.
- Do not eat green tomatoes, or the leaves or berries of the plants in the potato family.
- A number of people cannot tolerate hot chilli, either externally or internally. For those who can, a little is beneficial, but people who consume chillies in quantities of about 10 per cent of their dietary intake have a high incidence of mouth and oesophageal cancer.

I do not recommend it for young children or frail elderly people, as it is too pungent for the mouth and digestive tract.

Known therapeutic components

- A component in tomatoes (P-coumaric) protects the tomato against excess sunlight. In the human body this compound blocks the cancer promoting activity of nitrosamine.
- Lycopene is a cancer protective substance in tomatoes.
- Other cancer preventive compounds in this family include flavonoids, glucarates, coumarins, terpenes and phenolic acids.[75]
- Capsaicin is the main hot principle in hot chillies, and over 114 clinical studies in humans have shown that it is an effective external pain remedy.

Growing the potato family

It can be very rewarding to grow these because you often get a very high yield. Seeds and seedlings of these plants, as well as seed potatoes, are available through nurseries according to what will grow in your area at different seasons. There are many gardening books on growing your own fruits and vegetables, and these also give guidelines for the most appropriate times and regions for growing these crops.

How to use

Try potatoes sliced thinly, and grilled instead of fried. I brush over a little olive oil, grill to a golden brown, and serve with a light sprinkling of herbal vinegar and/or salt-reduced tamari.

Stuffed potatoes (Serves 2–4)

2 large potatoes, scrubbed and halved
½ teaspoon dried mixed herbs (or 1 dessertspoon finely chopped fresh herbs)
2 dessertspoons yoghurt or cream
2 dessertspoons soya or dairy cheese

1 Preheat the oven to 200°C.
2 Place the halves face down on a greased tray, and bake for 40 minutes.
3 Scoop out some of the insides, and mash together with spices and herbs, yoghurt or cream.
4 Return the filling to the potatoes, and sprinkle the tops with cheese.
5 Bake or grill until the tops are golden brown.

Vegetarian shepherd's pie (Serves 6)

1 cup brown lentils
1 cup chick peas
4 cups water
2 onions, finely chopped
½ cup shelled peas
2 vegetable stock cubes
1 small handful of finely chopped fresh herbs (or 1–2 teaspoons dried mixed herbs), such as parsley, sage, thyme, basil, mint, oregano, ginger, turmeric, chilli, tarragon and garlic
4 large potatoes
½ cup milk or yoghurt
½ cup chopped chives
1 cup grated tasty or soya cheese

1 Soak the chick peas and lentils overnight in the water.
2 Preheat the oven to 180°C.
3 Add the onion, and bring to the boil. Simmer until the chick peas are soft (you can shorten the cooking time by using a pressure cooker or a microwave oven).
4 Stir in the peas, the stock cubes, and the herbs (but not the chives).
5 Leave to stand with the lid on, while you cook the potatoes.
6 Strain, and mash the cooked potatoes with the milk or yoghurt, then mix in the chives.
7 Pour the cooked lentils and chick peas into a baking dish with a capacity of about 2 litres, and spread the mashed potatoes evenly on top.
8 Sprinkle the cheese over the top.
9 Bake for 30 minutes.
10 Gently brown the top under the griller before serving.

Vary the ingredients to suit your taste. If you are a vegetarian, add some barley, rice, nuts and seeds; if a non-vegetarian, add some beef mince or minced cold meats. Tomatoes and zucchini are always good in such recipes. Be creative!

When I cook legumes such as lentils and chick peas, I usually make twice the quantity so that I can freeze some for future use in soups, casseroles and rissoles (use within two months). Label and date the container.

Stuffed capsicums (Serves 2–4)

2 large firm capsicums, halved and seeded
boiling water: 1 tablespoon for stuffing; 2 litres for baking
1 tablespoon virgin olive oil
1 cup finely chopped onion
1 clove garlic, peeled and crushed
1 cup finely sliced small mushrooms
1 dessertspoon salt-reduced tamari
1 tablespoon water
2 tablespoons fresh mixed herbs (or 1 teaspoon dried herbs)

1 cup cooked brown rice (or ¾ cup barley or oat
    flakes, plus ¼ cup boiling water)
1 lightly beaten egg
4 slices tomato
½ cup grated soya or cheddar cheese

1 Preheat the oven to 200°C.
2 Place the capsicum halves in a large baking dish,
   and add boiling water to a depth of about 2 cm.
3 Bake for 10 minutes while you prepare the
   stuffing.
4 Gently heat the oil in a large frying pan, and add
   the onions and garlic, cooking to a light golden-
   brown.
5 Add the mushrooms, tamari, and water, and stir
   in the herbs, rice and egg.
6 Mix thoroughly, then stuff the capsicum halves;
   top with a slice of tomato and grated cheese.
7 Return the stuffed capsicums to the dish of
   water, and bake for 30 minutes at 180°C.

Ratatouille (Serves 4–6)

500 g peeled and chopped tomatoes (it is easier to
    peel tomatoes if you pour boiling water over
    them first; I am not a gourmet though, I leave
    the skin on)
1–2 cloves garlic, peeled and crushed
2 tablespoons oil
2 small onions, sliced
1 red capsicum, cut into squares
250 g sliced zucchini
1 small eggplant, peeled and cubed
1 teaspoon lemon juice
1 dessertspoon salt-reduced tamari
pepper to taste
a little hot chilli (optional)

1 Gently heat the oil, add the onions and garlic,
   cooking until a light golden brown.
2 Add the remaining ingredients, bring to the boil,
   and simmer gently with the lid on for 15 minutes.

Serve as a sauce over a meat or nut loaf, or with
grilled meat or fish.

Tamarillos (tree tomatoes) (Serves 2)

2 tamarillos
2 cups boiling water
1 dessertspoon honey or rice syrup

1 Soak the tamarillos for about 5 minutes in boiling
   water, then remove the bitter-tasting skins.
2 Slice, and cover with honey or rice syrup.
3 Leave to stand in the fridge.

Serve on cereal or as a dessert.
    Peeled, sliced tamarillos give a tangy, comple-
mentary taste to chicken.

Suggested intake

One or two servings a day of one of the plants in
the potato family.
    Hot chilli should be considered a medicine or
culinary flavouring herb rather than a food. I suggest you have a maximum of one small fresh chilli
a day, or about ¼ teaspoon dried chilli powder.
Do not give to children or frail elderly people.

Summary

I recommend edible foods in the potato family
for their nutritional and therapeutic properties.
Include them regularly in your diet, unless you
are allergic to them.

Sea vegetables

The main sea vegetable
products are nori,
kombu and wakame.
Arame and hijiki are
also available, mainly
from Asian and health
food stores.

Nori is usually sold in the form of paper-like
sheets, and is best known for its use in sushi
dishes. It is derived from species of *Porphyra*.

Kombu is the general name for a type of kelp; the main edible species is *Laminaria*. It is prepared in various ways, and is commonly used as a seasoning or as part of soup stock.

Wakame is produced from *Undaria pinnatifida*, and is popular in Asia as an additive to soups, noodles and rice dishes.

Arame (*Eisenia bicyclis*) and **hijiki** (*Hizikia fusiforme*) are often sold in fine dried strips, which are then soaked in water before adding to salads or cooked dishes. They are quite mild tasting.

Dulse (*Palmaria palmata*, *Alaria esculenta*) is a good source of iron. In common with most sea vegetables the easiest method of use is to cut the dried dulse finely, and add to other foods while they are cooking.

Irish moss (*Chondrus crispus*). The carageenans derived from this are widely used in food processing, cosmetics and some pharmaceuticals.

Rockweeds (species of *Fucus*) are also classified as kelp, and these are the source of kelp tablets.

Giant brown kelps can grow to 70 metres, and have been described as 'sequoia forests beneath the sea'. They are harvested for algin, an emulsifier used in some processed foods.

A number of products derived from seaweeds are used in the food processing industry, and prepared for use in cooking. Agar has a strong gelling effect, and is used in jams and canned meats; it is sold as flakes or powder for culinary use. These types of gelling agents act like pectin; they can also bond with toxic metals such as lead, and help carry them out of the body.

Background

Seaweeds have been found in Asian archaeological sites dating from about 10 000 years ago. From the twelfth century seaweeds were used as agricultural fertilisers, so early farmers must have recognised their nutritional value. Mountain people in Peru and Tibet carried little bags of kelp to help sustain their energy at high altitudes and, presumably, as an iodine supplement.

In Europe, Russia and Asia various seaweeds have a long history of medicinal use.

Edible seaweeds are now in such high demand in Japan that they are being cultivated, and there are many different products on the market in that country.

Australians are only just beginning to eat sea vegetables. Be on the lookout for Tasmanian products now available in some forms, as these are presumably much less polluted than those from overseas.

Specific health benefits

A Japanese study showed that eating a seaweed extract significantly increases intestinal levels of bifidobacteria.[76] Bifidobacteria are 'friendly' bacteria necessary for intestinal health.

The cancer protective role of edible seaweeds has been established by a number of animal and laboratory studies.[77] Population surveys confirm that people who habitually eat these foods have a lower incidence of cancer.

People who eat seaweeds regularly also have lower blood fats (including cholesterol), as well as a lower incidence of high blood pressure and atherosclerosis.

Natural therapists sometimes prescribe a herb called bladderwrack (*Fucus vesiculosis*) to treat fluid retention and excess weight.

In addition, sea vegetables contain elements that are antibacterial, antifungal and antiviral.

General health benefits

An important feature of seaweeds is that they contain vitamin B12 (100 g nori contains between 13 and 29 mcg). One study showed that vegans who consumed nori and/or chlorella (a seaweed powder or tablet) had serum vitamin B12 concentrations twice as high as those not using these seaweeds.[78] The only other plant foods that have been independently verified to contain this essential vitamin are mushrooms and tempeh. Vegans and vegetarians who become chronically fatigued should have a blood test to check if they have iron or vitamin B12 deficiencies.

Seaweeds are also a good source of other B vitamins, carotenoids and vitamin C. Nori contains very high levels of beta-carotene. Sea vegetables contain more carotene, thiamine, riboflavin, niacin, pantothenic acid, pyridoxine, folic acid, vitamin B12 and vitamin C than any land vegetable or fruit.

Sea vegetables are rich in minerals, notably iodine and potassium. All seaweeds have a very high calcium content, especially hijiki, wakame, arame and kombu. In fact, they have a higher calcium content than any other food, but it is not yet known whether this form of calcium is efficiently absorbed in the body. The iron content is between two to ten times more than that of egg yolks and spinach. Overall, sea plants contain ten to twenty times the mineral content of land plants, which is hardly surprising, given that minerals in the soil are constantly being leached out and carried to the ocean.

The carbohydrates in seaweeds are considered to be poorly absorbed in the human digestive tract, and this partly explains why they are considered a diet food. These types of carbohydrate absorb fats in the intestinal tract, and have a gentle laxative effect. Seaweeds are very low in kilojoules. My personal experience is that seaweeds are helpful for digestion.

Although relatively small amounts of seaweeds are consumed, they contain a wide range of amino acids (protein building-blocks). Some are of particular interest. Wakame, for instance, is very high in glycine, so it might be helpful for herpes. Nori is rich in taurine, which is good for the liver, helps control cholesterol and is protective against gallstones.

Japanese people live longer, on average, than any other race. Those that live the longest come from Oki Island, where they eat plain food and the diet is high in soya and sea vegetables. Women who dive in the sea for abalone, sea

urchins and algae often work productively when they are over seventy. Haemorrhagic strokes and high blood pressure are very rare in these areas.

Seaweeds can increase the lifespan of animals with leukaemia. These foods also prevent gastric ulcer and are useful liver tonics.

Cows that graze on sea vegetables are reported to have sleek coats, better general health and produce better quality milk than animals that feed on land products only. Japanese women say that eating seaweeds gives thick, glossy hair, a clear complexion and wrinkle-free skin, and it is not surprising that cosmetic companies around the world are beginning to use seaweeds in their products.

Cautions and adverse effects

- Not all seaweeds are edible. Even if you can definitely identify them, do not eat any unless the area is far away from human habitation and industry, as seaweeds naturally attract heavy metals, such as arsenic.
- People with thyroid problems should not eat sea vegetables or kelp products without the knowledge of their health practitioner, because the very high iodine content of these products may be detrimental to their condition, or affect the medication they have been prescribed. People in Japan who eat *excessive* sea vegetables have an associated higher incidence of what is called 'coast goitre'.[79] You can have goitre (thyroid) problems because of iodine excess or deficiency, which explains why you must be careful with kelp supplementation.
- Seaweed powders are concentrated, and should be used sparingly.

Known therapeutic components

- Fucoidon has the capacity to lower the level of blood fats and reduce blood coagulation, and has antitumour effects.
- Alginates reduce intestinal absorption of

heavy metals, have antitumour effects, lower cholesterol, and lower blood pressure.
- Beta-homobetaine also lowers cholesterol.
- Eicosapentaenoic acid is an essential fatty acid that helps prevent atherosclerosis (clogged arteries).
- Fucosterol prevents thrombosis.
- Beta-sitosterol and other sterols are well recognised as cholesterol lowering agents, and, although seaweeds may not be an effective treatment by themselves because the quantities consumed are relatively small, foods containing these types of plant sterols should be considered helpful support therapy.
- The polysaccharides in green seaweeds assist anticoagulation (reduced clotting of blood).
- Bromophenols have antibiotic and anthelmintic (worm-killing) properties.
- Acrylic acids and tannins are antibacterial.
- Terpenes are antibacterial, and some are antifungal.
- Laminine is the component in kombu that lowers blood pressure.
- Porphyosin (in nori) protects the stomach lining against ulcers.

Seaweed supplements

Kelp and chlorella are available in tablet or powder form. Follow the label dosages.

Do not give these concentrated products to children unless prescribed by a health practitioner.

How to use

Basic instructions are nearly always given on the packaging, but you can adapt these to suit your taste. A few products seem to be a little 'sandy', so I suggest rinsing them thoroughly before use. For those products that have to be presoaked, I recommend that you also use the soaking water because this is rich in minerals. Once the packets are opened, keep the remainder in airtight containers.

I must confess that I found my first seaweed meal difficult, and would not have tried it again had I not been a guest. Now, I really look forward to a few servings a week, and use various types of flakes and powder as seasonings.

People who have developed a taste for seaweeds say that sea vegetables have only a faint flavour if harvested from the sea, immediately washed to remove some of the salt, and eaten straight away. I have not tried this myself, because when I have been in a clean ocean environment I was not confident about my ability to identify edible seaweeds

Kombu stock recipes are given in Japanese cookbooks, but it is more convenient to buy the kombu in powder form and simply add it to vegetable or chicken soups at the end of the cooking time. I cut kombu into strips, and cook them with legumes or rice for flavouring. I remove the strips if I have visitors, but keep them to add to salads or other foods. (I don't waste anything!)

Nori sheets with salmon (my favourite recipe) (Serves 2 as an entree)

1 large fillet Atlantic salmon
juice of 1 lemon
1 dessertspoon salt-reduced tamari
1 pkt nori sushi sheets, cut into segments about 5 cm x 18 cm
1 cup hot or cold cooked rice or barley (I prefer black glutinous rice for this recipe)

1 Preheat the oven to 180°C.
2 Place the salmon in a baking dish, and sprinkle with the lemon juice and tamari.
3 Cover, and bake for 20–30 minutes (depending on how well cooked you prefer your fish).
4 Carefully remove all the bones, flake the fish with a fork onto a dish, and add the sauce from the baking dish.

Serve the plain cooked rice or barley in another dish.

Each person can then make their own sushi by placing about 2 teaspoons each of fish and rice at one end of a nori sheet, and rolling it up.

You can adapt this recipe to incorporate many different soft foods. See Japanese cookbooks for more elaborate recipes.

Suggested intake

I suggest you have two servings a week — perhaps 2–3 sheets sushi nori each serving or 4–6 strips dried seaweeds in soups or other dishes. If you are a vegan, use twice these quantities. Give children proportionately less according to age (see pp. 4–5).

For seaweed powders use about 1 teaspoon per serving.

Summary

Sea vegetables are a valuable, underutilised food, and guaranteed 'clean' products would be a particularly valuable addition to your diet.

In conclusion

There is no doubt that fruits and vegetables are health enhancing. A scientific review of 206 human surveys and 22 animal studies showed that there is a protective effect against cancer from eating raw vegetables, the garlic family of plants (including onions, chives and leeks), carrots, green vegetables, the cabbage family (including broccoli and cauliflower) and tomatoes. Vegetables and fruits are also beneficial against cardiovascular disease, diabetes, stroke, obesity, diverticulosis and cataracts.[80]

Components in fruit and vegetables are able to reduce cancer and other degenerative diseases in various ways. They can

- act as antioxidants
- increase the activity of enzymes that detoxify carcinogens
- block the formation of cancer-causing substances, such as nitrosamines
- beneficially affect hormone metabolism
- decrease abnormal cell multiplication
- maintain a healthy intestinal environment
- enhance DNA repair and functioning
- improve circulation, skin and organ functioning.

Basic vegetable recipes

A real salad

a selection of grated raw vegetables (beetroot, carrot, celeriac, fennel root, kohlrabi and cucumber)
pumpkin seeds or cashews
mixed sprouts
mushrooms, finely chopped
mixed fresh herbs (such as rocket, parsley, chives, sweet basil and mints)
tomato
avocado
grated soya cheese

SALAD DRESSING
herbal balsamic vinegar
a small quantity of salt-reduced tamari

OTHER OPTIONAL EXTRAS
cold, cooked wild rice or chick peas (after cooking, the chick peas are tastier if they are roasted in the oven with a little olive oil and salt-reduced tamari)
finely chopped cabbage (this is better prepared at least 30 minutes in advance of the meal, and sprinkled with a little lemon juice or vinegar to help with digestion)
cold, cooked cauliflower or broccoli (these are too hard to digest raw)
cold, cooked broad beans or green beans
bite-size pieces of cold, cooked soya burgers
cold hard-boiled eggs
cold, cooked fish

This makes a chewy, filling salad, rather than just boring lettuce leaves, tomato and cucumber with an oily dressing. I don't feel that a salad is successful unless it contains about twenty ingredients!

An interesting way of using lettuce leaves is to serve them whole at the table, and let each person put hot or cold food in them. It can be somewhat messy, but children sometimes eat salads and other foods if they are given choices. Mignonette and similar types of lettuce are the right size, but you can break Imperial or other types of lettuce into suitable sizes for this purpose.

If you use oils on a salad, add them at the table. Any leftovers should be stored in the fridge for that day only — the combination of plants and oils can cause harmful bacteria to multiply.

Vegetarian crumble (Serves 6)

2 cups water
1 cup pearl barley
1 onion, finely chopped
2 vegetable stock cubes
1 egg, lightly beaten
1 chopped red capsicum
2 cups broccoli, cut into in small segments
1 cup cauliflower, cut into small segments
1 cup sliced baby mushrooms
3 chopped tomatoes
$\frac{1}{2}$ cup chopped fresh herbs — parsley, mint, chives, basil, thyme, oregano (or 1 dessertspoon dried mixed herbs)
1 cup grated soya cheese

TOPPING
2 tablespoons tahini
$\frac{1}{2}$ cup sesame and sunflower seeds
$\frac{1}{2}$ cup walnut pieces
1 dessertspoon finely chopped parsley
1 cup millet meal

1 Preheat the oven to 200°C.
2 Place the water, barley and onion in a large saucepan, bring to the boil, and simmer for 20 minutes. (I like onion well cooked, as it avoids digestive problems!)
3 Mix in the stock cubes, and leave stand for 20 minutes with the lid on.
4 Stir in the egg.
5 Spread the barley and egg mixture evenly over the base of a lightly greased baking dish.
6 Spread the vegetables evenly over the barley.
7 Sprinkle the cheese over the top.

8 Heat the tahini gently, then thoroughly mix in the rest of the topping ingredients. Spread this mixture evenly over the top of the cheese.
9 Bake for 20 minutes.

This recipe is quite rich, so is best served with something plain, such as steamed or grilled fish.

How to increase your fruit and vegetable intake

1 In summer, cut salad vegetables into bite-size pieces, sprinkle with lemon juice and herbs, and keep in a container for snacks. You can also use them as entrees, so that you are less likely to fill up on unhealthy foods. In winter indulge in vegetable soups.

2 Eat more international dishes, such as stir-fries, curries and pasta. Modify some by using less oil, and substituting wholegrain pasta.

3 Each week have at least a few vegetarian meals using whole grains and legumes, instead of meat, cheese and eggs.

4 Include a piece of fruit with your breakfast, and eat pieces of fruit as snacks. Try chilled melon as an entree.

   In summer, chill bite-size pieces of fruit for children. They are more likely to eat wedges of peeled oranges or other fruit than if they have to prepare it themselves.

   In winter, make hot fruit desserts, for example, baked apples.

5 Substitute dried fruit for confectionery, or make your own sweets and biscuits with generous portions of dried fruit.

6 Instead of soft drinks, buy fruit or vegetable juices. Make ice blocks of fruit juices to add to water.

7 Aim to buy one new fruit or vegetable each week.

8 Be creative with salad and vegetable dishes.

The downside of fruits and vegetables

Pesticide residues and other harmful chemicals are found in most foods. These are offset to a large extent by the beneficial natural components in plants. However, I recommend that you wash or peel all fruits and vegetables to remove at least some of the residues. Unfortunately, other residues are systemic (they penetrate inside the plant).

Examples of residues found in common foods*

	No. of different pesticide residues found in a particular food	Total quantity of those residues (mg per kg)
Apples	13	2.83
Bean, green	9	9.32
Capsicum	15	2.09
Celery	11	2.12
Grapes	8	2.83
Lettuce	12	11.29
Peaches	13	6.96

* These figures are from *The 1994 Australian Market Basket Survey* (AGPS, Canberra).

To avoid harmful residues and contaminants in foods, I recommend that you:

1 Buy organic fruit, vegetables and other foods if you can afford it.
2 Avoid processed foods and drinks as far as practicable.
3 Grow some of your own food.
4 Drink filtered water.

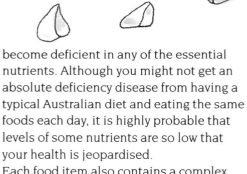

CHAPTER 2

Six super grains, legumes and seeds

- Buckwheat
- Lentils
- Linseed
- Millet
- Rice
- Soya beans

This is my selection of the six best foods in this category. Other highly recommended foods in this group include amaranth, barley, beans, chick peas, cornmeal, oats, rye, and sunflower and pumpkin seeds. I do not recommend refined grains.

What's wrong with wheat?

Wholegrain wheat is a valuable food. However:
- Some people consume it excessively. For example, it is very easy to have wheat cereal or toast for breakfast; sandwiches for lunch, pasta for dinner, plus biscuits for morning and afternoon tea. Perhaps this is why the number of people I treat who are allergic or sensitive to wheat is increasing.
- Wheat is the Western world's largest mono crop. Mono crops tend to require large quantities of fertilisers, pesticides, weedicides and chemicals used for post-harvest storage. Some sensitivity reactions may relate more to the chemicals than to the grain itself.
- Each food item has its own unique and extensive range of nutrients. If you eat a variety of foods, you are less likely to

become deficient in any of the essential nutrients. Although you might not get an absolute deficiency disease from having a typical Australian diet and eating the same foods each day, it is highly probable that levels of some nutrients are so low that your health is jeopardised.
- Each food item also contains a complex mix of various natural plant chemicals.
- If you develop a sensitivity to wheat, it is extremely difficult to switch over to other foods if you have built your diet around that one food. A few of my patients have become very frustrated when I have suggested that they go off all wheat products for three weeks to see if their health problem markedly improves by the end of that time.
- Although wheat fibre (bran) added into a typical Australian diet may help prevent constipation in some, it it often causes gas and does not alleviate the constipation. Wheat bran is water insoluble, reduces the uptake

of minerals in the digestive tract, and interferes with other beneficial plant components.[1] In addition, the bran contains a very high level of chemical residues that the body may not handle well, especially if your diet is poor. Unless you have an allergy or a sensitivity problem, whole wheat is a recommended food as long as you do not consume it excessively. It is delicious sprouted.

Many Australian speciality food stores and supermarkets now sell pasta made from vegetables or various grains and legumes. It is becoming easier to buy non-wheat cereals and breads. Many other carbohydrate foods are available, such as potatoes, rice and legumes. In normal circumstances you should not rely on only one food.

Whole grains versus refined products

Many of the forty-five essential nutrients contained in grains are markedly reduced when they are refined. Although a few of the nutrients (for example, thiamine, riboflavin, niacin and iron) are sometimes replaced in processed foods, this does not compensate for the decreases in almost *all* the essential nutrients, as you will see from the examples in the table.

When you eat any whole grain, you are getting more vitamins and minerals than found in refined (milled) grains. The nutritional differences depend on the degree of milling. For example, in very refined rice the mineral content may be reduced to 23 per cent of the levels in brown rice. Rough rice contains 12 g fibre, brown rice 0.9 g, and milled rice 0.1 g.[2] However, there are other factors that should be considered:

- If you eat refined grains, although they have lower levels of vitamins and minerals the minerals are absorbed more effectively.

Key nutrients in wheat (per 100 g)		
Nutrient	**Wholemeal flour**	**White flour**
Thiamine	510.00 mcg	220.00 mcg
Riboflavin	0.09 mg	0.05 mg
Niacin	4.10 mg	1.30 mg
Pyridoxine	0.50 mg	0.15 mg
Vitamin E	1.00 IU	0
Calcium	0.37 mg	0.20 mg
Iron	3.20 mg	1.40 mg
Potassium	370.00 mg	90.00 mg
Fibre	9.60 g	3.40 g

- Refined grains can be stored for longer than whole grains.
- Refined grains contain less fibre. Fibre is important for preventing constipation, and fibre-rich diets are associated with a lower incidence of obesity and degenerative diseases.
- Whole grains have higher levels of vitamins and minerals, but they also contain phytate, which reduces the absorption of minerals. Short-term studies do not reflect the full picture of phytate, because initially there is a high degree of interference with mineral absorption. However, the body adapts with time, and mineral absorption improves.
- Phytate is only a problem if you are not eating a varied diet.
- Some researchers now believe that phytate has the capacity to reduce free radical activity and tumour growth.[3] In other words, this compound, which most nutritionists have been telling us is harmful, may actually be a cancer preventive.
- The fibre part of whole grains contains lignans, which have a beneficial role in male and female hormone metabolism, as well as cancer preventive properties. I discuss lignans in detail under **Linseed** in this chapter. The outer fibrous layers of grains also contain potentially beneficial phenolic compounds, phyto-oestrogens and antioxidants.

- Population studies support the contention that whole grains are protective against cancers and cardiovascular disease.[4] Now all we need is a major effort to reduce the chemicals used on most grain crops.
- A few people with diverticular disease and diarrhoea may not be able to tolerate whole grains, although it is worth trying the grains in finely powdered form.

To sum up, whole grains (and whole foods generally) have more advantages. People on a poor diet who simply add a fibre supplement may avoid constipation, but they will not otherwise improve their health status.

If you are changing to whole grains, I suggest that you do this slowly to allow your digestive system time to adapt. You may also need to chew your food more thoroughly. Food is absorbed in microscopic fragments (molecules), so if you see hunks of recognisable foods in your bowel motions you are not effectively absorbing nutrients. Some foods, such as the outer part of corn and seeds, are not absorbable but you should chew them sufficiently to release the inner portion.

Vegetarians and food combining

Legumes, eggs and dairy products are the main alternatives to meat for vegetarians. A good vegetarian diet can provide all the essential nutrients, as well as lowering the incidence of most of the major degenerative diseases, including cancer, diabetes, heart and circulatory diseases.

Vegans, who do not eat eggs or dairy products, run the risk of becoming deficient in vitamin B12. All categories of vegetarians are at risk of being somewhat deficient in protein and other nutrients if they do not eat a varied diet. I use food combining to ensure that I get enough protein.

Protein is made up of amino acids, many of which are manufactured by your body. However, there are nine essential amino acids (see the Glossary). In this context 'essential' means that you have to eat these components because they are not made by your body. Furthermore, in order for these essential amino acids to be efficiently used in your body, *they must be combined in one meal*. Some groups of plant foods, such as legumes and grains, are relatively low in the amino acid methionine, whereas this is more abundant in brazil nuts, pumpkin seeds, other seeds and nuts. Grains are relatively low in lysine, but lentils have a higher level. Therefore, if you make, say, a barley and lentil curry and serve it with yoghurt, plus a side salad with a handful of pumpkin seeds mixed through it, your body is able to produce more utilisable protein than if you had eaten barley for breakfast and lentils for dinner. The main groups of foods that have this complementary effect are

- grains and legumes
- grains and dairy foods
- seeds and legumes.[5]

This type of food combining is important only for vegetarians.

Other types of faddish food combining that advise you to eat only, say, fruit in one meal simply do not make sense.

In recipes many grains can be fully or partially substituted for each other. I often use pearl barley instead of rice, or use cornmeal to thicken a bean casserole. When I make bread or muffins, I commonly use about five types of flour, but this makes the foods much 'heavier' because the gluten in wheat flour acts to lighten the dough. You could also partially substitute flours made from legumes for wheat flour, especially if you are vegetarian.

Weight problems

You need food to keep your energy level high. If your energy level is not good, your metabolism slows down. When your metabolism slows down, you put on weight and/or get tired; fatigue then lowers your resistance to disease. However, not all of us are meant to be reed-slim.

Example of a protein-rich hot vegetarian meal	Example of a protein-rich cold vegetarian meal
ENTREE **Corn** on the cob.	**ENTREE** Nori with cold savoury **rice**.
MAIN COURSE **Barley** and **lentil** curry. *Optional:* Add coconut milk, sultanas and various vegetables. Top with plain, low-fat **yoghurt** and finely chopped chives. Serve with broccoli and carrots.	**MAIN COURSE** Mixed salad with herbs, **pumpkin seeds** and mushrooms. *Optional:* Avocado or **yoghurt** dressing; **rye** biscuits with dairy or **soya** cheese; or fruit and **yoghurt**.
DESSERT Baked apple, stuffed with chopped **walnuts** and dates.	

(The main protein foods are indicated in **bold type**.)

Basically, *you should be able to eat as much as you like* (varied, whole foods spread over three meals a day), but not necessarily what you like. If you eat for emotional reasons, find non-food ways for consolation and celebration.

Buckwheat
(*Fagopyrum esculentum*, the main species of edible buckwheat))

Although many people think buckwheat is a type of wheat, it is a shrub in the Polygonaceae family that produces grain-like, triangular seeds that are chewable — once the outer fibrous shell is removed. Sometimes buckwheat is called kasha, although this is really the name of a particular buckwheat recipe.

Background

The buckwheat plant originated in Asia. It was being cultivated in Eastern Europe by the four-teenth century, and became a basic food item in Poland and Russia.

Specific health benefits

Aside from its use as a carbohydrate food, buckwheat is a rich source of rutin, quercetin and other flavonoids. Naturopaths use it as part of the treatment for all conditions related to weak blood vessels, including haemorrhoids, varicose veins, chilblains and bruising. It is recommended as an adjunct remedy for hypertension, and for helping weak eyes and connective tissues.

As flavonoids have anti-inflammatory activity and strengthen blood vessel walls, buckwheat should be a useful adjunct in conditions such as lymphoedema (fluid retention that sometimes occurs following surgery and radiation cancer treatments). One study showed that for patients with varicose veins who drank buckwheat tea this reduced the accompanying fluid.[6] However, I do not recommend buckwheat tea because you would obtain more of the therapeutic components from eating buckwheat as a food.

Animal studies show that buckwheat is more effective than soya beans for lowering LDL cholesterol.[7]

General health benefits

Buckwheat does not contain gluten because it comes from a shrub. It is therefore a suitable wheat substitute for people with coeliac disease or grain sensitivities.

Buckwheat is relatively high in the amino acid lysine; when this is combined with grains, more effective protein utilisation takes place in the body.

Key nutrients in buckwheat (per 100 g)	
Protein	11.7 g
Fat	2.4 g
Fibre	9.9 g
Calcium	114.0 mg
Magnesium	252.8 mg
Iron	3.1 mg
Niacin	4.4 mg

Laboratory experiments suggest that some buckwheat components have effects on enzymes that relate to growth factors; they are potentially useful for reducing some forms of tumour, psoriasis, atherosclerosis and inflammatory conditions.[8] Although this may or may not be proven in the human body, no one has suggested that these types of advantages are possible with wheat, so here is yet another reason to diversify your diet.

Cautions and adverse effects

- Although suggested as a flour substitute, buckwheat does not contain gluten, and therefore cannot be totally substituted in recipes such as scones, unless you like really heavy foods.
- Buckwheat is bland tasting, and is best cooked with flavoursome ingredients.

Known therapeutic components

- Buckwheat has been used naturopathically for centuries — between 3–8 per cent of its total weight is rutin, a flavonoid that helps strengthen blood vessels.
- When you cook buckwheat, you will see that it turns slightly pink. This is due to a mixture of pigments known as fagopyrins, and there is some evidence that these may be potentially useful as anticancer compounds.[9]

Growing your own buckwheat

Although buckwheat grows quite easily as a shrub, without special equipment you will find it difficult to remove the dark-coloured fibrous husk surrounding the seeds.

How to use

Buckwheat seeds can be milled into flour, or the seed cracked to make 'groats'. The taste is mild, and the seeds or groats are tastier when lightly roasted.

The flour is often used to make pancakes, and it can partially replace wheat flour in most recipes, especially to increase protein utilisation in the body. You can also use it as a thickening agent in casseroles and savoury dishes.

Buckwheat porridge (Serves 2)

$1/2$ cup buckwheat groats
1 cup water
1 peeled and grated (or finely diced) apple
handful of raisins

1 Place all the ingredients in a saucepan, and bring to the boil.
2 Simmer for a few minutes; then stir.
3 Turn off the heat, and leave to stand with the lid on for 5–10 minutes.

Serve with a light sprinkle of cinnamon, and yoghurt.

Buckwheat muffins (Makes 12 small muffins)

1 cup buckwheat flour
$1/2$ cup self-raising wholemeal wheat flour
$1/2$ cup sesame or sunflower seeds

½ cup sultanas
½ cup walnut pieces
1 dessertspoon olive oil
1 cup soya milk
1 green apple, peeled and grated
1 teaspoon cinnamon

1 Preheat the oven to 200°C.
2 Combine all the dry ingredients.
3 Add the soya milk, and mix thoroughly.
4 Spoon the mixture into well-greased muffins tins.
   (As most muffins are quite 'heavy' it is better not
   to make them too large.)
5 Sprinkle the apple and cinnamon over the tops.
6 Bake for 20 minutes at 200°C, then for
   10 minutes at 180°C.

Buckwheat banana pancakes (Serves 2)

¼ cup buckwheat flour
2 eggs
¾ cup soya milk
1 tablespoon lemon juice
1 small ripe banana

SUGGESTED TOPPINGS
½ cup berries or grated apple lightly cooked in
   1 tablespoon concentrated apple or pear juice
or ½ cup maple or rice syrup, or honey
or your favourite jam

1 Blend the ingredients to a smooth batter.
2 Cover, and leave to stand for 30 minutes.
3 Pour 2–3 tablespoon of batter onto a heated and
   lightly greased griddle or heavy pan.
4 Cook the pancake until light brown underneath,
   then turn it over and brown the other side.
5 Fold, and serve with the topping of your choice.

You can use buckwheat seeds as thickeners, although
they need at least 5 minutes' cooking time. I use
them as nut substitutes in biscuits, and also add
them to rissoles, stuffings and other savoury dishes.
If you make bread, add them at the end of the
kneading process to give your bread a very crunchy
crust.

   Commercial buckwheat biscuits, noodles and pasta
are available.

Suggested intake

For therapeutic purposes, I suggest a serving of
about 1 cup cooked buckwheat every second
day; otherwise have a few servings each week.

   Serve children proportionately less according to age (see pp. 4–5).

Summary

Buckwheat is a gluten-free grain substitute that
is therapeutically useful for high cholesterol,
and for circulatory and connective tissue weaknesses.

Lentils (*Lens culinaris*)

Lentils are in the
legume family, and all
produce pods. They
come in different
colours: brown,
yellow or red. Edible
plants in this family,
which includes peas, beans, chick peas and
fenugreek, are often referred to as pulses.

Background

Remnants of lentils were found in Turkey,
together with the remains of sickles and
pounders, from a site dated at about 5500 BC.
They were a common food of the ancient
Greeks, Jews, Egyptians and Romans. The
preparation of lentil soup is depicted in a fresco
of the time of Ramesis II of Egypt. Red lentil
broth is mentioned in chapter 25 of the Book of
Genesis.

   Although esteemed highly by the ancient
Egyptians and extensively cultivated, lentils
and other legumes have been somewhat dis-
paragingly classified as 'poor man's meat'. In
India lentils have a long history, and are

commonly served as dahl to accompany rice. The old Greek saying, 'Now he doesn't like lentils any more', implies that when people become wealthy they prefer to eat meat. The trouble is that when people become wealthier they do not necessarily become healthier.

Specific health benefits

It is well established that legumes lower LDL cholesterol (the most harmful cholesterol). They also favourably influence the body's fat metabolism in a way that is preventive against heart disease.

Lentils and other legumes are being increasingly recommended because their phyto-oestrogens help to balance oestrogens in the body and to reduce menopausal symptoms. The overall hormonal effect is to reduce the likelihood of hormone dependent cancers such as breast and prostate.

No one can give you a guarantee that if you eat lentils regularly you will not get cancer or heart disease, but there is now abundant evidence that legumes are one of the food groups that will reduce your risk of these diseases.

General health benefits

In common with other pulses, lentils are a recommended food for vegetarians because they are low in fat and provide a reasonable source of protein, fibre and other nutrients. When the brown lentils are cooked they resemble cooked beef mince, which also makes them ideal meat extenders.

Cautions and adverse effects

- Lentils are the easiest of the dried legumes to digest. However, all legumes need to be soaked in water and cooked until really soft to reduce the components in them that are antinutrients or indigestible.[10]
- If you are not used to eating legumes, it

Key nutrients in dried, boiled lentils (per 100 g)	
Protein	6.8 g
Fat	0.4 g
Cholesterol	0
Carbohydrate	9.5 g
Sodium	8.0 mg
Potassium	220.0 mg
Calcium	17.0 mg
Magnesium	25.0 mg
Iron	2.0 mg
Zinc	0.9 mg
Thiamine	0.08 mg
Riboflavin	0.06 mg
Niacin equivalents	1.80 mg
Retinol equivalents (vitamin A)	1.00 mcg

takes at least four weeks for your digestion to adjust, so start with small servings. Most people can handle the quantities that would be used in soups.
- As lentils and other legumes shunt cholesterol into bile, which then has to be excreted through the gallbladder, it may not be advisable to eat legumes regularly if you are at risk of developing gallstones or have a current gallstone problem.
- Lentils do not contain vitamin C unless you sprout them. Sprouting also makes them more digestible and improves the flavour.

Known therapeutic components

- Lentils contain all the essential amino acids (the necessary building blocks for the body to make protein), although methionine is low.[11]
- The fibre content is about 4 per cent and insoluble.
- Isoflavones and lignans are overwhelmingly acknowledged as having benefits for hormone metabolism, and are particularly recommended for menopausal women and to prevent prostate problems. As you will see

under **Soya beans** in this chapter, these plant compounds have cardiovascular benefits and are a cancer preventive.
- The types of phytosterols (hormone-like substances) in legumes have beneficial effects on the metabolism of blood fats.

Growing your own lentils

It is not feasible to grow lentils in a domestic garden because they are so slow to mature, and the crop is relatively small.

Lentils are excellent sprouted; this reduces the cooking time.

How to use

Basic cooking method (Serves 6)

1 Soak 2 cups lentils overnight in 3 cups water.
2 Strain, discarding the soaking water.
3 Wash the lentils in a fine sieve.
4 Place the lentils in a further 2 cups water and bring to the boil; simmer for 1 hour.
5 Add seasonings, and leave to stand with the lid on for 10 minutes.

Note: If you are using a microwave oven or pressure cooker, adapt the cooking times to suit. My experience is that legumes usually need a longer cooking time than specified in most recipe books.

Once you are used to eating legumes, do not discard the soaking water.

Precooked plain lentils can be added to many savoury dishes, such as rissoles, casseroles and meat loaves. This is an ideal way of introducing legumes to the family.

Easy lentil and barley curry (Serves 8)

2 cups brown or red lentils
4 cups water
2 cups whole or pearl barley
2 onions, finely chopped
4 cups water or stock (or add 2 vegetable stock cubes to the water)
curry paste or powder (to taste, and how hot you want it to be) (a home-made curry formula is given under **Turmeric** in chapter 3)

1 Soak the lentils overnight in 4 cups of water.
2 Drain the lentils, and place in a saucepan; add the barley and onions, plus the remaining water or stock.
3 Bring to the boil, and simmer for about 1 hour. If you use a pressure cooker or microwave oven, reduce the cooking time by half. If you use pearl barley, add halfway through the cooking time.
4 Stir in the curry paste, and simmer for a few minutes.

OPTIONAL EXTRAS
coconut cream, sultanas, tomatoes, fresh or dried herbs; you could add vegetables near the end of the cooking time.

Serve with a topping of plain yoghurt and chives, together with separately cooked vegetables such as carrots and broccoli.

Freeze any leftovers for later use. I spread this curry hot or cold on toast or in a sandwich, because it is moist and does not require butter or margarine.

For a good vegetarian topping for pasta, substitute a generous quantity of juiced tomatoes for the curry paste.

Suggested intake

Cholesterol-lowering effects are achieved on 33–100 g dried legumes daily. In a healthy diet you would be eating other foods that contribute to beneficial levels of blood fat; for this reason I recommend an intake of about 1 cup cooked legumes every second day, proportionately less for children according to age (see pp. 4–5).

Summary

In common with all legumes, lentils are a healthy vegetarian food and a meat extender.

Other legumes

Dried beans and chick peas

These legumes can be used in similar ways to lentils, although they need a somewhat longer cooking time. I pre-soak and cook chick peas until soft; then roast them in a baking dish with a little olive oil and salt-reduced tamari. I serve them cold as snacks, or added to salads.

Linseed *(Linum usitatissimum)*

Linseed is in the Linaceae family, and is not a legume. It is also known as flaxseed.

Background

Linseed was originally grown in Egypt and the Middle East for the leaves that were used to make linen. Ancient Egyptians and Cherokee Indians valued linseed as a food for its nourishing and healing properties. European herbalists still use it hot as an external healing poultice. Modern science has widened its use, and we now know that its oil content and a special class of compounds known as lignans have specific beneficial effects in the body.

Specific health benefits

Linseed oil is a good source of omega-3 fatty acids, with lesser quantities of omega-6. These omega-3 oils are helpful in treating arthritis, premenstrual syndrome, fatigue, eczema and other skin conditions, as well as heart disease and lipid (fat) metabolism. In one study linseed oil, compared to sunflower oil, reduced blood stickiness.[12]

Linseed meal is one of the healthiest rem-edies for constipation. You could use the whole seeds for a laxative effect in foods or drinks, but they are difficult to chew and not very palatable taken this way. Rather than using the seeds as roughage, I suggest that you grind the seeds in a blender so that the valuable components can be more readily absorbed, or buy the seeds already ground and sold as linseed meal.

Lignans in linseed are helpful for menopause symptoms because they have oestrogenic effects. Lignan-rich foods are also recommended as part of the treatment of pre-menstrual symptoms for their oestrogen-balancing effects.

It is important to note that these plant oestrogens (phyto-oestrogens) are not like your body's own hormones. Human tests indicate that women who have high levels of lignan breakdown products in their urine have the lowest incidence of breast cancer. Animal studies support this finding, and confirm that linseed suppresses the initiation and growing phases of breast cancer.[13]

For hormone dependent cancers it seems rational to recommend linseed as a preventive food and as support in cancer treatment, because these types of plant lignans have been shown to be effective, not only in animal trials but also in laboratory studies and in dietary surveys.

General health benefits

Because of its antioxidant properties, linseed is one of the foods that is likely to improve your overall health status and wellbeing.

The types of oils found in linseed also have a tendency to increase metabolic rate and to improve immune functioning.

Children with behavioural problems and attention deficit disorder tend to have lower levels of omega-3 fatty acids, so adding the oil or linseed meal to their diets may help reduce the problem.

Cautions and adverse effects

- Linseed oil that is prepared for treating timber is *not* edible.
- The edible oil should be purchased in small, dark-coloured bottles, and stored in the fridge so that it does not become rancid.
- If the oil is heated, it loses most of its therapeutic value.

Known therapeutic components

- Linseed is the richest known source of unsaturated alpha-linolenic acid (one of the omega-3 fatty acids) necessary for physical health but lacking in many foods that most people eat regularly. Omega-3 fatty acids are compounds, also found in oily fish, that are now considered to be protective against many common degenerative diseases. These fatty acids are anti-inflammatory and help modulate a number of metabolic processes in the body. It is estimated that a typical Australian diet contains about twenty times more omega-6 oil than omega-3, and that our ancestral diet had these oils in equal proportions.
- Fresh, unrefined linseed oil contains lecithin and other phospholipids that help emulsify fats and oils in the body, therefore helping with their digestion. It also contains carotene and vitamin E, which are necessary to preserve the oil in both the bottle and the body.
- The mucilage (gel-like) content of linseed is about 12 per cent. Linseed is a non-irritant laxative because it swells to about twenty times its dry weight, is soft and slippery, and soothes the intestines. In addition, mucilage buffers excess acid, so it may help inflammatory conditions of the digestive tract, including ulcers. It also increases the amount of cholesterol excreted, and helps to stabilise intestinal bacteria.
- A special category of lignans was discovered in 1980, and linseed is by far the best source of these valuable plant compounds. The lignans found in linseed have antiviral, antifungal and anticancer properties. In the intestines they are converted to hormone-like compounds (phyto-oestrogens) that have some of the benefits of human oestrogens, but without the abnormal cell growth effects. These lignans are mainly concentrated in the outer layer of the plant, which means that the oil contains less of them. The most remarkable feature of these types of lignans is that they have the capacity to balance oestrogens in the body, and numerous scientific studies give weight to their protective role in breast, prostate and colon cancer.[14]

The way plant hormones can act as oestrogen balancers is described under **Soya beans** in this chapter.

Growing your own linseed

It is not feasible to grow your own linseed in a domestic garden because relatively few seeds are produced on each plant, and it is very time-consuming to separate the seeds. Although these types of oily seeds can be sprouted, I do not find them very palatable.

How to use

The healthiest option is to buy organic linseeds, and grind into a meal as required. Linseed grinds down easily in a coffee grinder or blender. Once ground, the oils in linseed tend to become rancid quite quickly. However, I often buy linseed meal and have not noted any signs of rancidity; I get small quantities at a time, store it in the fridge in an airtight container, and use it quickly.

The easiest way is to buy commercial bread or biscuits containing linseed, as many of these are now available.

Linseed oil

Along with virgin olive oil, linseed oil is recommended as a dietary oil, but if it is heated so that the colour changes you lose the benefits.

Basic salad dressing

QUANTITY PER PERSON
1–2 teaspoons linseed oil
1–2 teaspoons lime or lemon juice
1 teaspoon salt-reduced tamari

OPTIONAL EXTRAS
¼ teaspoon mustard, a little pepper, salt alternatives (such as a pinch of kelp)
a little crushed garlic
finely chopped herbs (chives, thyme, sage, oregano, basil, mint, rocket) — although I prefer to use green herbs somewhat more generously in the salad vegetables rather than a tiny quantity in a dressing.

Lignan-rich vegetarian loaf recipe (Serves 8)

2 cups water
1 onion, finely chopped
1 cup linseeds   ⎤ (For this recipe I blend
1 cup pumpkin seeds ⎦ these seeds)
1 or 2 vegetable stock cubes
1 cup corn kernels
1 cup peas
1 cup sunflower seeds
1 cup plain wholemeal rye flour
1 cup grated raw carrot
1 cup finely chopped green herbs (parsley, chives, basil, rocket, oregano, fennel, etc.), or
    1 dessertspoon mixed dried herbs
1 teaspoon ginger powder, or 1 dessertspoon grated raw ginger root
1 teaspoon turmeric powder
4 eggs, lightly beaten
3 tablespoons sesame or caraway seeds

SAUCE
1 dessertspoon linseed oil
1 large onion, very finely chopped
2 large tomatoes, finely chopped
1 tablespoon finely chopped fresh chives or basil
2 tablespoons finely chopped mushrooms
1 tablespoon salt-reduced tamari
½ cup water

1 Preheat the oven to 180°C.
2 Place the onion and water in a large saucepan, bring to the boil, and simmer for 5 minutes.
3 Add the corn, peas and stock cube; stir, then turn off the heat.
4 Mix in all the other ingredients (except the sesame or caraway seeds).
5 Pour the mixture into a greased baking dish or a pie dish with a capacity of at least 2 litres.
6 Form the top into a loaf-like shape, and sprinkle the sesame or caraway seeds over the top.
7 Bake for 40 minutes.

To prepare the sauce:
8 Heat the oil gently, and add the onion. Cook until the onion is a light golden-brown.
9 Add the remaining ingredients, and bring to the boil.
10 Simmer for 5 minutes.

Serve the loaf hot, sliced, with the sauce.

Optional flavourings: a little chilli, and/or
    1–2 crushed garlic cloves.
Variations: 1 cup of sliced brazil nuts (especially recommended for vegetarians because these nuts are rich in methionine, an amino acid that is relatively low in a typical vegetarian diet), or
    1 cup cooked, mashed chick peas or kidney beans. Vary the ingredients according to your taste, and what is available.

The seeds and rye flour provide most of the lignans; they are also high in kilojoules (as are all nuts, seeds and oily foods), so I would use a recipe like this about once a month.

Freeze any leftovers; they can be served later, reheated with a fresh sauce.

Try this loaf cold with a salad, or broken up into bite-size pieces and added to a mixed salad.

Suggested intake

I recommend about 10–20 g linseeds or linseed meal every second day.

Linseed oil is high in kilojoules, so use no more than 1–2 teaspoons daily.

Young children can choke on seeds. Give linseed meal or ground seeds proportionately according to age (see pp. 4–5).

Summary

Make linseed a regular part of your diet because it helps balance the body's oestrogens, probably helps prevent cancer, maintains healthy intestines and a healthy skin, improves blood flow and blood lipid levels, and may even strengthen emotional wellbeing and resistance to infections.

Other plants containing beneficial plant lignans

Pumpkin, sunflower and similar seeds
Legumes (beans, peas, etc.)
Black tea
Whole grains
Berries
Cabbage family, carrots, garlic

Population studies and animal tests indicate that the lignans in these and other foods are important health enhancing components that play a significant role in preventing atherosclerosis and cancer.[15]

Although scientists at this stage are unable to give the precise quantities that are required for prevention of disease, it seems sensible to recommend that you include them in your diet on a regular basis.

Millet

A number of types of millet grow in temperate to tropical regions. The one most commonly grown in Australia is white French millet or proso (*Panicum miliaceum*). Compared to other grains, millet is small and round, with an extremely hard outer coat.

Background

This grain probably originated in Africa or the Middle East, although the first known cultivation was in Asia and Eastern Europe. Millet has been used for about 5000 years, and before the introduction of potatoes and corn it was an important carbohydrate food in Europe. It will grow in poor soils, is drought resistant, and is often associated with marginal agricultural lands and lower socioeconomic regions of the world. For millions of people it is a major part of their diet — during times of need people have survived for long periods with millet as their sole food.

Specific health benefits

An important advantage of millet is that it is gluten free.[16] It is therefore an alternative carbohydrate food for people with gluten intolerance (coeliac disease). It is far less likely to cause allergy and sensitivity problems than wheat, and is also relatively easier to digest.

Unlike most grains, millet is not acidic.

General health benefits

Compared with other grains it is relatively high in iron and a good source of the B vitamins (except vitamin B12). Millet is superior to wheat, rice and corn in protein quality, although it is somewhat low in lysine, an essential amino acid. This could be offset by having it in the same meal with legumes, fish or dairy foods.

Millet is actually reputed to be alkaline residue in the body, and may be an ideal food for people with arthritis. Apparently Russian athletes use millet as an energy food because it reduces lactic acid levels in the body — lactic acid is produced following vigorous exercise; it causes the muscle soreness and pain you would have experienced following unusual or strenuous activities.

Cautions and adverse effects

- Although millet does not contain gluten, people with coeliac disease are sometimes sensitive to it so they should try it cautiously.
- Flour from grains that do not contain gluten does not rise, which is why millet is used to make flat breads and griddle cakes.
- Unhulled millet is virtually impossible to cook, although some recipes suggest roasting it first in a little oil. I've never been able to cook unhulled millet successfully as it maintains its birdseed-like texture. You can sprout unhulled millet for a few days before cooking it — sprouting puts vitamin C into grains and legumes.

Known therapeutic components

Millet contains catechin tannins — useful antioxidants.

Growing your own millet

In common with all grains, it is not feasible to grow millet in a domestic backyard because of the space required to produce a useful quantity, and the time it takes to produce the seeds.

How to use

Millet is available as a grain, a flour, ground to a meal, and as a pasta.

Basic recipe for plain millet grain
(Serves 2–4)

1¾ cups water
1 cup hulled millet

1 Bring the water to the boil, and add the millet.

2 Simmer gently for 25 minutes, without stirring. (Check that it is not burning by gently pushing a spoon down to the bottom of the saucepan.)
3 Turn off the heat, and leave to stand with the lid on for 10 minutes.
4 Fluff up the millet with a fork before serving.

Plain millet has a subtle, sweetish flavour. I prefer it served with curried vegetables.

Easy 'pastry treat' (Serves 6)

200 g cream! (this is the 'treat' part) (or yoghurt or coconut cream)
1½ cups plain wholemeal wheat flour
½ cup millet meal (for a mild, nutty flavour)
4 cups fruit or savoury filling of your choice

1 Preheat the oven to 250°C.
2 Mix the cream into the dry ingredients.
3 Knead the mixture, and form into a ball.
4 Sprinkle some millet meal on a flat surface, and roll out the pastry to a circle to fit a 14 cm flan tin.
5 Add the fruit or savoury filling.
6 Knead and roll the offcuts of the pastry, and cut into strips to decorate the top of the filling.
7 Bake for 5 minutes at 250°C, then for 20 minutes at 200°C.

My favourite pastry filling is dried apricots and sultanas soaked in water for a few hours, then heated with just enough added concentrated pear or apple juice to moisten the fruit.

Millet-stuffed pumpkin (Serves 4)

2 small butternut pumpkins, cut in half lengthwise, and deseeded
1 dessertspoon virgin olive oil
1 onion, finely chopped
1 crushed clove garlic
2 cups cooked millet
2 cups sliced baby mushrooms
½ cup grated soya cheese
2 tablespoons finely chopped fresh parsley and chives

2 tablespoons pine nuts or chopped cashews
1 dessertspoon lime or lemon juice
1 dessertspoon salt-reduced tamari
2 litres boiling water

1 Preheat the oven to 200°C.
2 Place the pumpkin halves face down on a lightly greased baking dish, and bake for 20 minutes.
3 Heat the oil gently, and cook the onions and garlic until light golden-brown. Remove from the heat, and add all the other ingredients, mixing well.
4 Turn the pumpkin halves over, and fill with the mixture.
5 Add boiling water to a depth of 2 cm, and bake, uncovered, for 30 minutes.

Millet meal

Millet meal enhances the taste of most recipes that use wheat flour, and is excellent added to muffins, biscuits, and as a partial substitute for wheat in most recipes. You can also use it as a substitute for breadcrumbs in many recipes. Millet and linseed meal can be combined to make porridge, but as it is somewhat gluey you may prefer to add this combination to a barley or oat porridge.

In parts of Africa millet is used to make couscous and unleavened bread, although the bread will not bind unless the millet flour is pre-soaked in hot water.

Suggested intake

About 1–2 cups cooked millet a week, proportionately less for children according to age (see pp. 4–5); and as a partial substitute for wheat flour.

Summary

Millet is a nutritious, gluten-free grain that is a healthy option for people who cannot tolerate wheat.

Barley — a wheat substitute

- Barley is another healthy wheat substitute that is relatively easy to digest. However, it is not gluten free.
- Pearl barley is readily available, and is traditionally used in soups. I prefer whole, organic barley, although this takes longer to cook and is quite 'chewy'. Generally, you can use barley in the same way as rice.

  Make a damper bread with some millet flakes in it, and knead in barley flakes — this makes the exterior very crusty when cooked. Barley flour can be partially substituted for wheat flour in most recipes, or used as a thickening agent. Barley and oat brans in breakfast cereals are helpful for people with sluggish bowels.
- You can sprout whole barley, wheat and other grains. Another option is to sow the whole grains in small trays of soil. Harvest it when the crop ('grass') is about 8 cm high. I chop a handful into salads.

  You can also make these young, green grain shoots into juice. After the first growth is cut you will get another crop, although the second and third batches are not as sweet. (Millet is not successful for this purpose — it is tough, and tastes like grass.)

Rice (*Oryza sativa*)

Rice is now grown in over a hundred countries, and it is estimated that there are about 100 000 varieties of rice. 'Improved' semi-dwarf plant varieties are now commonly cultivated.

Background

Rice has been cultivated in China for about 5000 years, and no doubt before that time people ate wild rice. Rice is popular throughout the world. Many Brazilians, for instance, use rice and beans as their main protein food.

In some Asian cultures rice is a symbol of life and fertility — hence the custom of throwing rice at weddings.

About 2.5 billion people depend on rice as their staple food — in Asia the annual consumption per person is about 85 kg per year, compared to about 4 kg in other countries.

Specific health benefits

Remarkably few people are allergic to rice, so it is a convenient option for many people with grain allergies.

A survey of over 3000 Chinese women showed that eating rice — and fish — reduced the risk of insulin resistance syndrome (a pre-diabetic condition where the body's insulin does not work properly).[17]

Rice bran, and to some extent unrefined rice, lowers cholesterol.

General health benefits

Rice is relatively easy to digest. It is a remarkable food, given that millions of people living in poor conditions manage to live relatively long, healthy lives with rice forming the bulk of their diet.

Cautions and adverse effects

- Rice bran and rice bran oil have higher levels of pesticides and other toxins compared to refined rice. This is because many chemicals are retained in fatty tissues (of plants, and of people), and also because of contamination by surface sprays and environmental toxins. I do not use rice bran oil, and, as far as possible, I buy organic rice products.

- Major crops such as rice and wheat are subjected to heavy pesticide spraying because they attract particular pests and diseases. These crops are often stored for long periods of time in large quantities, so further chemicals are needed to protect them.

Known therapeutic components

- Rice bran has a high content of soluble fibre, in contrast to wheat bran, which contains mainly insoluble fibre. Studies show that rice bran is more effective than wheat bran in improving the function of the intestinal wall and bowel bacterial balance.[18] Generally, I recommend whole grains rather than the isolated fibres, but if you need to take bran for constipation then I recommend organic rice bran should be added to one meal a day only.
- Gamma oryzanol is found in the outer part of rice grain — it is not present in white rice. This component is classed as a phytosterol (a hormone-like substance that occurs in plants); it is antioxidant, antifungal, and reduces the amount of cholesterol produced by the liver.[19]

Key nutrients in rice (per 100 g) *			
Nutrient	**Whole grain**	**White rice**	**Rice bran**
Protein	7.7 g	6.7 g	13.1 g
Fibre	3.5 g	1.5 g	23.0 g
Calcium	30.0 mg	20.0 mg	75.0 mg
Iron	2.7 mg	1.5 mg	25.0 mg
Zinc	1.7 mg	1.4 mg	15.0 mg
Thiamine	4.5 mg	0.06 mg	1.8 mg
Riboflavin	0.09 mg	0.04 mg	0.3 mg
Niacin	0.44 mg	0.19 mg	38.3 mg
Vitamin E	1.7 mg	0.15 mg	9.0 mg

* These are average levels, taken from various authoritative reference texts. Calcium, for instance, can vary from 10 mg to 50 mg per 100 g rice.

- Beneficial lignans are also found in the fibre part of grain, and details about these plant components are given under **Linseed** and **Soya beans** in this chapter. In addition, rice bran contains a form of vitamin E that is a potent antioxidant.

Growing your own rice

This is generally not feasible, but you can sprout whole rice — the sprouts are sweet — and this markedly reduces the cooking time.

How to use

There are many different forms of rice, including basic brown, polished, basmati, or glutinous rice — my favourite is wild rice.

You can also buy rice vinegar, wine, biscuits, noodles, cracker snacks, and various fermented products. Rice syrup is a substitute for sugar and honey.

Basic recipe for cooking wholegrain (brown) rice (Serves 4–6)

2 cups wholegrain rice
4 cups water
1 dessertspoon salt-reduced tamari, shoyu or miso

1 Wash the rice in a sieve, and drain.
2 Put the rice in a large saucepan with the water.
3 Bring to the boil, and simmer with the lid on for about 45 minutes (or until all the water is absorbed).
4 Stir in the tamari, shoyu or miso.
5 Leave to stand with the lid on for a further 5 minutes.

Serve this plain rice with curries, stir-fries or similar foods.

Depending on how you want to use the rice, stir in a little dark sesame oil, herbs or vegetables at the end of the cooking time.

Alternatively, gently fry the raw rice in a little oil, or dry roast it in the oven, and then cook as above, adding herbs, spices and vegetables in the last 15 minutes of cooking time.

Wild rice is cooked in a similar way to whole-grain rice.

White rice needs less cooking time, and most packets have cooking instructions on the label. It is the best form of rice for making dessert dishes. Try the following: mix chopped cashews into the cooked rice, roll the mixture into balls, and pour over them a sauce of strawberries blended with yoghurt or cream.

Cook **sticky white rice**, allow to cool, then mix it with desiccated coconut into balls, chill and serve with segments of rock melon.

Although hot rice puddings are not as popular as they used to be, try baking the rice with soya milk and dried fruit.

Stuffed pawpaw (Serves 2)

In Papua New Guinea pawpaw is cooked before it is ripe, and eaten as a vegetable.

1 medium pawpaw (pale yellow but not soft), peeled, halved and deseeded
2 cups cooked rice and cooked mixed vegetables such as onion, corn and peas
1 teaspoon dried mixed herbs
½ cup coconut cream or yoghurt
2 litres boiling water

1 Preheat the oven to 180°C.
2 Fill the centre of the pawpaw halves with the rice, vegetables and herbs.
3 Pour in the coconut cream or yoghurt (this will prevent the rice and vegetables from drying out).
4 Place in a large baking dish, and add the water to a depth of about 2 cm, and bake for about 30 minutes (or until the pawpaw is soft but not mushy).

Suggested intake

Three or four cups of cooked rice a week; proportionately less for children according to age (see pp. 4–5).

Summary

Rice deserves its popularity because of its nutritional and therapeutic components.

Soya beans (*Glycine max*)

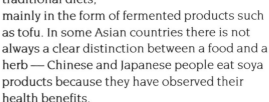

Background

For more than a thousand years Asians have eaten soya beans as the staple food in their traditional diets, mainly in the form of fermented products such as tofu. In some Asian countries there is not always a clear distinction between a food and a herb — Chinese and Japanese people eat soya products because they have observed their health benefits.

Specific health benefits

Oestrogen balancing

Although the phyto-oestrogens in soya beans are much weaker than your body's own hormones, some of these phyto-oestrogenic isoflavones have the capacity to balance oestrogens — they take up some of the absorption sites in the body, thereby crowding out the body's stronger hormones. In other words, when the blood levels of oestrogen are high, these phyto-oestrogens lower the overall oestrogen load in your body.

In other words, plant oestrogens can reduce the body's oestrogens by crowding them out. This is why they can help prevent hormone dependent cancers.

On the other hand, when your body's oestrogens are low, as in menopausal women, phyto-oestrogens are taken up to a certain extent and thereby reduce menopausal symptoms, such as flushing and dryness in the vagina.[20] When your body does not produce much of its own oestrogen, plant oestrogens perform some oestrogen activity but they do not reproduce cells in the same way and to the same extent as natural or pharmaceutical oestrogens.

To sum up, depending on the oestrogen levels in your body, the relatively weak plant oestrogens can lower the overall oestrogen load or produce some types of oestrogenic activity, so they are one of the few known substances that can truly be classed as 'balancing'.

Cholesterol and heart disease

A survey of thirty-eight clinical studies confirmed that consumption of soya protein significantly reduced total serum cholesterol levels by 9.3 per cent, LDL cholesterol by 12.9 per cent, and serum triglyceride levels by 10.5 per cent.[21]

In addition, some of the phyto-oestrogens in soya beans act as antioxidants that protect LDL from oxidising[22] — the body's version of rusting. LDL (low density lipoprotein) is the harmful cholesterol linked to atherosclerosis and other heart diseases.

Some studies show that soya products act as a gentle blood thinner.

Cancer

Japanese people, who regularly include soya products in their diet, have a markedly low incidence of prostate, breast and pancreatic cancers.[23] Of course, traditional Japanese consume very little animal foods, and their diet is high in vegetables and fibre, and low in fat. Vegetarian women also have a lower incidence of breast cancer, and this, too, is linked to the phyto-oestrogens in soya protein and other plant foods. Numerous scientific studies have shown the connection between dietary plant oestrogens and low cancer risk.

Genistein, one of the isoflavonic plant oestrogens, prevents the growth of cancer cells in laboratory studies, and probably has protective effects for hormone-related and other cancers in humans.[24]

Dr H. Adlercreutz is probably the world's leading expert on plant oestrogens. His summary is:

> Our interest has been focused on the cancer-protective role of some hormone-like phyto-oestrogens of dietary origin, the lignans and isoflavonoids. The precursors of the biologically active compounds originate in soybean products as well as whole grain cereals, seeds, probably berries and nuts. The plant lignan and isoflavonoid glycosides are converted by intestinal bacteria to hormone-like compounds with weak oestrogenic and antioxidative activity; they have now been shown to influence not only sex hormone metabolism and biological activity but also intracellular enzymes, protein synthesis, growth factor action, malignant cell proliferation, differentiation and angiogenesis, making them strong candidates for a role as natural cancer protective compounds.[25]

Bone health

A few controlled human studies and animal tests show that soya has the potential to improve bone mineral density.[26] Whether it will be a significant treatment for osteoporosis will not be known until 1999 when long-term trials are completed. In the meantime I consider that soya, along with appropriate mineral supplementation and lifestyle adjustments, warrants a year's trial, and is worth discussing with your health practitioner. I currently use soya to support the main treatment for increasing bone mineral density.

Antioxidant

Fermented soya products such as tofu, tempeh, miso and soya sauces are effective antioxidants; they help break down the hydroxyl radical, which is one of the most toxic of the oxidising agents, commonly known as free radicals.

General health benefits

All beans and other types of legumes do not contain cholesterol, and they are a good source of fibre and essential fatty acids such as linoleic acid. Using soya protein or soya beans to partially replace other protein foods may help to maintain normal body weight — you don't see many obese vegetarians or Japanese — sumo wrestlers aside. In a British study of people with kidney diseases 50 per cent less calcium was excreted in the urine when soya beans replaced meat. This means that less calcium passed through the kidneys. Soya may help to reduce the incidence of both kidney stones and osteoporosis.

Key nutrients in cooked soya beans (per 100 g)	
Protein	13.5 g
Fat	6.7 g
Fibre	7.2 g
Potassium	420.0 mg
Sodium	9.0 mg
Calcium	76.0 mg
Magnesium	71.0 mg
Iron	2.2 mg

As discussed in the Introduction, I recommend food combining for vegetarians to ensure quality protein absorption, although some researchers in America maintain that soya beans will provide all the essential amino acids that the body needs.[27]

Cautions and adverse effects

- Soya in any form is a common allergen — bloating and other digestive upsets being the most common symptoms. However, the problem is not always an allergic reaction, because it takes the digestive system time to adjust to eating soya beans and foods such as dried beans and chick peas, which is why I recommend starting with very small quantities and ensuring that they are thoroughly cooked. (In my experience, most recipes do not give a long enough cooking time — I like all dried beans to be presoaked and cooked until really soft.)

  In their raw state all types of dried beans contain substances that cannot be broken down by human digestive juices, as well as an antitrypsin factor that prevents the absorption of protein. Cooked soya sprouts, tofu and tempeh are the most digestible forms of soya.

  The theoretically indigestible carbohydrates in legumes are raffinose, stachyose and verbascose but intestinal bacteria such as bifidobacteria can digest them for you. If you get bloating from eating legumes, they are not being cooked properly or you are allergic to them, or your 'friendly' intestinal bacteria are inadequate.

- Do not feed soya in any form to your pets, as most animals, especially cats and birds, are extremely sensitive to them (and to many other common human foods). They are no more appropriate for them as a diet of fresh mice or unhulled raw seeds would be for us.

- There has been some criticism and concern about the side effects of phyto-oestrogens in soya, especially regarding its use for infants and young children. A recent article in the *Medical Journal of Australia* stated:

  > Irvine et al. state that soy formulas contain high levels of the phyto-oestrogens daidzein and genistein, and assert these may be potentially harmful. Discussions in Australia, the United Kingdom and New Zealand have suggested placing warning labels on these foods. We believe these comments are inaccurate, alarmist and an inappropriate assessment of current data on phyto-oestrogens ... Breastfeeding is the 'gold standard' in infant nutrition but formula feeding may be necessary. We are not aware of any epidemiological or clinical evidence to support the contention that the current level of exposure of human infants to isoflavones from natural diets or soy formulas has adverse effects. Indeed, it is possible that a moderate level of exposure is beneficial.[28]

- There have been a few reports of reduced thyroid activity in people who consume excessive soya in any form. Refer to the suggested intake on p. 66. If you are taking pharmaceuticals for a thyroid problem, discuss your soya intake with your medical practitioner, as drug reference texts advise that it can interfere with the thyroid hormone, thyroxine. (Early signs of lowered thyroid activity include fatigue, weight gain, cold sensitivity, constipation and mental confusion, but a blood test is necessary to confirm thyroid hormone levels.)

- Because of the possibility of interference with the metabolism of thyroid and reproductive hormones, I suggest that, until we can get a guarantee from growers and manufacturers, infants and young children should not be given soya in any form unless there are no other options.

- Soya products are becoming increasingly popular throughout the world, and no doubt some crops are being pushed along with genetic technology, chemical fertilisers and pesticides. If you are worried about this, buy organic products.

Known therapeutic components

- Over 490 different compounds have been identified in soya beans.[29] Seven different substances (phytates, flavonoids, carotenoids, coumarins, triterpenes, lignans, phenolic acids) have been provisionally designated as cancer preventive.[30]

- Saponins and protease inhibitors also have anticancer properties.[31]
- The lecithin and omega-3 fatty acids in soya have benefits for the body's fat metabolism, and are helpful for cardiovascular and skin problems.
- Soya contains more phyto-oestrogens than any other plant. The most therapeutically useful phyto-oestrogens are genistein, daidzein and equol. Genistein and daidzein help stabilise oestrogen levels in women and testosterone levels in men.[32]
- More than 200 scientific studies have been published on genistein, mainly on its anti-cancer actions. Laboratory studies show that when genistein is added to cancer cells, cancer growth is inhibited in a wide range of cancers. Although clinical trials have not been done in humans, nutritional surveys of large numbers of people give further support to the cancer preventive potential of soya. Genistein is an antioxidant and has gentle blood thinning activity.
- Daidzein and other isoflavonic phyto-oestrogens in breast milk may have some cancer preventive potential for the breast-feeding infant.[33]
- Phyto-oestrogens may help reduce bone mineral loss in postmenopausal women — without the adverse effects associated with pharmaceutical therapies. This may partly explain why Chinese and Japanese women, who do not eat dairy foods and have a low calcium intake, sustain fewer fractures than women in most European countries. Vegetarians also have a lower incidence of osteo-porosis.
- Phytosterols (other hormone-like substances) may reduce skin cancers; they also help lower cholesterol.
- Soya beans contain both soluble and insoluble fibre, as well as complex carbohydrates. Some of the carbohydrates (fructo-oligosaccharides, or FOS) can stimulate the growth of friendly intestinal bacteria. This may partly account for the lower incidence of bowel cancer amongst many Asian and vegetarian groups.

Soya supplements

Concentrated soya supplements and isolated phyto-oestrogens are now on the market. Until we have more information (my guess is in about ten years) I suggest that you get your intake from soya foods unless you are going through menopause. For menopausal symptoms, use the label dosages of these supplements for up to three months, unless otherwise directed by a health practitioner.

Growing your own soya beans

In subtopical or tropical climates soya beans grow easily, although they take many months to mature. An additional benefit is that the plants produce their own nitrogen, and the crop residue can be dug into the soil as a natural fertiliser.

Soya beans will grow in a temperate climate if you sow them in November, but they will not produce bean pods if you have a cold summer.

I sometimes grow them in small trays of soil, and harvest the young green shoots when they are about 10 cm high to use as a salad vegetable.

How to use

Dried soya beans

Presoak the beans in water overnight, and then cook until soft. Drain and add to soups, casseroles and similar dishes. Dried and reconstituted beans are useful as meat extenders.

I cook presoaked soya beans in a pressure cooker for about an hour — or you could use your microwave oven — otherwise you will need about three hours' cooking time. This is in addition to the cooking time in recipes.

You can dry roast cooked soya beans in the oven (for half an hour at 180°C), perhaps with the added flavouring of some dried herbs, a little oil and tamari. Cool, and add them to salads or other dishes, or use as healthy snacks.

Fresh soya beans

The pods are smaller than those of peas. Soak the pods in boiling water for a few minutes to make them easier to open. Cook fresh beans for 10 minutes only. They are surprisingly tasty.

Soya flour

About 20 per cent soya flour can be substituted in recipes that use wheat flour. Soya flour can be used as a thickening agent in casseroles.

Soya flour and seed bread (Makes 1 small loaf)

This is an excellent combination for obtaining utilisable protein.
  I prefer this bread toasted.

1 cup soya flour
1 cup self-raising wholemeal wheat flour
$1/2$ cup millet flakes
$1/2$ cup corn meal
1 cup mixed sunflower seeds, sesame seeds and
  linseeds
$2^{1}/2$ cups soya milk
1 tablespoon caraway seeds

1 Preheat the oven to 200°C.
2 Sift the flours together in a large mixing bowl.
3 Stir in the millet, corn meal and mixed seeds.
4 Stir the soya milk into the dry ingredients,
  mixing well.
5 Pour the mixture into a well-greased loaf tin, and
  sprinkle the caraway seeds on top.

6 Bake for 45 minutes, by which time the bread
  will come away from the sides of the tin.

Optional additions: tasty grated cheese, fresh or
  dried herbs (especially thyme), or dried fruit.

Soya cakes (Makes 12–15)

1 cup soya flour
1 cup rice flour or self-raising wholemeal wheat flour
$1/2$ cup sultanas
$3/4$ cup soya milk
1 tablespoon honey or rice syrup
2 egg whites, very stiffly beaten

1 Preheat the oven to 180°C.
2 Sift the flours together, then add the sultanas.
3 Mix the honey or rice syrup into the soya milk,
  and stir into the dry ingredients, mixing well.
4 Fold in the egg whites.
5 Drop dessertspoons of the mixture onto a lightly
  floured non-stick tray.
6 Bake for 25 minutes, or until lightly browned.

Soya pasties (Makes 4)

1 cup soya flour
1 cup buckwheat flour
$1/2$ cup millet meal; plus extra for dusting the
  benchtop
$3/4$ cup soya milk
1 dessertspoon olive oil
4 tablespoons thickened curried vegetables (or other
  filling)

1 Preheat the oven to 200°C.
2 Combine the dry ingredients.
3 Add the soya milk and oil, and stir into the dry
  ingredients, mixing well.
4 Knead the pastry lightly, and cut into four even
  segments. Roll each one into a ball and place in
  a damp tea towel; refrigerate for 30 minutes.
5 Roll out the pastry on a bench that is heavily
  dusted with millet meal.
6 Cut the pastry into circles about the size of a
  small saucer.

7   Put the filling in the centre of each circle, leaving the outer 1.5 cm edge free.

8   Fold the pastry over in half, firming the edges together with the reverse side of a fork; prick a few holes in the top of each pasty, and place on a lightly floured baking tray.

9   Bake for 30 minutes.

Soya grits

Cook with savoury rice dishes, or add to curries or soups. Use about 1 tablespoon soya grits per person.

Soya flakes

Add these flakes to porridges, biscuits or rissoles. Use about 1–2 dessertspoons soya flakes per person.

You could add a cupful of flakes to a batch of biscuits or cakes.

Tofu

Most people need to try tofu a few times to adjust to the texture and taste; some people love it, but I find it fairly tasteless, and recommend that it be added to other flavoursome foods.

There are three different types of tofu:

Soft tofu has a texture somewhat like firm custard.
- Use in milk smoothies, together with fruit.
- Add to salad dressings, blended with avocado and chives.
- Mash into burgers.

Standard tofu has a texture like soft rubber.
- Slice thinly, and marinate in herbs and salt-reduced tamari before adding to stir-fries.
- Mash in rissoles or crumble into soups, casseroles and chilli dishes.
- Cut into cubes, and dry roast with a little oil and tamari; then add to salads or other dishes.

Dried tofu has the texture of rubber tyres. It is sometimes called bean curd.
- Soak in water for at least 15 minutes before cooking, and then slice thinly and use in stir-fries or savoury dishes.

Before cooking tofu, marinate it as follows: Mix ½ teaspoon ginger powder, ¼ teaspoon turmeric powder in a little water, and add 1–2 dessertspoons salt-reduced shoyu or tamari. Pour this over slices of tofu, and leave to stand for 10 minutes; turn the slices so that the marinade coats both sides, and leave to stand for a further 10 minutes.

Various other herbs and flavourings could be used in the marinade. Coriander is a good choice in Asian recipes, but this, too, is an acquired taste.

Tempeh

Use tempeh in a similar way to tofu, although it would not be suitable in a smoothie as it is salty and has the consistency of cold sausage meat.

Before cooking, marinate tempeh as for tofu (see above).

My favourite way of using tempeh is sliced thinly and stir-fried, together with plenty of herbs, mushrooms and cashew nuts. Tempeh and mushrooms both contain vitamin B12, so this is a good combination for vegetarians.

Miso

A fermented product made from soya beans, sea salt, water and beneficial micro-organisms. It comes in different forms and resembles Vegemite in texture. Miso makes an excellent flavouring in cooked foods, or can be spread on bread.

It can be heated; however, boiling destroys the beneficial bacteria and enzymes.

The sodium content is very high, so use it in small quantities.

Shoyu and tamari

These are high-quality, naturally fermented soya sauces used for flavourings — I prefer the flavour of tamari.

As they are high in sodium, I recommend salt-reduced forms.

Textured vegetable protein (TVP)

These types of products are mainly used as meat substitutes or meat extenders. The soya protein products often resemble chunks of dried meat or mince.

Before use, soak in water or marinate.

Soya sprouts

Sprouted soya beans are the richest known source of beneficial phyto-oestrogens. Their hormone content reaches its peak on the ninth day, but you don't have to wait this long to use them.

It is quite difficult to sprout these dried beans. If you haven't tried sprouting, don't begin with soya beans. Start the sprouting in warm weather (the dried beans will not germinate in cold localities or during cold weather). Soak the beans for about 5 hours, then rinse and thoroughly strain the sprouts at least three times daily for about five days.

Before using, steam the sprouts for about 5 minutes. They are surprisingly delicious cold in salads or added to stir-fries.

Soya cheese

You can buy this in various flavours. The texture is somewhat rubbery, but it is excellent grilled or grated into salads.

Soya milks and yoghurt

Many types are now readily available, including low-fat ones.

Tofu icecream

Use in the same way as dairy icecream.

Soya pasta

Cooking instructions are on the packets, and are basically the same as for other pastas.

Snacks

Soya chips and other products are now on the market.

Suggested intake

1 glass soya milk daily — use fat-reduced products if you have a weight problem — and 2–3 tablespoons soya products every second day.

Give proportionately less to children according to age (see pp. 4–5). As mentioned under **Cautions and adverse effects** above, it might be prudent not to give infants and preschool children soya in any form unless there are no other options.

Summary

Populations with high soya intakes have lower rates of coronary artery disease, breast cancer, prostate cancer and osteoporotic fractures. The plant hormones in soya beans help to stabilise both oestrogen levels in women and testosterone levels in men.

I classify soya beans as a health function food, meaning that there are compounds in it that are remarkably therapeutic.

In conclusion

A variety of whole grains, legumes and seeds gives you energy, nutrients and valuable phytochemicals.

CHAPTER 3

Fourteen super medicinal herbs

Aloe	Ginseng	Milk thistle
Cat's claw	Gotu kola	Pau d'arco
Chamomile	Hawthorn	St John's
Echinacea	Kava	wort
Ginkgo	Liquorice	Withania

There are hundreds of medicinal herbs, but I have chosen these fourteen because of their particular therapeutic values and to give a selection from various parts of the world. Some of these herbs are relatively new to Australia; other common herbs that are now known in nearly every household, such as echinacea and milk thistle, would have been considered mysterious even twenty years ago.

Some herbalists believe that we should use the plants that grow naturally in the area in which we live. However, some of us have been transplanted into different environments. I, with my 'Celtic' skin, now live in a hot, dry climate. Should I use only traditional Celtic herbs or should I use Aboriginal medicines? Why not take the best that the world has to offer?

Modern herbal medicine

Herbal medicine today is a blend of traditional herbal medicine, folklore and recent clinical experience, plus scientific evaluations of the individual components in plants and some scientific, controlled studies of herbal remedies.

The whole plant versus isolated components

Herbalists are trained in the use of the whole plant. This does not necessarily mean that every part of the plant is used, because for some plants we use only the flowers, or the leaves or the root. It means that a particular substance in that plant is not isolated and used — isolated compounds are more in the nature of pharmaceuticals. If you take, say, an alkaloid out of a plant to use as a medicine, that alkaloid might represent less than 1 per cent of the total weight, or be one of 500 compounds in that particular plant.

In general, scientists now tend to study smaller and smaller components. They are also

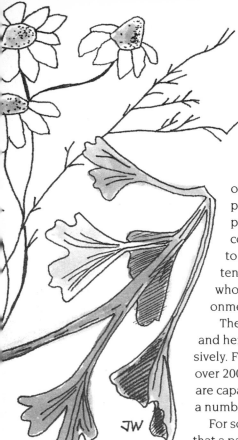

on the lookout for single compounds that could become pharmaceutical drugs. Single compounds are relatively easy to test and measure. Herbalists tend to look at whole plants, whole people and the total environment.

The components in many foods and herbs have been studied intensively. For example, garlic contains over 200 unusual compounds that are capable of protecting us against a number of diseases.

For some plants scientists tell us that a particular compound is the most therapeutic for a specific activity, but often a group of compounds is considered to be therapeutically active. If a particular medicinal herb does not contain any of the purported principal therapeutic ingredient, then that particular remedy will not be effective for treating some conditions. For instance, if feverfew does not contain any parthenolide, then it is unlikely to help migraines; feverfew has to be prepared in a specific way to retain parthenolide.

Nutrients in herbs

In most cases the nutrients in herbs are irrelevant simply because the herbs themselves are used in such low doses. There are a few exceptions to this, such as selenium in garlic.

Toxicity

All plants contain toxins, but not all are harmful. There is a distinction between a toxin and a hazard. Parsley, for example, contains myristicin, which is toxic if enormous quantities are eaten, but when consumed as a culinary herb it is not dangerous — otherwise tabouli eaters would not last long! However, I would not recommend that you make parsley juice, although a handful juiced would not present a problem.

Sometimes, moderation in everything is sensible advice.

Naturally occurring toxins in edible foods and herbs are in minute quantities, and the body's natural detoxification system can take care of these. It has even been suggested that these keep our detoxification enzymes activated.

Isolated reports of adverse reactions need to be kept in perspective. If one person in many thousands or millions has a bizarre reaction to a pharmaceutical drug, it is unlikely that it would get the massive publicity that happens every year or so with a natural therapy. Occasionally, individuals are extremely sensitive to particular compounds, and this is very unfortunate, but it does not mean that the plant should be banned.

Medicinal herbs cause remarkably few adverse reactions — this is based on the clinical experience of practising herbalists. Some scientists write book about herbs, emphasising how dangerous they are, but I can tell by about page two of these books that the author has never used them personally or on anyone else for that matter. Why don't these scientists write scary stuff about foods? Because they eat foods every day that contain toxins, and they know that these foods are not dangerous when consumed in reasonable quantities.

There is no doubt in my mind that if peanuts or potatoes were herbal medicines they would have been banned decades ago because the aflatoxins and alkaloids in them are extremely toxic.

Dosages

There is no international agreement on dosages of herbal remedies, although some texts such as the *British Herbal Pharmacopoeia*, *The Complete German Commission E Monographs* and the monographs of the European Scientific Cooperative on Phytotherapy are considered authoritative. In the absence of professional herbal training or a clinical consultation, you should follow the label dosages for all remedies.

Duration of use

Herbal medicine is generally slow acting. For instance, for menstrual and arthritic problems the remedy must be taken for three months or longer. Some herbs, like ginkgo, are helpful for the circulation and act as antioxidants, so I recommend some people, especially the elderly, take them continuously. Other remedies such as echinacea probably work more effectively if taken for about a week to relieve problems such as flu symptoms.

Herbal formulas

Sensitive, allergic or reactive people should always try only one new remedy or new food at a time.

Interaction with pharmaceutical drugs

There is very little precise information on combining herbs with pharmaceuticals. I always ask my patients what they are taking, and hope I am open enough for them to be truthful.

To a large extent, common sense applies. For instance, if you are taking a pharmaceutical sedative, you would not take a herbal sedative as well. On the other hand, if you were being weaned off that pharmaceutical sedative, then, with the help of a health practitioner, you could take a more gentle natural sedative to help avoid withdrawal effects.

Herbal systems

The Chinese and Indian (Ayurvedic) systems commonly use combination remedies, sometimes the formulas contain up to seventeen herbs. The patients are often given dried plants to make up into teas or decoctions, although some formulas are now being made up as liquid extracts and tablets. The traditional Chinese and Indian systems of herbal medicine are more holistic, and they tend not to be so concerned with the name of the disease; they

attempt to balance the individual according to factors, such as where the energy is deficient or excessive, and to consider the nature of the person being treated. European herbalists now use some Asian herbs within the European system.

The European system is more or less divided into two groups. In Germany, France and Italy, in particular, medicinal herbs have been successfully integrated into the official health care systems, and are prescribed by doctors. This often means that guaranteed potency herbs are prescribed for a specific complaint. For many herbs, there are now official prescribing guides, such as the German Commission E monographs, which are largely based on the main therapeutic component in the plants. When European doctors use herbs, many of the secondary plant components are not considered, and each herb tends to be prescribed singly for a narrow range of conditions.

Professional herbalists may be aware of the main therapeutic component or components, but they also consider the historical and clinical use of herbal formulas — and this may be the collective wisdom of hundreds, even thousands, of years. Within this group there are those who prescribe, say, 15 ml daily in divided doses, and who recognise the science that is now available, while the other group tends to prescribe in drops and rely more on the historical evidence and factors such as the patient's personality and the life force or energy of the plants.

The information in this chapter covers mainly the European system of herbal medicine, even though many of the herbs originate elsewhere.

Growing and making your own remedies

The first step is to make sure you are using the correct plant. From my experience as a professional horticulturist in Australia, commercial seeds and plants are labelled correctly — I have not seen one case of a toxic plant with a label indicating it was edible.

Knowledge of therapeutic components is

important. For example, if the aromatic oils are considered to be important therapeutically, you should appreciate that these oils are volatile — they come out of the plant into the air (or steam) when heated. Obviously, they should not be boiled, and, if you make them into a tea, they should be covered during steeping.

Drying and preserving herbs requires care. Herbs must be dried carefully, and stored in a dry, dark and cool place. As a rule, herbs retain their therapeutic value if they still possess their original colour and smell.

When herbal manufacturers make extracts, tinctures and tablets, they are guided by pharmacopoeial textbooks that give instructions on the most appropriate manufacturing process for each herb. These technical details are beyond the scope of this book, and very few, if any, of the general public would have the necessary equipment.

If you are making herbal teas and decoctions (simmering the herbs in water), do not use aluminium teapots or saucepans.

Miracle cures?

In my twenty years' experience as a health practitioner I have found that most herbs do bring about health improvements, although results often take weeks, or even months, to become evident. The therapeutic effects are often due to the body being strengthened in some way, rather than from a specific biochemical effect.

Aloe

There are 300 types of aloe, the main medicinal species being *Aloe vera* or *barbadensis*, A. *ferox*, A. *aborescens* and A. *striatula*. A. *vera* is

the species most commonly grown and used in Australia.

Background

In the New Testament (John 19:39) reference is made to myrrh and aloe being used to embalm the body of Jesus. The use of aloe for medicinal purposes has been part of ancient medical history in all the continents of the world.

Egyptian papyrus scrolls more than 3000 years old refer to aloe, and the Greeks also recorded many applications for its use 2000 years ago. Alexander the Great was said to have conquered an East African island for the purpose of obtaining sufficient amounts of aloe to use as a wound-healing agent for his soldiers. Marco Polo recorded that the Chinese used aloe for stomach ailments and skin disorders; in Java, the juice was massaged into the scalp and hair to improve its condition and to stimulate growth.

Unfortunately, in recent times exaggerated and unfounded claims have been made for aloe. Scientific researchers tend to shy away from plants that are tagged as 'miracle cure-alls', and that may explain why much of the very good research in the 1930s to 1960s has not been followed up with modern scientific studies. However, since the fourth century BC there has been persistent and continuous agreement that aloe possesses healing properties.

The part used

At present I recommend the gel (the clear jelly-like substance found *inside* the leaves) or products made from the gel.

The latex or the juice obtained from the outer part of the leaves contains more of the specific polysaccharide (acemannan) that is considered to be particularly therapeutic for the immune system, but it also contains most of the anthraquinones that can cause diarrhoea, bloating and abdominal pain.

Therapeutic use

External

Aloe is recommended for household burns, sunburn, minor wounds, acne and dermatitis, and to reduce scarring. Researchers concluded from a study on mice that stabilised aloe cream appeared to be an effective treatment for first- and second-degree burns.[1] Of course, you must get medical advice for serious burns.

An eight-month controlled trial on patients with slight to moderate plaque-type psoriasis showed that aloe externally was markedly successful; 83 per cent improved on the aloe, compared to only 8 per cent on the placebo.[2] In this trial the gel was mixed with mineral and castor oils to form an ointment that contained 0.5 per cent of aloe. Perhaps the castor oil externally had some effect, as the quantity of aloe seems too low. My experience in using aloe for skin problems is that the inside gel causes remarkably few adverse reactions, although for sensitive skins I usually combine it with a non-allergenic cream during the early stages of treatment.

Herpes simplex (cold sores) and *Herpes zoster* (shingles) have also been helped by the external application of aloe gel.

An aloe preparation has been used successfully in Russia to treat periodontal disease (swollen or bleeding gums, and loose teeth). If you have a severe dental problem, see your dentist, but for general mouth hygiene and minor gum problems you may find it helpful to use aloe as a mouth wash. Some toothpastes contain aloe.

In 1935 aloe was reported as being helpful for treating acute radiation dermatitis. Studies and case reports provide support for the use of *Aloe vera* in the treatment of radiation ulcers and stasis ulcers in humans, and burn and frostbite injuries in animals.[3] As far as I know, no one has tested aloe as an external remedy for cancer patients who suffer skin burns from cancer radiation treatments. It would be relatively easy for

a hospital to do a trial for this purpose, as half the patients could be given aloe as an additional therapy and half the standard medical treatment.

One of the lesser-known side effects of radiation therapy, and surgery, is fluid retention, and aloe has been helpful for this in laboratory animals.[4]

As aloe is anti-inflammatory, a wound healer, antibacterial, antipruritic (itching), antifungal, antiarthritic, moisturising, a skin softener, and antiageing, it is likely to be helpful for a wide range of skin problems. I recommend it, mixed into a high-potency vitamin E cream, before and after surgery, but only after the possibility of infection has passed.

Internal

Herpes simplex, herpes zoster, influenza and other viral infections may be relieved by aloe.

Animal and preliminary human studies suggest that the use of acemannan (an isolated compound in aloe) may reduce the amount of the drug AZT required to treat AIDS by as much as 90 per cent.

A number of animal studies have shown that aloe as an internal remedy reduces joint inflammation. In traditional herbal medicine, aloe has been prescribed for arthritis and fluid retention.

Some early studies in Russia and America showed that aloe gel used internally could successfully heal peptic ulcers, and that it has a soothing effect on the linings of the stomach. The juice can reduce stomach acid. Aloe gel may be helpful in treating asthma and other inflammatory or allergy-related problems.[5]

Aloe can have a laxative effect, it stimulates the gallbladder and promotes bile flow, and may help prevent gallstones. It is a traditional digestive remedy, which may be due to its anti-inflammatory and wound-healing effects.

In addition it is immune modulating, and therefore useful for a range of infections.

Cautions and adverse effects

- Aloe gel contains a small quantity of anthra-quinones, which may have a laxative effect in some people when used as an internal remedy. All laxatives should be used with care, and aloe is no exception.

  Any laxative that causes watery bowel motions should be avoided. If you have watery bowel motions, this not only upsets your body's natural fluid balance but it means your intestines have not had time to absorb essential minerals and other nutrients. In addition, diarrhoea leads to inflammation of the intestinal wall, which can lead to what is known as 'leaky gut' — that is, the linings of the intestines do not filter correctly, and your body can then absorb a whole range of substances that would normally be eliminated. These substances subsequently get into your blood circulation, resulting in allergic reactions, inflammatory and immune disorders.

  Aloe may be helpful as a short-term remedy for a lazy bowel, but it is a habit-forming laxative. It is never recommended for spastic colon conditions such as irritable bowel. Generally, bulk-swelling laxatives such as rice bran and psyllium are healthier, together with dietary modifications, a high fluid intake and exercise.
- Any substances that stimulate the intestines may also reflexly stimulate the uterus, so aloe must never be taken internally during pregnancy. However, it may be helpful lightly massaged onto the abdomen to reduce stretch marks.

Known therapeutic components

- Aloins and hydroxyanthracene derivates are responsible for the laxative effect.
- Polysaccharides, including mannose; acemannan, a form of mannose, is currently being tested as an antiviral agent, and it has other beneficial effects on the immune system.
- Prostanoids are considered to be responsible for the wound-healing effects of aloe.
- Aloctin A is a glycoprotein component that has anti-inflammatory and antioedema activity.
- A number of enzymes, such as carboxypeptidase and bradykinase, have useful therapeutic properties, and this may account for aloe's reputation as an antiallergy and anti-inflammatory remedy.

  It is probable that the beneficial properties of aloe gel are due not to one isolated component but to the synergistic effect of many of the plant's compounds.[6]

Aloe products

Aloe is available as juice, extracts and capsules. It is also incorporated in many cosmetics, shampoos, toothpastes and other products.

Hopefully, future products of the whole leaf will contain high levels of acemannan plus the other beneficial components, but with the irritant laxatives removed. Meantime, I recommend products made from the gel.

Growing and making your own remedies

Aloe grows easily in containers or in the ground in most parts of Australia, and the plant is available in most nurseries. It needs good drainage, and should not be overwatered.

If possible, harvest the leaves that are over two years old, because they have more therapeutic activity than young leaves. The leaves have large prickles on them, so cut them open carefully, and scoop out the clear inside gel. Store the gel in the fridge, and use it within two days because the therapeutic components break down very quickly.

Note: Commercial products are stabilised so they do not lose their therapeutic activity.

Dosages and duration of treatment

If you use aloe as an internal remedy, follow the dosages recommended by the manufacturer, but always reduce the quantity at the first sign of loose bowel motions, and do not continue taking it if diarrhoea persists.

When I use fresh aloe internally, I take a daily dose of 1–2 teaspoons aloe mixed into a little soft mashed fruit, yoghurt, or soft cooked food; I swallow it quickly to avoid the bitter taste. You could use somewhat more, but only if it does not give you diarrhoea.

As an internal remedy, I recommend it for occasional short-term use or for a maximum period of two to three months for serious disorders such as arthritis, repeating if necessary after at least a two-week break.

I do not recommend aloe as an internal remedy for children.

You can use aloe freely and indefinitely as an external remedy for adults and children, but always try a test skin patch first just in case you are one of the few people allergic to it.

Summary

Aloe is one of the best natural external healing remedies. Its main internal therapeutic activity relates to reducing inflammation and enhancing the immune system.

Other useful external healing herbs

Calendula   Comfrey   Golden seal

Cat's claw

This vigorous vine grows in the rainforests of South America. It is called cat's claw (*uno de gato*) because claw-like hooks on the branches enable the plant to climb upwards.

Uncaria tomentosa is reputed to be the most therapeutic species, and is the one that is available in Australia. U. *guianensis* is also used as a medicinal herb in South America.

Background

Cat's claw has been used in Peru and other South American countries for about 2000 years. Traditionally, Peruvians recommended it for about thirty different conditions. The tribal people known as Ashaninka consider the vine to be 'life giving', and it is their treatment for many illnesses, including arthritis, rheumatism, tumours, digestive problems such as gastric ulcers, urinary infections and various inflammatory disorders. They make a tea from the shredded bark, and may drink a litre a day for three months for serious conditions, or a cup a week as a general preventive. They drink the fluid from the centre of the vine, and use the leaves externally as a fresh poultice, or dried and powdered as a wound treatment.

A number of early explorers were impressed with the healing effects of cat's claw. The first serious European research was done in the 1970s by Dr K. Keplinger, who introduced it to Austria and then to other countries. He is still studying the plant and its constituents.

As with many traditional herbs, there are accounts of miracle cures. Nicole Maxwell, a Fellow of the Royal Geographical Society, writes of a man with terminal cancer who was given ten days to live. After using a herbal treatment containing cat's claw, his condition improved, and after thirty days on the remedy he went back to work.[7]

The parts used

The root, bark and leaves.

Therapeutic use

Internal

Cat's claw has a number of different effects, including antioxidant, antiviral, antitumour, anti-inflammatory, and healing of the digestive tract. It is also considered to be a general metabolic tonic.

It can be useful for treating arthritis and other inflammatory joint problems, cardiovascular problems such as mild hypertension, varicose veins and haemorrhoids. Herbalists report its value in the treatment of chronic fatigue syndrome and systemic candidiasis associated with leaky gut (faulty intestinal functioning). Other problems that are helped by this herb include irritable bowel syndrome, diverticulitis, gastritis, and as a support treatment of gastric ulcers.

In studies on rats both a water and an alcoholic extract of cat's claw showed protective activity against the formation of gastric ulcers. A concentrated extract produced a 69 per cent inhibition of arthritic inflammation.[8]

Doctors in Austria have been using standardised root products for cancer patients, and have found that those who use this herb tolerate chemotherapy and radiation far better than those who have the medical therapy alone. The standardised products available in Europe are recommended for diseases mainly caused by 'malfunctioning of the immune system', and this also includes rheumatoid arthritis, allergies, and as support therapy in the treatment of cancer and herpes. As a support therapy for cancer it is as yet unproven, because there have not been enough people using cat's claw products under medical supervision, nor have controlled study results been published in medical journals. However, there is enough evidence to show that specific alkaloids in this herb can beneficially increase the immune system so that the body is better able to ward off infections and fight abnormal cells. A number of herbal remedies work in this way, that is, they do not directly kill the 'bug' that is causing the problem but rather work to get the body's immune system functioning more effectively.

A standardised cat's claw root extract has been used on some AIDS patients in Europe, and the results of immune function tests were quite promising; herpes, and vaginal and oral fungal infections were eradicated in some AIDS patients.[9] Again, large controlled studies have not been done, nor have results been published in English-language medical journals.

In an eight-day trial cat's claw was given to a smoker and a non-smoker. The smoker's urine showed mutagenic (cancer potential) activity before taking the tea, but the non-smoker's urine was clear. At the end of eight days the smoker's urine showed a significant decrease in mutagenic potential, which persisted for a further eight days after the treatment.[10] This suggests that the folklore may have some substance, and the herb may have the ability to help the body resist cancer-causing compounds.

In general, cat's claw can be used whenever the immune system is weakened. Experiments show that the immune stimulatory effect varies between 10 and 40 per cent, depending on whether a tea, an extract or extract powder is used, but generally the root is the most potent. In normal people who consumed the root tea the number of active monocytes (part of the body's defence system) increased from 33 to 50 per cent in one week.

Cat's claw can also be used for preventive purposes. When the standardised root extract was used, red blood cells were less susceptible to breakdown, and the number of malformations greatly reduced.

Cautions and adverse effects

Doctors in Europe have prescribed cat's claw for over eight years without any signs of toxic effects, even at triple the usual dosages. However, there are some warnings:

- Allergic reactions are always a possibility.
- Do not use for children under three years of age; nor during pregnancy or lactation.
- Do not use for haemophiliacs or anyone who has had organ transplants, skin grafts, or about to have these procedures.
- Do not combine with vaccines, hormone or medical immunotherapies.

Known therapeutic components

Immodal Pharmaka GmbH in Austria produce a standardised alkaloid product from cat's claw called Krallendorn.* Based on Dr Keplinger's decades of research, this company maintains that the phytochemicals known as pentacyclic oxindole alkaloids

> enhance the mechanism of auto-control of human defence by regulating the rate of proliferation of T- and B-lympocytes. Resting lymphocytes are activated whereas lymphoblasts are inhibited.

In other words, these particular alkaloids should be standardised when serious immune disorders are to be treated.

- Other alkaloids have a variety of therapeutic effects, including lowering blood pressure by dilating arteries, lowering blood cholesterol, lowering heart rate and reducing fluid reten- tion.
- Triterpenes and quinovic acid glycosides are potent anti-inflammatory agents, and show some antiviral properties.
- Catechin tannins are inactive by themselves, but stimulate the alkaloids in the herb.
- Cis-epicatechin is more powerful than vita- min E as an antioxidant.
- Proanthocyanidins and polyphenols also have antioxidant activity.
- Polyphenols tend to exert antifungal effects.

Cat's claw products

Liquid extracts and tablets of cat's claw are available in Australia from professional herbal- ists, and are just becoming available in some retail stores.

---

* Krallendorn can be obtained by post, together with prescribing information, from Immodal Pharmaka Bundesstrasse 44, 6111 Volders, Tirol, Austria, only if you have a doctor's prescription.

Growing and making your own remedies

Cat's claw plants are not available in Australia.

Dosages and duration of treatment

The recommended liquid extract dose is about 2.5 ml, three times daily. Dosage of the tea is between 2–6 g per day, and the tablet dose is on the label.

Cat's claw is not recommended for children under three years of age; for children over three use dosages proportionately according to age (see pp. 4–5).

The traditional use of the herb suggests a maximum medicinal dose for no longer than three months, although a low dose could be used indefinitely. Your health practitioner will give you advice if you have a serious illness.

Standardised root extracts used by European doctors contain 1.3–1.75 per cent oxindole alka- loids. The usual dose of the extract powder is 20 mg, and sometimes 60 mg per day. The liquid extract contains 81 mg oxindole alkaloids per litre; adults should take 20 drops, three times daily. Additionally, in Europe, products are available that omit the dark-coloured tannins, while leaving in the clear ones — the clear tannins enhance the activity of the alkaloids. Some patients have taken this remedy for up to two years.

Summary

Recommended for diseases that relate to a mal- functioning of the immune system and inflam- mation, including rheumatoid arthritis, digestive problems, and as a support therapy for cancer.

Recommended reading

Jones, K. *Cat's Claw: Healing Vine of Peru*. Sylvan Press, Seattle, 1995 (219 references).

Chamomile
(English or Roman chamomile (*Anthemis nobilis*); German chamomile (*Matricaria recutita* or *M. chamomilla*))

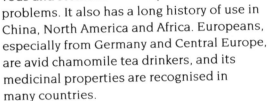

Background

Herbalists from the sixteenth century to the present day have recommended chamomile for nervous and stomach problems. It also has a long history of use in China, North America and Africa. Europeans, especially from Germany and Central Europe, are avid chamomile tea drinkers, and its medicinal properties are recognised in many countries.

The part used

The flowerheads; also the aromatic oil, but as an external remedy only.

Therapeutic use

Internal

For millions of people around the world chamomile tea is a popular, gentle sedative. It has other properties, including anti-inflammatory, antispasmodic (relaxant to body tissues), antiseptic, mild antibacterial and mild antifungal.

Herbalists recommend chamomile for digestive problems, especially those associated with nervous problems and stress. For gastric ulcers it is helpful support therapy, and many herbalists include it in extract formulas for gastritis, colic, flatulence and irritable bowel syndrome. Some people find it reduces nausea, but only if they like the taste of chamomile — I suggest combining it with

ginger for this purpose. Although chamomile tends to reduce stomach secretions and activity, it improves gallbladder functioning and, according to animal studies, it helps regenerate the liver.[11]

Chamomile has a long history of use as a gentle antianxiety remedy, and it is thought that the flavonoid apigenin is responsible for this action. Traditionally, it has been recommended for painful periods, insomnia and tension headaches.

Due to its mild antibacterial and antifungal effects, chamomile is a useful adjunct to the treatment of respiratory and candida fungal infections.

For teething problems in babies drop a few teaspoons of tepid chamomile tea into the baby's mouth or add to milk. Alternatively, use chamomile in prescribed homoeopathic form.

External

Both the oil and the flowers have anti-inflammatory, antifungal, antibacterial and healing properties.

Chamomile creams and ointments have been used successfully for eczema, nappy rash and various minor infections and wounds. A trial in Germany showed that a chamomile wash and ointment improved varicose ulcers. See p. 79 for my recipe for chamomile ointment.

Use a strong tea as an inhalation to help clear the nose and throat of excess mucus; and as a facial cleanser. You can also use the cooled, strained tea as a gargle and mouth wash.

One study found chamomile extract throat preparation effective against mucositis (inflamed and painful throat) caused by chemotherapy. Chamomile is one of a number of herbs that improve the health of the gums; some 'natural' toothpastes contain chamomile.

Chamomile extract gargle

25 ml liquid chamomile extract
25 ml glycerine
tepid water

1 Combine the chamomile extract and glycerine in a screwtop bottle, seal, and label.
2 Shake the bottle vigorously before use.
3 Add 1 teaspoon of the chamomile and glycerine to ½ cup tepid water, and gargle this quantity three times daily.

This gargle is helpful for all throat problems where there is excess mucus or irritation.

One study showed that in cell culture chamomile inhibits herpes virus (cold sores).[12] I recommend a cold chamomile tea bag for herpes, although you have to lie down while the tea bag is on your cold sore! You can also use a cold chamomile tea bag for puffy eyes.

Use aromatic chamomile oil on the skin or in a bath — it has an apple-like aroma; it is often helpful for inflamed skin conditions such as acne. Blue chamomile oil gives the best results, but it is expensive. A therapeutic quantity is 6–10 drops, and it can be diluted in a plain oil or an external cream, or applied undiluted on small problem areas such as pimples.

One study showed that the inhalation of chamomile oil improves emotional wellbeing.[13]

Blue chamomile is one of the oils I use for ear infections and glue ear, usually combined in a mullein oil base with lavender, rose, tea tree and lemon oils.

Cautions and adverse effects

- People with eczema, asthma and those generally sensitive to ragweed, daisy plants and pollens might be allergic to chamomile both as an internal and external remedy. One case of fatal anaphylactic shock has been reported. This potential for allergies needs to be considered in the light of an estimated million cups of tea that are consumed worldwide each day, and that between 1887 and 1982 only five cases of allergic reaction were reported.[14]
- If you harvest your own chamomile, always make sure that you have identified the plant correctly, because there are many similar 'daisy' flowers. Feverfew flowers, for instance, are the same size and colour as chamomile, but have quite different constituents. Only the leaves of feverfew are used therapeutically.

Known therapeutic components

- The aromatic oils from chamomile are the most important constituents, and they are responsible for the anti-inflammatory and spasmolytic actions. German chamomile contains (–)-a–bisabolol, which is responsible for many of the therapeutic effects.
- Apigenin, quercetin and other flavonoids have antihistamine and anti-inflammatory activity.[15] In addition, apigenin has distinct antianxiety activity and produces sedative effects.
- A bitter glycoside, anthemic acid, aids digestion.
- Valerianic acid is a sedative.

Chamomile products

Chamomile tablets, capsules and teas are available in retail stores. Professional herbalists often prescribe liquid extracts.

In Germany there are over ninety licensed preparations of chamomile. An external remedy (Kamillosan) made from the extract of German chamomile flowers has been tested successfully as a treatment for eczema and skin reactions to radiation therapy. It is also recommended for nappy rash, cracked nipples and inflammatory skin problems. It has been shown to accelerate the healing of skin injuries.[16] Mouth sprays and bath additives are also available in Europe. A professional herbalist could make similar types of remedies specifically for you.

Growing and making your own remedies

Chamomile grows readily in most areas of Australia, but prefers temperate climates.

Harvest only the flowers for therapeutic purposes, so make sure you buy either German or English chamomile, and check that you do not buy the variety that is non-flowering, which is used for cultivating a lawn.

Fresh, rather than dried, chamomile flowers may have the most effective anti-inflammatory effects.

When you make a tea for therapeutic purposes, keep the lid on while the tea is steeping; if you let all the steam escape, you will lose the aromatic oils. Use the teas as a hot drink or as a steam facial. A cooled tea also makes an effective gargle for laryngitis, or a mouth wash.

If you harvest the flowers for later use, try my system of drying them: put the flowers on shadecloth or similar screen-like material pulled tightly over bricks so that it is off the ground, away from wind but well-ventilated. Dry the flowers in a warm, dry, protected area but not in direct sunlight. You will know if you have dried them properly because they will have no moisture in them if they are crushed, and they will have retained much of their colour and aroma.

Store the dried flowers in a dark airtight glass jar in a cool place. The dried flowers will retain their therapeutic properties for up to a year; if they no longer emit their characteristic odour, they have lost their therapeutic value.

Chamomile flower ointment

2–4 tablespoons hot water
50 g aqueous cream or plain ointment base
1–2 tablespoons fresh, finely chopped fresh or dried chamomile flowers

1 Place the flowers in a jar, adding just enough hot water to cover the flowers. Dried flowers could be used but they are not as effective.
2 Put the lid on, and leave to stand for an hour.
3 Strain the liquid through a small piece of cotton cloth into a 50 g jar, and squeeze out all the juice.
4 Stir in the aqueous cream (available from pharmacies) or plain ointment base.

As the remedy contains no preservative, it has a short life, and should be kept in the fridge. After a month, if you have not used it all for therapeutic purposes, use the remainder as a hand or body cream.

A simpler way of making external remedies is to buy a base cream, and stir in a herbal liquid extract that has been preserved with alcohol. To make a strong remedy, use 5–10 ml extract in a 50 g jar of aqueous cream or other plain ointment base. Alternatively, stir in about 10 drops of an aromatic oil. These types of remedies will last for many months.

You can use many other herbs in this way, as long as they are appropriate for external use. However, both the extract and aromatic oils may be too strong for very sensitive skins.

Chamomile wine

contents of 8 chamomile tea bags (about 20 g)
8 teaspoons honey
grated rind of 1 lime or lemon
750 ml red or white wine

1 Combine the contents of the tea bags, honey, lime or lemon rind, and wine in an airtight, screwtopped jar.
2 Leave the jar on its side for two weeks, turning it periodically.
3 Strain carefully, and bottle the liquid. Date and label before storing.

Drink one small wineglass of the wine either before or during a meal. Vacuum wine savers will keep the wine fresh in the bottle after opening.

Sedative honey

200 g honey
10 g powdered chamomile flowers

1   Gently heat (don't boil) the honey in a small saucepan.
2   Add the chamomile flowers.
3   Turn off the heat, and leave to stand for 30 minutes. Then reheat, and pour the honey into a small jar.
4   Seal, date and label.

Use 1 teaspoon honey on food, or as a remedy one to three times daily.

Optional: Use 10 g mixed sedative herbs (such as verbena, betonica, linden, scullcap). I do not recommend valerian for this purpose, as the taste may be too strong.

Dosages and duration of treatment

As a tea use 2–3 g, three times daily. Increase to twice as much for external applications or inhalations.

Liquid extracts are usually prescribed in doses of approximately 2 ml, three times daily.

Tablets and capsules are available in various strengths, so be guided by the label dosage.

Children could be given weak chamomile tea or proportionate dosages of remedies according to age (see pp. 4–5). Homeopathic chamomile remedies are especially useful for children because they are very dilute and virtually tasteless.

Summary

Chamomile is an underutilised medicinal herb that acts as a gentle sedative and digestive aid as an internal remedy, as well as an external treatment for inflammation and to accelerate healing.

Echinacea
(*Echinacea purpurea, E. angustifolia, E. pallida*)

Echinacea angustifolia is considered to be somewhat superior therapeutically, but it is in quite short supply, and very expensive. The additional therapeutic value may not be all that important as the other species contain components with similar medicinal properties. Purple cone flower is one of the common names given to this plant, but nearly everyone calls it echinacea.

Background

The American Indians were using this herb long before European settlement.

By 1887 echinacea had been introduced to the medical profession, mainly by doctors in the USA known as 'The Eclectics', who used herbal medicine in their practices. Professor John King wrote in 1898:

> A crushed hand, thought to be beyond aid, with the intolerable stench of putrid flesh, was saved by the application of echinacea. It has given equally satisfactory results in alarming cases of venom infections from the bites of rattlesnake, tarantula and other spiders and from the stings of scorpions, bees and wasps.[17]

The Eclectic doctors often used massive doses of echinacea when treating severe infections. Today, for these types of life-threatening infections and wounds we rush to the nearest hospital. We use echinacea to boost the immune system, while leaving the treatment of serious micro-organisms and major wounds to the doctors.

One famous American formula of the nineteenth century was Meyer's Blood Purifier — a combination of echinacea, wormwood and hops. Dr Meyer (a lay doctor) was said to have allowed a rattlesnake to bite him, after which he bathed the parts with some of the mixture, took a drachm (about 5 g) internally, and laid down and slept. Upon waking, he found all traces of swelling had disappeared. Dr Meyer claimed to have cured numerous diseases with this remedy, including malaria, typhoid, ulcers, haemorrhoids, eczema, tonsillitis, and a long list of infections and wounds.

In the early part of this century echinacea was medically prescribed in America for many serious infections and injuries.[18]

The parts used

Commonly the root, but the above-ground parts also have therapeutic actions.

Therapeutic use

Internal

There is no doubt that echinacea is effective as a preventive and treatment for coughs, colds, influenza and sore throats.

It is also recommended as part of the prevention and treatment of acne, bronchitis, cystitis, herpes, skin diseases, benign prostate hypertrophy, otitis media (middle ear infection), candida (thrush), and a wide range of serious infections.

Over 200 supportive scientific papers have been published on echinacea. Much of the scientific work has been done in Germany using Echinacin, a stabilised juice of *Echinacea purpurea*. The following are some of the trial results.

Echinacea is not classed as a cure, but it has been shown in a number of trials and in practice to reduce influenza symptoms, such as weakness, chills, sweating, sore throat, muscle and joint pains and headaches, and to decrease the frequency of flu infections, as well as the length

of time the symptoms last. A German trial of 1280 children with acute bronchitis, using the juice of E. *purpurea* resulted in a faster recovery compared to those who were given antibiotics.[19]

In a study of 203 women with recurring vaginal thrush it was shown that those women who applied a medical antifungal cream had a recurrence rate of 60 per cent, whereas those who took E. *purpurea*, in addition to that cream, had only a 5–17 per cent recurrence rate.[20]

A small study showed that arthritic inflammation was reduced by echinacea. Although it was considered that the results were only half as effective as cortisone pharmaceuticals, there were no adverse effects from echinacea.

Recent laboratory studies showed that echinacea is able to increase natural killer cell activity and other immune parameters of the blood of people with AIDS and chronic fatigue syndrome.[21] All we need now are some large, human clinical trials for these and other devastating illnesses.

The antiviral effect of a product using the whole plant of echinacea was shown to be equivalent to the body's own interferon production.[22]

Echinacea also has mild antibacterial and anti-inflammatory properties. It is an immune stimulator that works by inhibiting hyaluronidase (a destructive enzyme); and activating phagocytic activity and increasing beneficial T cell activity and interferon. This means that its effects are more in helping the body fight infections rather than directly killing the 'bugs'.

External

Echinacea is one of the herbs in toothpastes and mouth rinses for effectively reducing plaque build-up and strengthening the gums so that there is less bleeding. I recommend it as a mouth wash to disinfect the teeth and gums. Some of my patients have found it helpful for treating mouth ulcers and gum infections. There are a few toothpastes available that contain echinacea, sage, myrrh and other herbs.

For both mouth and throat infections, buy the tea or powder, make a strong tea, let it cool, and use it as a gargle. If you take echinacea tablets, let them dissolve in the mouth, so that the remedy stays in your mouth and throat area for longer. The taste is rather unpleasant and bitter, but the direct contact of the herb with the throat and mouth tissues seems to be more effective than if you swallow the tablet and wait for it to be absorbed and circulated via the blood.

My preference is to combine a liquid herbal extract with glycerine in a small bottle. Shake this well before using 1–2 teaspoons of the mix in ½ cup tepid water as a gargle. If you can also obtain myrrh, sage and golden seal, combine them with a few drops of tea tree oil to make a powerful gargle. If you are prone to throat and gum infections, use a daily herbal gargle as an antiseptic and preventive.

For acne and minor wounds dab on undiluted echinacea liquid extract with a cotton bud or a dropper if small areas of the skin are involved. For larger areas, or as an antiseptic or healing wash, dilute the herb with a saline solution. For people who have poor immune systems or tend to get small injuries that develop into serious, long-lasting external wounds, I make up a combination of echinacea, golden seal and calendula extracts, plus tea tree oil, and recommend it be applied on the skin on any scratch, bite or wound. In my experience this works extremely well for prevention and early treatment.

To make external healing remedies mix echinacea and other herbal extracts into plain bases. These will keep quite well because the extracts are preserved with alcohol. You can use dried powdered herbs, but the resultant remedies tend to be somewhat 'gritty'; if you mix a strong tea into the base, it goes off after a relatively short time, depending on the temperature, the base and the herb.

External applications of echinacea may help prevent sun damage to skin. Many Australians have sun spots removed routinely; your herbalist could make up a strong echinacea cream specially for you to see if this reduces the number that occur. Because of its carotenoid content calendula could also be combined with it.

My experience is that as an external remedy echinacea is a useful antiseptic, anti-inflammatory and wound healer.

Cautions and adverse effects

- A German Commission E monograph states that echinacea should not be used in individuals with autoimmune illness and other progressive systemic diseases like tuberculosis and multiple sclerosis. As far as I know, there is no good reason for this caution.
- For sensitive skins, dilute echinacea in water or in an external base. In all cases, always do a test on a small area before applying any external remedy or cosmetic. For infections, dilute echinacea in commercial saline or distilled water from a pharmacy.
- Echinacea is about to join evening primrose oil as an overused remedy. It is not a cure-all. If you take it long term without a break, you might even develop a sensitivity to it — although only one case has been reported, in spite of wide usage throughout the world.
- Adverse effects are rare at medicinal doses; this is based on observations from hundreds of trials and millions of patients. It is possible that echinacea, in common with every other plant, could cause an allergic reaction. However, in my twenty years of prescribing herbal remedies I have not observed one allergic reaction to echinacea, nor have other experienced herbalists to whom I have spoken.

Known therapeutic components

- Polysaccharides stimulate T and B lymphocytes that activate natural killer cells and phagocytic macrophages — these polysaccharides help your body attack and destroy harmful bacteria, viruses and aberrant cells.

Interferon is also stimulated, which adds to the immune activity.

- Inulin is a polysaccharide that stimulates *Bifidobacteria* (bacteria necessary for healthy intestinal function). This compound is also thought to protect connective tissue and aid the body's immune defences.
- Glycoproteins also have immune enhancing effects.
- Echinacin B reduces inflammation and promotes wound healing; it may also help regenerate connective tissue.
- Echinacoside is a glycoside with slight antibiotic properties, and also helps protect the skin from damage by reducing collagen breakdown.
- Flavonoids have anti-inflammatory effects.
- Alkylamides are components with immune stimulatory effects. These components are responsible for causing a tingling sensation in the mouth known as 'the buzz'. This is not an adverse effect, but gives an indication of the herbal activity on the mucous membranes. Remember, the mucous membranes are your first line of defence against invading micro-organisms.
- Caffeic acid derivatives, notably cichoric acid, have the ability to increase the activity of particular white cells that are involved in fighting infections.
- Polyacetylenes and aromatic oils also provide therapeutic effects.

Echinacea products

Tablets, capsules, teas, powder and liquid extracts are widely available. The strengths of products are variable, so be guided by the label dosages.

Injectable forms of echinacea are available to medical practitioners in Europe.

A popular German remedy for treating infections is Esberitox, which combines echinacea with baptisia and thuja. My clinical experience is that combinations are more effective than single herbs.

A few companies are making so-called guaranteed potency products based on one therapeutic component. Since there are many therapeutic compounds in echinacea these are probably not worth the extra cost.

Growing and making your own remedies

Echinacea purpurea plants and seeds are available from most nurseries in Australia.

Make a tea using 1–2 teaspoons finely chopped fresh leaves to 1 cup water, plus 1 dessertspoon lemon juice to help extract the components from the plant. Cover the tea, and leave for at least an hour; drink it cold with added fruit juice. Add a little honey if necessary to make it more palatable. Drink 1 cup a day as a preventive dose, or 3 cups daily for about 7–10 days to treat an infection.

Alternatively, simmer 2 teaspoons cleaned, grated root in 2 cups water, together with 2 teaspoons apple cider vinegar and 2 teaspoons honey. Cover, and allow to cool. Sip this throughout the day, or take it in three doses after meals.

Another option is to make fresh plant juices from either the above-ground parts or the roots. These keep for about three days in the fridge. A dosage guide would be 2 teaspoons, three times daily, for 7–10 days. Take half that quantity long term, with short breaks of at least three days a month in the treatment.

Making extracts and tinctures is quite demanding, and not feasible for personal use.

Dosages and duration of treatment

In the light of all the studies, I recommend that you take echinacea in measured periods of time; not because it is harmful, but if echinacea is taken without a break the immune system seems to get used to it.

Note: For best results I recommend that echinacea be used somewhat differently depending on whether the infection is acute (sudden, severe) or chronic (long standing).

Acute infections

For acute infections, such as the flu, take 6 g tablets or 6 ml extract daily in divided doses — spread throughout the day in 3–6 doses if possible — for 6–10 days. This is a higher dose than on most labels, but it is short term. If the problem persists, take another remedy such as garlic and vitamin C for a few days before resuming the echinacea. If you are getting worse, always consult a health practitioner.

Chronic infections

For chronic infections, such as bronchitis, take 3 g (or 3 ml) daily in divided doses. Use for two weeks, then have a two-day break before continuing with the remedy. If your self-treatment is not effective, see a health practitioner or use additional remedies.[23]

As a preventive

I recommend alternating one course of echinacea with another natural therapy such as garlic, or whatever other remedy is appropriate for your main health problem.

Give children proportionately lower doses according to age (see pp. 4–5).

Summary

Echinacea enhances the body's resistance against infections, stimulates the lymphatic system and promotes healing. It is a valuable medicinal herb, but it suffers from exaggerated claims and overusage.

Ginkgo (*Ginkgo biloba*)

The common name is maidenhair tree, but it is now usually called ginkgo.

Background

The oldest Chinese herbal, dated 2000 BC, mentions ginkgo as benefiting the brain. Interestingly, the leaf (which has two lobes) does resemble a cross-section of the human brain.

In Germany and France guaranteed potency ginkgo leaf extracts and tablets are used by medical practitioners, and have been a common prescription medicine for many years. Worldwide, over 10 million prescriptions are now written for this herb each year.

The part used

In Western medical herbalism the green leaves are dried and processed.

Therapeutic use

Internal

Ginkgo is an effective remedy:
- It acts as an antioxidant and free radical scavenger by helping to break down toxic substances in the body, as well as reducing some harmful oxidative processes that occur naturally in the body.[24] One way that antioxidants work is by protecting red cells that carry oxygen and nutrients, and this may explain why ginkgo helps problems such as memory loss.
- Experimental evidence shows that its components have some neuroprotective effects in the brain and other nerve tissue, and that neurotransmitter (brain signal) activity is helped.

- It stabilises the body's membranes. These cell walls (linings) are the first line of defence against damage and invasion, and act as a filter to absorb beneficial substances, such as glucose and oxygen for energy, while keeping out toxins of various kinds. Nerve tissue and brain cells need particular protection because they have only small reserves of energy. When blood vessel linings are stabilised, fluid and mineral balance is improved. Excess fluid retention in the brain leads to a build-up of toxins, and is associated with an ageing brain.
- Blood vessels are strengthened, relaxed and dilated. Since the blood carries oxygen and nutrients, nothing will work efficiently in the absence of efficient arteries and veins.
- Blood flow is improved. The blood is less 'sticky', and the formation of clots and inflammatory substances is reduced. When blood flows freely through the arteries and veins, there is less likelihood of plaque build-up on the blood vessel walls (atherosclerosis).
- Biochemical benefits include an increase in brain chemicals such as dopamine, with a corresponding decrease in histamine. Dopamine is a beneficial brain chemical, while histamine has some necessary functions, though it can cause irritation, inflammation and allergic reactions. The absorption of choline by the brain also improves; choline is a B vitamin necessary for nerve and muscle function.

There are hundreds of published scientific studies on ginkgo, and a brief summary of a few of the double-blind controlled studies follows.

Clinical trials in Germany show that it is helpful for about one-third of patients suffering from mild to moderate primary degenerative dementia of the Alzheimer type and from multi-infarct dementia. There were improvements in memory, attention, mood, appetite, emotional stability, motivation and initiative, and a decrease in orientation disturbances, anxiety and depression.[25]

A trial of depressed people between 51 and 78 years of age, who had not been helped by pharmaceutical antidepressants, showed that ginkgo (in addition to the drugs) subsequently improved the symptoms of depression quite markedly compared to those who received the placebo with their medication.[26]

Fifteen healthy young people, average age 29 years, were given single doses of ginkgo for five days. They were monitored with sophisticated brain-monitoring equipment, and it was established that ginkgo enhanced vigilance and improved some cognitive (mental) skills. Other studies have shown that test results can be improved in young people if they take ginkgo about an hour before examinations. If you are using it for this short-term purpose, always do a little trial of the remedy beforehand just in case it does not suit you. It would be disastrous, for instance, if you had a severe allergic reaction during your exams, so always try anything new beforehand.

People with long-term blocked arteries in the legs were given ginkgo for four weeks, and subsequent tests showed a 38 per cent reduction in blockages.[27] Many other studies show that ginkgo improves circulation in the legs, as evidenced by people being able to walk longer distances with less leg pain.

The following is a list of other problems that may be helped by ginkgo, all of which are supported by scientific studies:

- short-term memory loss, mental fatigue, confusion, diminished learning capacity, dizziness and all conditions relating to poor brain circulation
- migraine and other headaches
- additional therapy or preventive for atherosclerosis, thrombosis, angina, some types of irregular heartbeats and congestive heart failure
- intermittent claudication (leg cramps brought on by walking a short distance, or aching fatigue in the calf muscle), haemorrhoids, varicose veins, Raynaud's syndrome,

and generally all problems relating to poor circulation anywhere in the body, because it has been verified that ginkgo increases blood flow in the tiny blood vessels
- cochlear deafness, tinnitus (ringing in the ears)
- impotence due to arterial deficits, but treatment is required for six months
- I recommend ginkgo as support or preventive therapy for the following: diabetic vascular diseases, and as a protective against macular degeneration
- all eye problems related to poor circulation, including diabetic retinopathy
- before and after surgery to improve blood flow, and to strengthen blood and lymph vessels
- recovery from stroke, accidents and head injuries.

Cautions and adverse effects

- In my clinic I have not observed any side effects with ginkgo leaf extracts or tablets, but there are reports from researchers of mild gastric upsets, skin rashes and headaches. These reactions occur in less than 2 per cent of patients, and are probably allergic reactions.
- If you are taking pharmaceuticals, consult your prescribing doctor before taking additional remedies. It is possible, for example, that ginkgo could increase the effect of blood thinning medication. While it is good to have the blood flowing smoothly through all the blood vessels, you don't want your blood to get too thin.
- All serious disorders should be supervised by a health practitioner. Ginkgo may be a support therapy only.

Known therapeutic components

- A number of scientific studies have confirmed that a concentrated, standardised

leaf extract works better than isolated constituents. However, it is commonly agreed that the most important therapeutic substances in the plant are the various types of flavonoids.
- Terpene lactones, in particular, are useful therapeutically. These include ginkgolides, which have the capacity to reduce inflammation, thin the blood and reduce the effects of toxic shock and allergies. In animal studies ginkgolides A and B reduced the size and percentage of damaged brain cells following lack of oxygen.
- Bilobalide is a terpenoid in ginkgo that protects nerve tissue from damage caused by an oxygen deficit.

Ginkgo products

The standardised extract used in many of the European clinical trials is very concentrated and contains 24 per cent flavone glycosides. Some products also guarantee 6 per cent terpenoids. There are varying qualities and strengths of ginkgo extracts and tablets. When EGb 761, a standardised product used in Europe, was compared to a ordinary herbal extract of ginkgo, the results were as follows:[28]

Therapeutic components of ginkgo	Standardised EGb 761 (%)	Ordinary ginkgo herbal extract (%)
Bilobalide	2.9	0.04–0.2
Ginkgolide	3.1	0.06–0.23
Flavone glycosides	24.0	0.50–1.80

This table shows that it is likely that common herbal extracts and tablets have only about one-tenth of the therapeutic activity of the remedies used in European trials. However, in a number of clinical trials this standardised product was used at a daily dosage of about 120 mg, whereas in my clinic I generally prescribe between 1000 and 3000 mg of a non-standardised product. My dosage gives a similar therapeutic value.

For sensitive or frail people with serious health problems, it might be worth paying the extra for a standardised product, rather than increasing the dose of a non-standardised product. This is because some standardised products have a low level of ginkgolic acid — the component considered to cause adverse reactions and allergies.

Growing and making your own remedies

Ginkgo is one of the world's oldest living tree species, and is native to China. It no longer grows in the wild, but is now cultivated in many temperate countries, including Australia. There are distinct male and female trees — the female tree produces a fruit that is smelly and messy when ripe. The pulp of its fruit is toxic, although the internal nut is not. In Chinese medicine the nut and the leaves are used in formulas.

In most Western countries nurseries sell the male species of ginkgo. It is a tall, deciduous tree, the autumn leaves colour yellow before they fall. In Western herbal medicine the green leaves are dried and powdered to make herbal extracts or tablets. I cannot recommend making your own remedies as there is no information on the medicinal use of the unprocessed fresh leaves — perhaps because they are too leathery to be digested and absorbed.

People with land might consider growing some trees as a future cash crop, but you would need to ensure that the area was chemically free and unpolluted. Ginkgo requires a good water supply in the hot weather, and takes about fifteen years to reach its full height. The tree has a very long life, but constant harvesting of the spring leaves may reduce this somewhat. Obviously, you would not strip the trees completely, but take a portion of the foliage, and perhaps give each tree a 'rest' year.

Dosages and duration of treatment

A typical dose of standardised products would be 40 mg, three times daily, taken consistently for at least twelve weeks. It takes time to rebuild blood vessel walls and nerves, and to improve cell functioning. In some trials a daily dose of 240 mg was used for up to six months, after which time the dose was lowered.

As there are so many different products now available, follow the label instructions for the dosage unless your health practitioner advises otherwise.

I have never prescribed ginkgo for infants or young children. However, there is no reason why it cannot be taken by school-age children if their health problems warrant it. As explained on pp. 4–5, give children proportionate dosages according to age.

Summary

Ginkgo is a remedy that can be taken indefinitely, especially for elderly people, because it not only helps circulation but acts as an antioxidant.

Ginseng

Asian ginseng
(*Panax ginseng*)

Background

Asian ginseng is one of the oldest natural remedies, and has a continuous history of use for at least 2000 years. In traditional Chinese medicine it is recommended to help strengthen the body, aid recovery from illness, improve the mind and mental functioning, and enhance the body's circulatory and organ systems. In other words, to promote *chi* (the flow of energy within the body).

It is probably the most researched medicinal herb, although much of the research has not been published in English. In Chinese medicine herbs are commonly prescribed in formulas or even as part of the diet, so the effects are somewhat different compared with the more recent Western use of Chinese herbs. In this section I will cover mainly the Western use of ginseng.

The part used

The root.

Therapeutic use

Internal

In general, ginseng is most useful as a periodic tonic to counter fatigue and stress, and to accelerate convalescence. It is also recommended to enhance mental and physical performance.[29] However, there is unlikely to be any improvement if these levels are already optimal, as the body can only reach its best. Athletes who have peaked may benefit from the antistress effects of ginseng, but each person should do a trial with ginseng before an event, just in case of allergic or sensitivity reactions.

A feature of ginseng is that it is classed as an 'adaptogen' (a natural non-toxic remedy that provides support during times of physical and mental stress, and helps balance the body's functions).

A few examples of clinical trials follow.

In a scientifically controlled study ginseng was shown to be effective in treating functional fatigue, anxiety or nervousness and poor concentration. In this study some basic low-dose vitamins and a few minerals were also included in the formula.[30] Another trial showed that for improving the quality of life Asian ginseng, together with a multivitamin, was more effective than a multivitamin alone. In addition, the

ginseng group had less weight gain and lower diastolic blood pressure.

A standardised ginseng extract was evaluated in patients who had difficulty maintaining normal occupations or social activities, and who could not function efficiently. After fifty-six days they showed improvements in mental alertness, memory, motivation, mood, sociability, co-operation, appetite and personal hygiene. The investigators considered that ginseng gave a good result in 96 per cent of cases.[31] Nurses who worked night shift improved in alertness, tranquillity, and in speed and co-ordination, compared to those who did not take ginseng.[32]

Eight weeks on Asian ginseng at 100–200 mg daily reduced fasting blood glucose levels and body weight in newly diagnosed non-insulin-dependent diabetic patients.[33] There were also improvements in mood, physical and emotional wellbeing. This is a very low dose but a very high quality, concentrated product was taken. People with early stage non-insulin-dependent diabetes would have to be tested under medical supervision, because only doctors can legally treat this condition.

Two preliminary trials with 150 men showed that ginseng can slightly increase testosterone levels, increase sperm count and motility, and improve some types of impotence. These hormonal increases occur only in cases of under-functioning.

In experimental animal studies, ginseng protected the liver from toxins, stimulated adrenal activity and increased white cell production. It may promote natural antioxidant activity, and was shown to inhibit various kinds of cultured tumour cells.[34] It is not known whether ginseng taken orally would effectively treat a tumour. However, Japanese laboratory experiments showed that components in ginseng can inhibit the growth of liver cancer cells and convert them to more normal cells.[35]

Ginseng is one of the natural remedies that could be useful for patients undergoing cancer treatments, as they are usually severely stressed emotionally and physically from both the disease and the medical treatment. Non-toxic natural remedies that have antioxidant and immune enhancing properties are likely to improve the health status of people with cancer.

Many trials have demonstrated that various physical and mental stresses are handled more effectively when ginseng is taken. You may be one of those people who find that when you are stressed you are more likely to catch infections. Antistress remedies indirectly improve immune functioning. The ability to prevent common infections and improve immune functioning is due to ginseng's action in strengthening the body's own immune system, rather than a direct attack on the micro-organisms. Laboratory studies showed that Asian ginseng improved the natural killer cells of patients with AIDS and chronic fatigue syndrome, but trials have not yet been done directly on humans suffering from these problems.

There is evidence that ginseng can reduce the damaging effects of radiation, viruses, some toxins, oxygen deprivation, hypobaric pressure, light or temperature stress and movement restriction. I recommend ginseng for meno-pausal stress, and a few tests show that it can improve vaginal tissue in older women.

Asian ginseng extract was shown to have beneficial effects on the cardiovascular system and blood lipids generally; it helps keep the blood thin, increases blood flow to the heart, and helps normalise blood pressure.

Components in ginseng act as free radical scavengers, and reduce harmful fat metabolism. In other words, ginseng has antioxidant activity, as well as promoting the body's own anti-oxidant system.

Cautions and adverse effects

- As for other tonics, I recommend you take ginseng daily, in one or two doses (after breakfast and after lunch), otherwise it may cause insomnia.

- No serious side effects have been reported from China and countries where the herb is used as a controlled medicine or according to established traditional use. Excess dosages, adulterated products and pro-longed or inappropriate use may well cause some of the adverse effects reported from Australia, England and the USA, where gin-seng is classed as a food supplement rather than as a medicinal herb.
- Ginseng is not recommended during preg-nancy because the effects are not known, nor should it be used during acute illnesses, such as influenza and other suddenly occur-ring infections, because it may stimulate the micro-organisms. It should not be taken by people who are on medication for hyperten-sion, or with stimulants such as caffeine.[36]
- Asian ginseng is known to increase the activ-ity of antidepressant medications, so people taking these should not also take this herb.
- Generally, ginseng is not appropriate for children.

Known therapeutic components

- Ginsenosides contain different types of triterpenoid saponin glycosides, about ten of which are thought to be significant in respect of the overall beneficial effects of ginseng. Oddly, some of the components have opposing effects, and Western scien-tists tend to consider that these offset each other; however, Asian researchers — and natural therapists — are of the opinion that the herb is utilised in the body according to the physical and mental state of the patient.
- Aromatic oils inhibit thrombocyte aggrega-tion (decrease excess blood clotting).
- Panaxanes have hypoglycaemic activity (lower blood sugar).
- Benzoic acid derivatives and flavonoids are antioxidants, and may be responsible for the tonic properties.
- Phenolic substances have antistress, anti-fatigue and liver detoxifying effects.

- Phytosterols produce beneficial hormonal effects in the body.

Ginseng products

Numerous ginseng products are available, including dried root, powders, capsules, tablets and liquid extracts of various kinds. Some standardised products are available, and may be worth the additional expense for people suffering from serious health problems.

Basically two types of Asian ginseng are available, so-called 'red' and 'white' varieties. They are dried and preserved differently, and there is no known difference in their therapeutic actions. Korean ginseng is the same herb.

Growing and making your own remedies

The plants are not sold outside Asia.

The root should be powdered and simmered in water to extract all the components. If you buy pieces of root, grate or chop it finely, and soak it in just enough vinegar to cover it. Add a little honey to make it palatable. Take 1 teaspoon daily of the remedy.

Dosages and duration of treatment

Follow the label dosages, because the products vary considerably in their strengths. Take for three months at a time only; then have a month's break before continuing the treatment.

I do not prescribe ginseng for children under the age of fourteen.

Summary

Ginseng is probably the best tonic and anti-stress herb in the world.

Recommended reading

Hobbs, C. *The Ginsengs*: A *User's Guide*. Botanica Press, Santa Cruz, Calif., 1996.

Siberian ginseng
(*Eleutherococcus senticosus*)

Siberian ginseng has qualities in common with Asian ginseng, notably its tonic and antistress properties. In my clinic I use Siberian ginseng more for younger people and women. It is one of the herbs I commonly prescribe as part of a menopause programme, because it helps the adrenal glands in particular.[37] Menopause is quite stressful because of the changing hormone pattern. The adrenal glands not only produce hormones to help cope with stress, they also make a hormone that the body can convert to oestrogen.

A number of Russian experiments have demonstrated that Siberian ginseng can improve athletic performance, reduce total disease incidence, lower blood sugar and help the body cope with various toxins. In one study of highly trained runners Siberian ginseng did not improve performance. However, in my clinic I have found that it seems to improve athletic performance. I am not seeing world-class athletes, so my conclusion is that it is helpful for people who have not yet reached their maximum performance level.

A number of studies show that it helps the immune system by increasing interferon and activating natural killer cells and macrophages, which explains why it can be helpful in treating serious diseases. Large-scale trials have been carried out on Russian workers, and those who received the ginseng had fewer incidences of influenza and other infections, and the attacks were less severe.[38]

Siberian ginseng is highly recommended to help prevent influenza and other infections, and as support therapy in treating high blood pressure.

Generally, it provides tonic effects similar to those of Asian ginseng, but its main therapeutically active components are eleutherosides.

Siberian ginseng is available in tablets, capsules and liquid extracts. I generally prescribe between 3–5 ml daily of a good quality extract, taken after breakfast.

I do not prescribe ginseng for children under the age of fourteen.

Other herbs considered to be adaptogens

Withania (*Withania somnifera*)
Astragalus (*Astragalus membranaceus*)
Holy basil (*Ocimum sanctum*)

Gotu kola (*Centella asiatica*)

Gotu kola is also known as Indian pennywort or hydrocotyle, and by various other common names. *Centella asiatica* and related species are native to India, Australia and other regions of the southern hemisphere.

This herb is sometimes confused with other plants in regard to plant names, plant identification and therapeutic effects. Unlike cola nut, it does not contain caffeine, and is not a stimulant.

Background

A Chinese sage who died in 1933 was said to have lived 256 years! It is recorded that he would have lived longer except for the rich food he consumed at a banquet honouring his 255th birthday. The sage claimed that he lived and ate simply, and that a herbal formula was partly responsible for his long, healthy life. Gotu kola is reported to be the main therapeutic ingredient in this formula. A Scotsman who knew this Chinese sage subsequently marketed the formula as Fo-Ti-Tieng — a blend of gotu kola, meadowsweet and African cola nut. Fo-Ti-Tieng has no meaning in Chinese, but is a registered name for a herbal formula that is commonly promoted as a tonic. Various products with similar-sounding names may or may not contain gotu kola.

In traditional Chinese medicine gotu kola is said to be cooling and detoxifying, and is used for upper respiratory and other acute infections, as well as for problems relating to excess mucus, inflammation, boils, jaundice and cirrhosis of the liver. Hawaiians use this herb for similar problems.

Gotu kola and its preparations have been used in the Indian (Ayurvedic) system of medicine, and in Madagascar, since ancient times. It was used as a treatment for many skin and nervous disorders, as well as for asthma and hypertension, and as a tonic. One researcher maintains that it is a favourite food of Indian elephants — which may explain why people began trying it to improve their memory!

The part used

The leaves.

Therapeutic use

Internal

Gotu kola is becoming increasingly popular with European herbalists because it is a nerve and general tonic, a learning and memory stimulant, a relaxant, an anti-inflammatory, and aids the formation of the body's connective tissue.

A major natural therapies textbook[39] lists the following general benefits of gotu kola:

- stimulates hair and nail growth
- improves the elasticity and strength of the skin
- increases blood flow to connective tissue
- increases the formation of healthy structural connective tissue — connective tissue includes joint structures such as cartilage.

Gotu kola helps with studying, memory and concentration. Two studies have shown it benefits mentally retarded children by improving their IQ and behaviour. Tests on animals also showed an impressive improvement in memory.[40] Gotu kola has been used with some success with children with attention deficit disorder.

Isolated components in gotu kola have mild tranquillising, antistress and antianxiety effects, and these may be partially responsible for the improvements in concentration. When you are agitated or upset, it is hard to concentrate.

A number of skin conditions have been treated successfully with gotu kola. These include cellulitis and other infectious inflammatory skin problems. (Cellulitis is not the dreaded, dimpled/citrus skin-like condition (cellulite) that affects the thighs and buttocks of some women, but it is a serious infection of the tissues lying just under the surface of the skin.)

Gotu kola has been used successfully to treat leprosy wounds, for burns, and following surgery. Obviously, these serious conditions were treated under medical supervision, but for minor household burns, and to help injuries heal without excessive scar tissue, this herb could be considered for both internal and external use. One study showed that gotu kola was helpful in up to 82 per cent of patients who have excessive scar formation, and that it was significantly beneficial before surgery as a preventive, that is, for getting the wounded tissue to repair more healthily. Unfortunately, in our high-tech medical system, it is almost impossible to get medical specialists to test natural therapies.

Enough evidence exists to support gotu kola as a skin and tissue strengthener, and it should therefore improve the quality of skin, hair, nails, gums, joints, blood vessels and other structures, and perhaps even bones.

The walls of the blood vessels are connective tissue, and gotu kola is therefore of benefit for a wide range of circulatory problems such as varicose veins and haemorrhoids. I recommend it be used internally, as well as in external applications. Visit a professional herbalist to get the external cream made up, and you should try a small test patch on your skin before use.

It is also a natural remedy that could be used as support therapy in the treatment of hypertension, as the herb has the capacity to relax and dilate blood vessels. Older studies showed that gotu kola helped with cirrhosis of the liver based on biopsy tests, but recent scientific tests do not appear to have been undertaken.

Some nurseries in Australia sell this as 'Arthritis Herb', with instructions to consume two leaves per day. There are anecdotal reports of this giving remarkable relief from osteoarthritis, but it may take up to three months to have any therapeutic effects. Although not used traditionally as an arthritis remedy, gotu kola has beneficial effects on connective tissue, and this is probably a good example of how science might lead to new ways of using traditional herbs. Gotu kola has also been tested on inflammatory joint problems, including scleroderma, and both the skin and joints showed improvements. Presumably, the herb works through its effect of normalising connective tissue.

I often include gotu kola in menopause formulas because it seems to help balance the nervous system. A number of researchers report that gotu kola can act as both a mental tonic and a gentle sedative. Other plants in the same plant family (notably aniseed, celery, dong quai and fennel) are recommended for their hormonal-balancing effect or to relieve arthritic symptoms.

External

Gotu kola is basically anti-inflammatory and wound healing. Laboratory studies show that constituents in gotu kola can stimulate the body's biosynthesis of types of connective tissue.[41]

This herb is underutilised as an external cream, poultice or compress for relieving inflammatory skin disorders and problems such as varicose veins. It may help some types of dermatitis, as well as skin problems associated with lupus and scleroderma.

In France in the 1960s a standardised gotu kola extract was used effectively in the treatment of patients with burns, either as an external application or as an intramuscular injection. Used in this way the extract prevented or limited the shrinking and swelling of the skin, inhibited scar formation, increased healing and decreased fibrosis (thickened tissue). Presumably better treatments are now available for serious burns, but the earlier medical use of gotu kola validates the recommendation that it be used for treating minor household burns and other injuries.

Cautions and adverse effects

- A test should be done on a tiny area of the skin before using any new remedy, especially for people with skin diseases and sensitive skins. My experience is that allergic or sensitivity reactions to gotu kola are extremely rare.
- A lay person promoting gotu kola leaves as a treatment for arthritis said that large quantities of the leaf as an internal remedy may cause dizziness and headaches. Given that gotu kola is used as a vegetable in some countries, presumably in small quantities, I wonder if these reported side effects relate to similar-looking plants.
- As an internal remedy, both the plant and its therapeutic components are regarded as safe by health practitioners and researchers throughout the world.

Note: One study on hairless mice in 1972 showed that skin tumours were caused by applications of the isolated constituent, asiaticoside. Asiaticoside represents about 1 per cent of the whole plant. I suggest that the external application of gotu kola be restricted to two months' treatment, and not used for people who have past or present skin cancers.

Known therapeutic components

- Triterpenes, including asiaticoside, are probably the most important components.

- Madecassoside, asiatic and madecassic acid.
- Volatile oils (mono- and sesquiterpenes).

Gotu kola products

Tablets and capsules are available over the counter. Most Australian herbalists use liquid extracts.

Centellase, Madecassol and TECA are some of the pharmaceutical forms of gotu kola that are available in Europe for treating circulatory and other disorders.

Growing and making your own remedies

Gotu kola (*Centella asiatica*) grows in the wild and in gardens, and spreads abundantly, especially in damp, sheltered places. In common with many plants, the leaves vary somewhat, and botanical texts describe them as 'broadly cordate or orbicular to reniform, entire, sinuate or crenate, glabrous or pubescent' — which means they are roundish or kidney shaped, the margins are either wavy or straight, and the texture is either smooth or lightly hairy! The leaves are similar to those of the common sweet violet, which explains why gotu kola is sometimes called Chinese violet. When in doubt about identification, ask the advice of a botanist.

Centella cordifolia also grows in many parts of Australia, and, as far as I can judge, is also sold as 'Arthritis Herb'. C. *cordifolia* has not been tested, but it is very similar in appearance and taste to gotu kola, so I presume the therapeutic effects may be somewhat comparable. The plant label recommends a dose of two leaves a day.

Gotu kola will grow quite well in a largish pot, but you must water it regularly, and keep it in the shade in summer.

If you have access to the plant, the fresh leaves are perhaps the best way to use this remedy, although the taste is unpleasantly bitter. Cut 2 cups of fresh leaves, and steep them in 475 ml apple cider vinegar. Take 2 teaspoons daily of this herbal vinegar on salad or vegetables.

Dosages and duration of treatment

I recommend 2 fresh leaves daily for three months, then 1 leaf daily as a maintenance internal treatment. Alternatively, take 2 ml, twice daily, of a liquid extract or tincture for three months, then half this dose for long-term use.

Use the label dosages for capsules and tablets, again full dose for three months, then half the dose indefinitely.

If the remedy has not produced an effect after three months, do not continue with it.

Do not use gotu kola externally on a daily basis for longer than two months.

Children's dosages are proportionately less according to age (see pp. 4–5).

Summary

Gotu kola is a useful herb internally and externally for skin, nervous, circulatory and joint problems.

Hawthorn
(*Crataegus oxyacanthoides*, *C. monogyna*, *C. laevigata*, and other species)

Other species are also used in traditional Chinese herbal formulas.

Background

Like many other European herbs, hawthorn's medicinal use can be traced back to the Greek herbalist Dioscorides in the first century AD. Over the centuries it has been used for a wide range of disorders, and as a food and wine. By the end of the nineteenth century European doctors were prescribing hawthorn for cardiovascular problems.

In 1919 a medical practitioner in the USA wrote: 'From these results my deductions are that *Crataegus oxyacantha* is superior to any other of the well known and tried remedies at present in use in the treatment of heart disease, because it seems to cure while the other remedies are only palliative at best'. He also recommended hawthorn for fluid retention.[42]

It is quite remarkable that, without knowing anything about hawthorn's flavonoid content and its specific therapeutic action, health practitioners in a number of different countries were able to pinpoint the medicinal value of this plant over a hundred years ago.

The part used

Australian herbalists have commonly used mature berries collected in autumn, but the flowers and leaves are now considered to be equally therapeutic. My preference is to combine the different parts of the plant.

Therapeutic use

Internal

Hawthorn may be helpful for some forms of hypertension, especially when the blood pressure is usually normal but rises excessively on exertion or from nervousness (technically known as vascular hyperreactivity). It should help mild cases of angina, and may strengthen the heart so that more blood is pumped and more oxygen carried. Generally, hawthorn could be considered for treating a wide variety of heart and circulatory problems, including regulating the heartbeat and helping to repair damaged blood vessels.

Hawthorn is an ideal treatment for elderly people who do not have a specific cardiovascular disease but who would benefit from a gentle long-term heart and circulatory tonic. It could be considered also as a suitable remedy for those in the early stages of congestive heart failure, as it is likely to slow down the rate of deterioration. Of course, people in these categories should be monitored regularly by a medical practitioner. Toxicological studies show that it can be used long term without adverse effects.[43] A German study on 136 patients confirmed that hawthorn is an effective and low-risk herb for patients with mild to moderate forms of cardiac insufficiency.[44]

In one study patients with early-stage congestive heart failure were given 160 mg hawthorn extract daily. After eight weeks they were able to do aerobic exercise for longer, and had increased endurance and wellbeing.[45] At least fifteen trials have shown that doses of between 160 and 900 mg daily can improve heart function, based on electrocardiogram measurements, shortness of breath, angina pain and recovery from exercising.[46] This means that the heart muscle is stronger, blood flow is improved and oxygen uptake is increased.

Chinese studies have shown that hawthorn is effective in lowering human blood pressure, blood triglycerides and cholesterol.[47]

The most relevant studies showing benefits to the heart and circulation have been carried out on humans in Europe with products that use extracts combining hawthorn leaves and flowers with a standardised flavonoid content, and taken for a period of at least four to eight weeks.

Hawthorn has alleviated some cases of menopausal flushing, possibly because of the effect of the flavonoids on blood vessels or because it is also a traditional mild sedative. In addition, the flavonoids in hawthorn are useful antioxidants.

Cautions and adverse effects

- Never use hawthorn if you are taking pharmaceutical medication for any heart or circulatory problems unless you get approval from your medical practitioner, because the combination might be too strong.
- All serious health problems, especially those involving the heart, require regular supervision by a medical practitioner.

Long-term oral studies and laboratory tests show that hawthorn extract is well tolerated, and that there is no evidence of toxicity or abnormal cell growth.[48]

Known therapeutic components

- The most important components are flavonoids (quercetin, rutin, hyperoside, vitexin), procyanidine, pentacyclical triterpenes and aromatic carbon dioxides. Evidence links flavonoids with an increased blood flow in the heart, lowered blood pressure and increased heart muscle action.
- Epicatechin and proanthocyanidin are the most potent antioxidants in hawthorn.
- The oligomeric procyanidins in hawthorn (commonly referred to as OPCs) are well absorbed. Experimentally, as separate components they also increase heart blood flow and heart muscle action, and have hypotensive effects.
- Epicatechin also has some of these effects.

Another feature of OPCs is a capacity to protect connective tissue such as that found in the walls of blood vessels. OPCs are the same components that are sold as grapeseed extract, which is used by European medical specialists for treating circulatory problems such as varicose veins.

As is the case with many herbs, the therapeutic effectiveness cannot yet be attributed to one component, but many of the scientific studies in Europe have used products that have a standardised level of some of the flavonoids.

Hawthorn products

Liquid extracts and tablets are not commonly available in retail outlets, although a few over-the-counter formulas contain small quantities.

Dried hawthorn berries are readily available, usually in the form of herbal teas.

Growing and making your own remedies

The hawthorn used medicinally grows wild throughout Europe, and is sometimes cultivated as a hedge. It was introduced into Australia and other countries, and is now naturalised in many temperate zones of the world.

Use 3–5 g daily of fresh, finely chopped spring leaves or flowers as a tea, or a slightly higher dose of the fresh berries.

Note: If you are harvesting the plants for your own use, ensure that you have correctly identified the medicinal species, as there are many plants called hawthorn.

Dosages and duration of treatment

Two doses of 160 mg daily is the commonly recommended dose of a standardised extract made from the hawthorn leaves and flowers. Higher doses are sometimes individually prescribed under medical supervision.

Herbal remedies made from berries and leaves are usually recommended in a dose of 3–5 g daily for treatment and preventive purposes.

Although some studies have been over a short period, most practitioners have observed that hawthorn is slow acting, and it might take more than two months to achieve a noticeable therapeutic effect. Where its use is warranted, it can be considered a long-term remedy, particularly for elderly people, because it has useful antioxidant effects.

Children should be given this remedy only if prescribed by a qualified herbalist.

Summary

Hawthorn is a non-toxic remedy for the heart and circulation.

Kava
(*Piper methysticum* ('intoxicating pepper'))

Background

At least from the eighteenth century onwards many Pacific Islanders have made an alcoholic drink from kava, and symbols, rules and procedures are associated with its preparation and consumption. It is still a social drink in many islands, used to welcome distinguished visitors, to celebrate births and marriages, to prepare for journeys, and for various ceremonial and ritual purposes. Kava was also used to cure illnesses and to remove curses.

Many Pacific Islanders believe that appropriate use of kava fosters friendship, and is therapeutic — just as many Europeans consider that a little wine is part of socialising and beneficial to health. In traditional island cultures kava was said to be helpful for respiratory and urinary tract problems, and it does contain at least mild antibacterial compounds.

Kava drinking has various effects:

> It gives a pleasant, warm and cheerful but lazy feeling, sociable though not hilarious or loquacious. The head is affected pleasantly, you feel friendly, not beer sentimental; you cannot hate with kava in you. Kava quiets the mind; the world gains no new colour or rise tint; it fits in its place and in one easily understandable whole.[49]

Others describe harmful effects similar to our alcoholic drinks, although it is reported that Kava does not give such a large 'hangover'. I have not tried kava as a drink, but most people say the first effect is numbness and dryness of the mouth.

People who drink kava excessively develop a number of serious health problems. *All* alcoholic drinks from *all* cultures are harmful in excess.

The European use of kava as a herbal medicine began about twenty years ago.

The *herbal* use of kava is not linked to the adverse side effects of kava drinking, just as the therapeutic use of, say, grapeseed tablets does not give the side effects of wine. Herbal kava is manufactured as a herbal medicine, and prescribed in doses of about 3–5 g daily, which is quite different from drinking a bowl, or more, of kava beverage.

The part used

The root.

Therapeutic use

Internal

The main use of kava is for anxiety and nervousness. Kava can reduce the tension in skeletal muscles as well as the smooth muscles in blood vessel walls, the bronchioles, digestive tract, and so on. It may be helpful, therefore, in treating a range of problems linked to physical and mental tension, including tension headaches, as well as some digestive disorders.

If you have mild depression you could try kava, as it tends to produce feelings of wellbeing. A controlled trial on 101 patients confirmed that kava gave significant results with people suffering from anxiety of non-psychotic origin.[50] This herb may be an alternative to antidepressants and benzodiazepines in anxiety disorders.

Kava improves mental performance and emotional stability without causing sedation.[51] It also alleviates insomnia — not as a 'knock out' but to promote deep restful sleep.

Laboratory tests showed that kava was active against a wide range of fungi (but *not* Candida), and this may partly explain its traditional use for urinary tract infections.

A German study on 84 patients with anxiety symptoms showed that an isolated kava lactone (kavain) improved vigilance, memory and reaction time. The same component was tested on another group of anxious patients, and measured against a pharmaceutical. Both treatments gave the same result, but the kavain did not produce any adverse effects — unlike the pharmaceutical.[52] Compared with a placebo, herbal kava reduced nervousness and anxiety symptoms, such as palpitations, chest pains, dizziness, headaches and stomach upsets, and no adverse effects were noticed.

In a placebo-controlled trial the herb improved mood and wellbeing in menopausal women — again, without side effects.[53]

Kava extract protected the brain tissue of animals from damage due to oxygen deficit.[54] It might therefore be helpful in recovery from stroke and head injuries.

These types of results have been confirmed in a number of trials, and it would be a pity if this valuable herbal remedy was banned simply because excessive intake of kava alcoholic drinks is harmful.

Research indicates that kava has some unusual non-opiate actions, and may help in pain states where other substances have not been effective.[55] Current investigations suggest that components in kava have the potential to be developed into anticonvulsive medications.

In general, herbal kava relaxes the body and mind, creating a feeling of 'mellowness' and general wellbeing. It is also a muscle relaxant (smooth muscles are found in the digestive system and blood vessels), as well as having mild antibacterial, analgesic and antifungal properties.

Animal studies show that tolerance does not develop.[56] You do not have to take larger and larger doses to get the same therapeutic effect, as happens with some pharmaceuticals prescribed for nervous complaints.

Cautions and adverse effects

- When kava is used as a herbal therapy at the recommended doses, trials of up to twenty-four weeks generally show no unwanted side effects. However, long-term, high doses of kava may cause a dry, scaly skin; this condition disappears when consumption is stopped. I have not seen any adverse effects in patients.

- Although some books warn that kava can cause impaired ability to drive and to handle machinery, a trial on forty people showed no significant changes when they were given medicinal doses of a standardised herbal remedy.
- There are also warnings about combining alcohol with kava, but a study showed that medicinal doses of kava tended to counter the adverse effect of alcohol on concentration. However, as there is evidence that alcohol worsens anxiety in the long term, it would seem prudent to avoid or markedly restrict alcohol, and not to combine it with any form of medication that has been prescribed for mental or emotional problems.
- Sedative and antianxiety pharmaceuticals should not be combined with kava, as the combination would make the treatment too strong.
- As kava is relatively new to European herbal medicine, it may be prudent to be monitored by a health practitioner while taking kava, and use it singly rather than in a formula until more clinical experience is accumulated.

Known therapeutic components

- Kava lactones are thought to be responsible for the antianxiety effects. German studies of the isolated components confirm that the relaxing effect of kava is not due to binding to receptor sites in the brain (as is the case for pharmaceutical sedatives and antidepressants). It is thought that kava acts on the limbic system of the brain, which is responsible for our emotional processes. Perhaps this is why some patients report that they have pleasant dreams and restful sleep when they take this herb, but they do not feel tired or groggy.

- A number of studies show that the therapeutic constituents are better utilised when the whole root is used rather than any isolated component.[57]

Kava products

Kava is available in Australia as a liquid extract, and as dried rhizome and dried root. Tablets are now available as standardised and non-standardised preparations, and in combination with other herbs. At present most kava products are available to health practitioners only.

Growing and making your own remedies

Not recommended.

Dosages and duration of treatment

Liquid extracts are prescribed in doses of 1–2 ml, three times daily.

Tablets are available in varying strengths, so follow the label dosages.

Generally, I suggest a maximum of three to four months' treatment. You could use it for a longer period with breaks in the treatment, depending on your symptoms and response.

I suggest that, because of our limited experience, kava be given to children only when prescribed by a qualified herbalist.

Summary

Kava is an effective treatment for mild anxiety and problems related to nervousness.

Further reading

Kilham, C. *Kava: Medicine Hunting in Paradise*. Inner Traditions International, Rochester, NY, 1996.

Lebot, V., Merlin, M. & Lindstrom, L. *Kava: The Pacific Drug*, Yale University Press, New Haven, 1992.

Liquorice
(*Glycyrrhiza glabra, G. uralensis*)

Glycyrrhiza glabra is used by European herbalists and is the species I cover in this section. *G. uralensis* is also used in traditional Chinese medicine.

Background

Throughout recorded history liquorice has been used as a medicine and for other purposes. The ancient Greeks and Romans drank the extracted black juice to quench their thirst. It is one of the most commonly prescribed herbs in traditional Chinese medicine, and is used for detoxification, digestive problems and inflammation. Herbalists in many countries have prescribed it for centuries to treat a wide range of health problems.

In the 1950s it was found that people with Addison's disease (underfunctioning adrenal glands) craved liquorice, and that this herb actually reduced the symptoms of this serious problem. However, this disease is now treated by cortisone and other prescription drugs.

A sample of liquorice was recently found that was 1240 years old. When it was tested, scientists found it still contained therapeutically active components. The enduring nature of the plant perhaps relates to its capacity to provide endurance to humans.

The part used

The root.

Therapeutic use

Internal

Herbalists class liquorice as an adrenal and immune tonic, anti-inflammatory, demulcent (soothing), antiulcer, mild expectorant (helps decongest coughs), phyto-oestrogenic, liver protectant, antiallergy and antioxidant. It also has antitumour activity, and weak antiviral and antibacterial actions. Some herbalists describe liquorice as having a natural cortisone effect, but it is markedly weaker than pharmaceuticals, and does not produce the major adverse effects of drugs.

In herbal medicine pure liquorice is used as part of the treatment for gastric and duodenal ulcers, heartburn and coughs. It may also help some cases of inflammatory intestinal and joint diseases such as Crohn's disease and arthritis.

Liquorice can alleviate symptoms related to chronic fatigue syndrome, including physical and mental weakness, bone and muscle pain, worsening of allergies and disturbed mood and sleep.[58]

It may be a worthy inclusion in the treatment of many viral diseases, as it inhibits virus growth and inactivates viral particles, and induces interferon activity.[59]

In a study on rats, liver enzyme changes suggested liquorice has a liver detoxification and potential anticancer effect. Glycyrrhizin (an isolated component of liquorice) has been used successfully in Japan to treat chronic viral hepatitis.[60] I often use liquorice extracts in formulas to treat hepatitis, but I monitor the patients regularly; it is not appropriate for people with fluid retention.

An isolated component of liquorice inhibits the tumour-promoting activity of two powerful tumour promoters (TPA and teleocidin).[61] The tumour-inhibiting effects of liquorice are supported in many scientific studies, and liquorice is on the list of plants determined by the National Cancer Institute of America to be potential cancer preventives.

Two studies demonstrated that the flavonoids in liquorice have a beneficial effect on blood stickiness and inflammation, indicating support for the use of liquorice for atopic dermatitis, as well as atherosclerosis and high blood fats.[62]

Animal studies show that glycyrrhizin, an isolated component of liquorice, can beneficially modify the immune system following burns.[63] Burn victims might also benefit from the adrenal tonic effects of liquorice, as the adrenal gland is the body's 'stress' gland.

A study on rats found that liquorice aided the clearance of excess immune complexes that are produced in a serious autoimmune joint disorder known as lupus, affecting joints, skin and organs.[64] Human trials have not been done, but it may be worth considering, as this inflammatory arthritic condition is painful, restrictive and difficult to treat. One problem with lupus is that most patients also suffer fluid retention, so liquorice treatments must be monitored by a health practitioner.

Despite its natural sweetness, liquorice is recommended as a mouth wash for treating mouth ulcers, and for gum and teeth hygiene. I sometimes combine a tiny portion of liquorice root with chewing gum to make the gum last longer, and for preventive purposes.

External

An article in a British medical journal suggested that glycyrrhetinic acid, as an isolated component, may assist the activity of external hydrocortisone creams.[65] As external cortisone tends to 'thin the skin' and have other adverse effects, a quality liquorice cream used at the same time may reduce or eliminate the need for the pharmaceutical.

In my clinic I have found that liquorice externally is helpful for a number of skin problems, including eczema, and the herbal cream rarely produces adverse effects. The side effects are invariably good, such as softening the skin. Liquorice, along with lemon balm herb, is beneficial as an external remedy for treating herpes.

Glycyrrhizin in a shampoo reduces dandruff, and such shampoos may soon become commercially available in Australia.

Cautions and adverse effects

- Large amounts of liquorice can cause potassium depletion, sodium retention, fluid retention, high blood pressure and weight gain. I have prescribed liquorice for hundreds of patients, and not noted any adverse effects. However, I do not use large doses, nor do I prescribe it long term. I always combine it in a formula with other herbs, especially dandelion leaf extract, which is very rich in potassium. And, of course, I do not prescribe it for people with fluid retention or high blood pressure problems. In addition, I always suggest a high vegetable intake, which amounts to a high potassium diet.
- A trial of eight people showed that there was less intestinal absorption of the glycyrrhizin in liquorice when it was taken as part of the whole root, compared to the isolated component, which suggests that the whole root extract is much safer.[66]
- Liquorice should never be taken in any form by pregnant women, or anyone who has high blood pressure, fluid retention, cirrhosis of the liver, or low potassium levels.
- People with serious diseases such as viral hepatitis should be guided by an experienced health practitioner, rather than treating themselves.

Note: Liquorice confectionery has none of the therapeutic properties of pure liquorice root, as it contains very little root and is largely flour and sugars. In Australia some popular brands contain less than 1 per cent of liquorice root, and also include a number of potentially harmful additives, such as a black colouring agent (that is banned in the USA) and aniseed oil. Some imported liquorice confectionery may contain up to 24 per cent of liquorice root. Adverse effects such as kidney damage, the reactions listed above, and, possibly, cancer-causing effects could be caused by eating quite small quantities of liquorice confectionery. Liquorice is a medicinal herb, not a food.

In Australia liquorice confectionery is often

sold in large bags. If you love the confectionery, buy only a very small quantity as an occasional treat. One researcher has suggested that a safe dose of liquorice confectionery is 5 g daily (1 teaspoon).

Known therapeutic components

- Glycyrrhizin is an amazing substance, and is responsible for the sweetness of liquorice. It is fifty times sweeter than sucrose. Two natural derivatives (glycyrrhizic and glycyrrhetinic acid) are considered to protect the liver.[67] Experimentally, this compound prevents some types of tumours.
- Glycyrrhizin significantly inhibits plaque growth and bacterial adherence to tooth enamel, in addition to its antibacterial action.[68] It is also anti-inflammatory.
- Liquorice contains isoflavonoids, some of which act like the components in soya beans (as discussed in chapter 2). Hormone-like compounds in liquorice possess at least two tumour inhibiting activities in breast tissue.

Liquorice products

Herbalists commonly prescribe liquid extracts of liquorice as part of a formula. Liquorice powders and teas are also available. The small quantities of liquorice in some over-the-counter tablet formulas should not present a problem, but I suggest that you should not take these indefinitely.

In some countries a deglycyrrhizinised liquorice is used to treat gastric and duodenal ulcers. In Japan a glycyrrhizin tablet and an intravenous pharmaceutical are prescribed for hepatitis and diseases related to the immune system.

Growing and making your own remedies

Liquorice plants are available in a few specialist nurseries.

As the dosage of liquorice is quite small, and it is not a remedy to be taken in the long term, it may not be worth the difficulty of cultivation, cutting the root, properly drying and storing it for your own use, even if your climate and soil are suitable.

External liquorice cream

10 ml liquid liquorice extract or 5 g finely powdered liquorice
10 ml distilled water
50 g external cream (I use a quality base that is not available over the counter, but any base that does not cause a reaction would be suitable, such as an aqueous cream from your local pharmacist; always test the base first in case of allergic reactions)

1 Gently simmer the liquorice and water in a small saucepan for 5 minutes, so that the alcohol in the extract evaporates. As the amount is small, you may need to tip the saucepan on its side.
2 Leave to cool, and then mix into the cream.
3 Label and date, and store in the fridge as it has no preservative; it should keep for a few months.

Dosages and duration of treatment

I recommend 3 g as a maximum daily dose of the root; do not use for more than three months without supervision by a health practitioner. Ideally, when you take liquorice root products you should also drink dandelion leaf tea or extract, eat plenty of fresh vegetables, and avoid obviously salty foods and added salt.

I suspect that herbalists rarely see adverse effects from the prescription of liquorice because they know when it should *not* be used and invariably recommend a healthy diet, which possibly offsets the potassium loss that may occur. Dandelion leaf is the best natural source of potassium.

Children should be given proportionately lower doses according to age (see pp. 4–5).

Summary

When used appropriately, liquorice is a medicinal tonic herb with proven anti-inflammatory action, and is highly recommended for its beneficial effects on the immune system. It is useful externally for inflammatory skin problems and as a skin softener.

Milk thistle
(also known as variegated thistle)
(*Silybum marianum* (formerly called *Carduus marianus*))

This plant is called milk thistle because the leaves are mottled milky white from the conspicuous white veins that run across the leaves. Liquid extracts of the plant develop a 'milky' colour the longer they are stored.

Some people call the plant St Mary's thistle, but this common name is best reserved for *Cnicus benedictus*, another 'thistle' that is used as a medicinal herb.

Background

About 2000 years ago milk thistle was recorded as a remedy 'for carrying off bile', and old herbal books refer to many medicinal uses of different preparations of milk thistle. There are various historical references to milk thistle as a treatment for jaundice and liver congestion.

It was also used as a food, and cooked like artichoke — one author wrote that the young spring leaves surpassed the finest cabbage (perhaps the writer was very short of vegetables?). I have not eaten it. If you were desperate enough for vegetables to try it you would need to be absolutely certain that the plants had not been treated with weedicides. Take out the spines from the leaves before cooking or using the leaves in a salad.

When I first began studying herbs about twenty-five years ago, milk thistle was not on the list of important medicinal herbs. Scientific research, particularly in Germany, has now confirmed that this plant actually possesses liver-protecting components, and so it has become an example of science restoring and confirming the historical use of a traditional remedy. Milk thistle certainly deserves its restoration and classification in the top fourteen medicinal herbs.

The part used

The seeds.

Therapeutic use

Internal

Milk thistle supports liver function generally, and reduces liver damage. It is known to have the capacity to reverse liver damage or toxicity caused by alcohol, drugs, toxins, pollutants, hepatitis or infections, and may also help with gallbladder functioning and reduce food intolerances. Signs of liver and gallbladder under-functioning include intolerance to fatty or oily foods, nausea, belching, bloating, constipation, upper abdominal discomfort, coated tongue and headaches. Pathology and other medical tests are used to diagnose specific liver diseases.

A number of studies have used the separated, therapeutically active components of milk thistle rather than products made from the whole seed, but many milk thistle products nowadays give the quantity of these silymarin compounds on the label.

Patients with chronic liver diseases taking silymarin have shown improvements in their liver enzyme levels compared to those who did not take silymarin.[69] Liver enzyme levels can be monitored by routine blood tests. When specific enzyme levels are high this indicates liver disease, malfunction or toxic stress. Liver enzyme levels also decreased in patients with chronic hepatitis after three months' treatment with silybin (one of the silymarins).[70]

Acute viral hepatitis B has also been helped by silymarin, and enzyme blood tests show that this compound can improve chronic forms of both hepatitis B and C.[71]

Trials on different types of hepatitis indicate that milk thistle and its isolated components are likely to be helpful for the majority of patients. Enlarged livers have also diminished substantially in patients taking standardised milk thistle products.

A study of 2637 patients with fatty infiltration of the liver, hepatitis or mild cirrhosis were given about 500 mg silymarin daily for eight weeks; 63 per cent of them reported a disappearance of their symptoms, which included nausea, itching, abdominal distension, lack of appetite and fatigue. Levels of liver enzymes were reduced by 34 and 46 per cent, respectively. Fewer than 1 per cent of the patients discontinued the programme because of side effects, which included stomach upset, nausea and mild diarrhoea.[72]

Herbalists consider that milk thistle has the capacity to reduce the liver damage caused by some pharmaceuticals. A trial of patients receiving long-term treatment with psychotropic drugs (butyrophenones and phenothiazines) indicated that silymarin reduced the liver damage.[73] I recommend milk thistle for all people on pharmaceutical and social drugs, as these commonly affect the liver. If you look in MIMS *Annual* or study the package insert of pharmaceuticals, you will note that many drugs have the potential to damage the liver. I suggest that milk thistle would be helpful for all patients who need these types of medications. Many people are not aware that even over-the-counter drugs such as paracetamol can cause liver damage.

Milk thistle is likely to be helpful for anyone exposed to any type of chemical toxin. This herb has not been tested for every possible liver toxin, but it is known that liver function has been improved in people who have been exposed to chemicals known as halogenated hydrocarbons.[74] Pesticides such as DDT, dieldrin, aldrin, heptachlor, and chlordane are in this category, and are known liver poisons. If you are at risk, your medical practitioner can organise a liver function test from a small blood sample.

Animal studies show that silymarin protects the liver against carbon tetrachloride, acetaminophen, galactosamine, heavy metals, phenylhydrazine, lipid peroxidation, poisonous fungi, and red cell breakdown.

Milk thistle is both protective and relatively curative from some poisonous mushrooms, including the deathcap mushroom (*Amanita phalloides*). In one European study people with accidental mushroom poisoning had mortality rates lower than any other known treatment when treated with Silibinin (an intravenous remedy of a milk thistle compound). With all cases of poisoning, you must seek emergency medical treatment.

A standardised extract of milk thistle (Legalon) used in Europe reduced the effects of alcohol-related liver damage in humans through its antioxidant activity, stabilising liver cell membranes, regenerating damaged liver tissue and preventing fibrosis. Furthermore, toxicological investigations have shown it to be practically non-toxic, with adverse effects being reported in only 1 per cent of cases — the main effect being mild laxative activity.[75]

Milk thistle protects the liver from alcohol damage. Rats given alcohol and milk thistle were compared to rats given only the alcohol; those receiving the herb had significantly lower levels of three enzymes that indicate liver toxicity.[76] A study of thirty-six people with alcoholic liver disease confirmed that silymarin has significant antioxidant activity. A four-year programme of 170 cirrhotic patients using silymarin resulted in a reduction in death rates among those who took the remedy.[77]

Of course, the wisest course is not to abuse the liver. I have patients whose liver enzymes become abnormal from the ingestion of only one glass of alcohol a day (based on symptoms such as upper gastric discomfort, nausea and standard liver function pathology tests). For sensitive people and alcoholics there may be no safe level of alcohol intake.

Animal studies show that silymarin may help protect the gastrointestinal tract from injury and ulceration.[78]

In my clinic I always use milk thistle as part of the treatment for high cholesterol, because most of the cholesterol in your body is actually produced by the liver, and excess cholesterol can be reduced by supporting the liver. This herb is also prescribed by herbalists for flatulence, constipation and digestive problems when these symptoms are linked to liver function. The bile produced by the liver is needed to digest dietary fats, and nearly all foods contain at least tiny amounts of fats or oils. If you cannot digest fats, you will suffer bloating and flatulence after eating them. Bile also gives a slippery quality to your bowel motions, and without it you can become constipated. This illustrates how a liver treatment can improve the digestive system.

Some people are sensitive to general anaesthetics, and milk thistle taken before and after surgery may help reduce the nausea and the detrimental increase in liver enzymes that sometimes occurs in surgery patients.

Evidence is now emerging that milk thistle may also be a helpful adjunct in treating chronic kidney diseases, and it is often part of herbal formulas for treating itching skin and other skin problems. A controlled trial showed that silymarin made an ideal addition to the treatment of insulin dependent diabetes secondary to alcoholic cirrhosis because blood and urine levels of glucose were lowered, as well as lipid peroxidation (harmful fat breakdown).[79]

Laboratory studies indicate that silybin (an isolated flavonoid in milk thistle) has some capacity to suppress ovarian cancer cells, as well as the capacity to reinforce the cancer-destroying capacity of two common chemotherapy drugs used to treat ovarian cancer.[80]

Herbal forms of milk thistle are strong enough for prevention purposes and for the treatment of mild liver upsets.

For serious disorders, standardised forms of this herb should be used when the isolated products are not available, and all remedies should be discussed with a health practitioner.

A competently functioning liver is essential for good health.

Cautions and adverse effects

- Milk thistle produces remarkably few side effects. However, my experience is that it tends to activate the liver, and so may cause temporary nausea, mild diarrhoea and other gastric upsets. Therefore, I recommend that a lower dose be taken for the first few weeks of treatment.
- Products made from silymarin only (the isolated flavonoids) tend to produce more adverse effects, but are more reliable for treating serious disorders. Most health practitioners now prescribe products with a guaranteed level of silymarin.

Known therapeutic components

- Silymarin is the most active ingredient in milk thistle, and it is a mixture of flavanolignans such as silybin, silydianin and silychristin. These compounds stabilise liver cells — the cells are somewhat protected from toxins, and are less likely to break down; in addition, silymarin helps develop healthy new liver cells. These two activities give the liver more capacity to continue its many important biological functions, including detoxification and lipid metabolism.
- Silybin is a more powerful antioxidant than vitamin E, and laboratory experiments show that silybin has anti-inflammatory and immune enhancing properties.[81]

Milk thistle products

Dried and powdered seeds, tablets, capsules and fluid extracts of milk thistle are available over the counter, some having a specified level of silymarin.

In Europe pharmaceutical products of silymarin are quite widely prescribed by medical practitioners. At least sixteen different silymarin pharmaceuticals are available in Europe, including Silibinin (a water-soluble product used intravenously). One German study showed Silymarin Z was the strongest therapeutically of the oral silymarin drugs, but the trial also showed that it caused a somewhat higher incidence of side effects such as gastric upsets and headaches.[82]

Growing and making your own remedies

Milk thistle is native to southern Europe, and has now been naturalised in many countries. In Australia it is classed as a noxious weed in most states as it grows vigorously and spreads rapidly by seed. The plant is not commonly eaten by stock unless they are very hungry — it produces high nitrate levels, which can fatally poison cattle. This toxicity for grazing animals may have led to negative beliefs relating to its usefulness as a medicinal plant.

The seeds are readily available if you wish to grow the plant in your garden, but you should check with your local council before growing it in case it is listed as a noxious weed in your area. Do not grow it if there is a possibility that it could spread to farmland.

If you wish to harvest it from someone's property, ensure that it has not been sprayed with weedicides. Seeds tend to accumulate toxins because they are oily. Wear gloves to separate the seeds from the plant.

Silymarin, the therapeutically active constituent, is not readily soluble in water, so making a tea of the powdered seeds is not very effective, and it is not very well absorbed in the gastrointestinal tract in this form.

Milk thistle decoction

10 g powdered milk thistle seeds
3 glasses water
juice of 1 lemon

1   Combine all the ingredients, bring to the boil, and simmer for about 10 minutes. (The acid in the lemon will help to extract the components from the powdered herb, and aid digestion and absorption).
2   Leave to cool.
3   Label and date, and store in the fridge.

Take over one to three days, perhaps adding some fruit juice to make it more palatable.

Milk thistle herbal vinegar

If you have access to unpolluted seeds, try making a strong herbal vinegar from the powdered seeds. When you make herbal therapeutic vinegars using seeds, you will find that the oils from the seeds coagulate after a month or so. When this happens, I strain the vinegar for use, because I presume that the vinegar has had time to extract the components from the plant matter.

Try ground seeds lightly roasted and powdered for use as a coffee substitute.

Dosages and duration of treatment

As a preventive, long-term remedy take about half the label dose.

For treating liver symptoms, take the full dose for three months, and then consult a health practitioner to be assessed.

Do not take liquid extracts of milk thistle if you have a liver disease, because these are preserved with alcohol.

Although I do not commonly prescribe milk thistle for children, it can be given when appropriate in proportionately lower doses according to age (see pp. 4–5).

Summary

Milk thistle is a valuable antioxidant remedy for protecting and restoring liver function.

Recommended reading

Foster, S. *Milk Thistle*. Botanical Series No. 305, American Botanical Council, Austin, Texas, 1991.

Other useful 'liver herbs'

Globe artichoke and bupleurum help restore and protect the liver.

Many digestive problems may be helped by milk thistle, but other herbs may be more appropriate for some people, including bitter herbs such as dandelion, turmeric and barberry bark, to stimulate bile flow as well as gastric and pancreatic enzymes.

Pau d'arco (also called Lapacho)
(*Tabebuia impetiginosa* or *avellanedae*)

Other species of *Tabebuia* are used medicinally in South America, and, in general, those with purplish flowers are considered to have therapeutic properties.

Background

This rainforest tree originated in Brazil, and subsequently spread to other South American countries. The South American Indians have used pau d'arco medicinally over centuries for many internal and external infections, as well as for arthritis, circulation disorders, tumours, and intestinal and respiratory problems.

In the 1960s a few Brazilian doctors began using pau d'arco as an unapproved medicine for some types of cancer and other serious diseases. However, once word spread of a few 'miracle cures' in terminally ill patients pau d'arco became the centre of controversy within the medical profession, and the trees themselves were threatened. As a consequence of the publicity and no doubt exaggerated stories, its use in hospitals in Brazil was discontinued, but a number of scientists continued studying the constituents in the bark and wood.

Pau d'arco has been used in Canada and the USA for twenty years, and there are many reports of successful 'cures' for a wide range of illnesses, including people who had already unsuccessfully tried many other treatments.

The tree itself is famous for its enduring timber, its resistance to insects and diseases, as well as for its beautiful flowers. Perhaps the plant's own ability to resist attacks by insects and fungal diseases was the initial reason why the South American Indians tried it centuries ago for human illnesses.

The parts used

The inner bark is considered to be the most medicinal part of the tree, especially for internal use, but the flaked wood and outer bark are also used in traditional South American herbalism.

Therapeutic use

Internal

One of the reasons why this plant has been used traditionally for a wide range of problems is because it helps with digestive weaknesses and disorders. Scientific tests confirm that lapachol (an isolated component from pau d'arco) can protect the stomach and intestines against ulcers. When digestion and absorption are improved, intestinal immune functioning is enhanced, unwanted toxins are more effectively excreted, nutrients are better absorbed, and therefore the overall functioning of the body improves.

People in tropical regions could take periodic courses of pau d'arco in addition to their preventive programmes against malaria and other tropical diseases.

Pau d'arco prevents and alleviates common respiratory problems, and is prescribed as part of the therapy for candida, herpes and other viral infections.

Isolated constituents of pau d'arco have anti-tumour properties, and also inhibit the Epstein-Barr virus.[83]

In North America pau d'arco has been successful for treating chronic fatigue and candidiasis. However, many of these patients have numerous sensitivities and allergies so an extremely low dose of even a few drops may be all that can be tolerated initially, gradually building up over one to two months to the full dose. Many people report that their allergies disappear after some months.

A few human trials have been done with lapachol on cancer patients; however, one trial was stopped because the blood became too thin. Another trial in South America showed shrinkage of tumours and pain reduction. As far as I know, no controlled studies have been done on the whole plant, but it should be helpful as support therapy for most cancer and leukaemia patients, and also for people with low immune function. Components in pau d'arco stimulate macrophage activity, which adds weight to its usefulness in treating infections and diseases that require immune support.

Animal studies confirm that pau d'arco can increase macrophage activity (an important part of the immune system), and that mice can tolerate doses of 2 g per kg bodyweight of the bark extract — that is, 140 g in a 70 kg human or seventy times higher than the recommended dose. Obviously doses of this magnitude would never be used on humans, and early studies on animals demonstrated that extreme dosages were actually less effective.

At least twenty-three animal and laboratory studies support the traditional use of pau d'arco as an antitumour agent, and some of these studies showed that extracts of the bark, as well as isolated components, reduced tumour size or the spread of cancer cells: 'The normalisation of blood cell counts was repeatedly witnessed by South American physicians who examined cancer patients who were taking pau d'arco.' This also occurred in leukaemia patients, and the South American experience suggests that this plant acts in a non-specific way, and that the treatment needs to be continued in the long term.[84]

We can only wonder why more studies are not done on this, as for many other herbs, given that current cancer medical treatments carry a heavy burden of adverse effects. In spite of billions of dollars spent on research, many cancer patients die or might survive in varying degrees of health, but there is no cure, and so people are mostly in a state of stressed uncertainty. Perhaps the answer does not lie in looking at smaller and smaller bits of chemicals and cells but in whole plants and whole people. It does not cost billions to research herbs or to do some small trials with cancer patients to see if pau d'arco or other no-harm remedies can strengthen the immune system, improve the recovery from the disease itself — and help the patient survive the medical treatment!

External

For use as an external wash on skin infections and scabies or on a tampon for vaginal candida, simmer the bark in water, then cool and strain it. This decoction is helpful as a mouthwash or gargle for infections of the gums, mouth and throat; see the recipe on p. 108. I have used a cool compress on *Herpes zoster* (shingles) cases with some success in relieving pain and itching, and seemingly reducing the time it takes to recover.

Cautions and adverse effects

- This herb is relatively new to Australian herbalists. Although there are some concerns about the potential toxicity of its individual therapeutic constituents, few side effects have been reported by people who have taken pau d'arco in its herbal form.

- I use it fairly frequently as part of an anti-fungal internal formula, so my experience is based on low dosage for a maximum of six to eight weeks.

  When you read about the side effects of a particular constituent in a plant, remember that an isolated component is in the nature of a pharmaceutical. It may have a specific beneficial activity, but it is also likely to cause adverse reactions that are apparently offset if it is combined with all the other components in the plant. If this were not so, then *all* plants would give us adverse effects. The whole plant may have weaker therapeutic activity, especially for a specific complaint.
- Do not use pau d'arco during pregnancy.
- Pau d'arco should not be used if you are taking blood-thinning medications.

Known therapeutic components

- Thirty different types of quinones have been identified in pau d'arco, the most important being lapachol. Some reports say that commercial products of pau d'arco may not actually contain any lapachol and therefore may not be therapeutic; however, studies show that the isolated components do not seem to work as well as the whole herb, and the naphthoquinones in general have a number of therapeutic properties.[85]
- Lapachol has been studied more than other components in pau d'arco. It has antibacterial, antifungal, antimicrobial, antiparasitical and antiviral activity. In addition it has anti-inflammatory effects.[86]
- Xyloidone has proven antibiotic and antiviral activity, and furanaphthoquinones have immune enhancing and antitumour properties. Plant quinones tend to have antioxidant effects in the body, and these give at least a measure of cancer preventive activity.
- Pau d'arco contains saponins, and in general these components increase the solubility of nutrients and other substances, therefore making them more easily absorbed.

- Tannins, flavonoids and benzoic acid have anti-inflammatory, antioxidant and immune enhancing properties.

  Tannins also tone and strengthen the body's linings and skin, but in excess they can be drying and irritating.

Pau d'arco products

Pau d'arco tablets and extracts are available in Australia.

Herbalists have access to various forms of pau d'arco, and stores are beginning to stock tablets and dried products that can be simmered in water as a decoction (see below).

Growing and making your own remedies

The pau d'arco plant is not available in Australia.

Pau d'arco decoction

2–4 tablespoons pau d'arco bark or flaked wood
4 cups water
1–2 teaspoons lemon juice or apple cider vinegar

1 Combine all the ingredients, bring to the boil, and simmer for about 5 minutes.
2 Leave to cool, and then strain.

Drink the fluid throughout the day, flavoured with juice if preferred.
Note: The therapeutic components of pau d'arco are not well extracted in water, so buy the bark in small pieces or as a powder. Lemon juice or apple cider vinegar help to draw out the therapeutic components.

If you are to use the decoction for external use, simmer the mixture for at least 10 minutes.

Dosages and duration of treatment

Liquid extract, 2 ml daily if self-treating; tablets, according to the label; decoction, 3 cups a day is a therapeutic dosage.

For serious conditions, take pau d'arco consistently for at least two months.

Use externally while your symptoms last, with a maximum of two applications daily for three weeks, as it can dry the skin.

I do not prescribe pau d'arco internally for preschool children. For older children give proportionately lower doses according to age (see pp. 4–5).

Summary

A good digestive and immune strengthener, pau d'arco should be considered at least as support therapy for a number of serious diseases.

Recommended reading

Jones, K. Pau d'Arco: Immune Power from the Rain Forest. Healing Arts Press, Rochester, Vermont, 1995.

St John's wort
(Hypericum perforatum)

'Wort' is the old English name for herb.

The plant is native to Europe, and a number of regions in the northern hemisphere, but it has been introduced into America, New Zealand and Australia. Unfortunately, it can spread rapidly, and is declared a noxious weed in some Australian states. It is toxic to grazing animals, and cows, in particular, can develop a red, itchy, flaky skin condition, which can advance into slow-healing raw areas.

Background

From the time of the ancient Greeks and throughout the Middle Ages St John's wort has been part of herbal folklore. People used to say that red spots appeared on the plant on the day that John the Baptist was beheaded, and in Europe it was hung over house doorways or was put under the pillow for protection against evil spirits.

St John's wort was recommended for all respiratory and bladder complaints, diarrhoea, bleeding, jaundice and nervous depression. In the 1973 British Herbal Pharmacopoeia this herb was specifically recommended for menopausal neurosis; also for painful nerve problems such as sciatica, fibrositis and neuralgia. It was also a popular external remedy. You will see below how many of these traditional uses are supported by modern scientific investigations.

The part used

The whole herb.

Therapeutic use

Internal

St John's wort possesses properties that are antiviral, antidepressant, antimicrobial, anti-inflammatory, antianxiety, wound healing and mild antibacterial. It is a gentle tonic with analgesic properties, and anticancer potential.

Many reliable studies and controlled trials confirm that for the treatment of mild to moderate depressive disorders, St John's wort is as effective as pharmaceuticals, but with far fewer side effects.[87]

An assessment of twelve clinical trials confirmed that St John's wort was superior to a placebo, and its therapeutic effects were similar to those of pharmaceutical antidepressants. There was a low incidence of adverse effects and overdosing compared to pharmaceuticals.[88]

Most of the trials on depression have been in Europe, using a daily dosage of up to 4.5 g standardised herbal product containing 1–2.7 mg hypericin (probably the most therapeutically active component relating to the nervous system). When people are depressed they are usually lethargic, and do not have the motivation to do anything. Treatment with this herb can gently motivate depressed people.

In cold climates some people experience seasonal affective disorder because of lack of exposure to light during long winters. The symptoms are depression, insomnia, fatigue with restlessness, increased appetite and sugar cravings. A study showed that St John's wort helped this condition just as much as 'light therapy'. Of course, we should all get at least a little sunlight exposure because it is necessary for good health.

Natural therapists find that St John's wort is also helpful for anxiety and insomnia, and acts as a gentle tonic. I sometimes add it into formulas for menopausal symptoms. In a study on healthy people St John's wort was shown to have a soothing effect; brain function was stimulated and performance tests under stress were enhanced.[89] This reinforces the concept of traditional herbalists who have categorised some herbs as nervine tonics (the capacity to calm the nervous system without causing fatigue).

St John's wort is likely to relieve certain types of viral infections, including AIDS, herpes, Epstein-Barr virus, hepatitis B, and some types of colds, and possibly some strains of influenza.

Since 1989 a number of informal studies with HIV-positive people have been done using St John's wort, and the patient outcomes have been favourable. A report presented at the 1993 International AIDS Conference indicated that a long-term clinical trial resulted in fourteen out of sixteen patients remaining clinically stable, and able to maintain their normal lifestyle and work. No serious viral infections were experienced, nor were any adverse effects encountered. In most of these patients some very specific immune cells were improved. This suggests benefits to the immune system generally. St John's wort may be therapeutically useful in many diseases that are linked to low immune functioning.

External

Traditional herbalists recommend St John's wort for its skin-healing properties, and animal studies confirm that it accelerates wound healing and new skin growth. External creams or compresses may help nerve pain, such as sciatica and neuralgia.

St John's wort oil is excellent for dry skin, especially in older people. The best way to use it is to mix the oil into a plain external base such as an aqueous cream available from a pharmacy.

Cautions and adverse effects

- Some herbal books warn that St John's wort can cause phototoxicity (sensitivity to sunlight), leading to skin discoloration and damage. This is based on experience with animals grazing on the plant. However, the latest report is that a dose thirty times above normal would be required to cause skin reddening in a human. I have only ever heard of one anecdotal report of such a reaction in a human.
- People with severe depression and serious infectious diseases should always be under the supervision of a medical practitioner, and should always tell their practitioner if they are self-treating with any remedies.
- If you are taking antianxiety or antidepressant medication, never add St John's wort or other natural nervous system remedies, unless guided by your practitioner.
- In recent times there have been a few reports from practising herbalists of various adverse effects, and this confirms my experience that some batches of this herb may contain more of certain components, which may be causing sensitivity or allergic reactions.

Known therapeutic components

- Hypericin and pseudohypericin (the red-coloured pigments found in the flowers and leaves of St John's wort) have antiretroviral activity. This means that they are effective against specific categories of virus, notably those covered under **Therapeutic use**, above. Synthetic hypericin, available in some countries, may not have any antiviral activity.[90]

If trials using hypericin are not successful, perhaps we should question whether the natural or synthetic substance was used. Many herbalists believe that plants contain an energy or life force that cannot be replicated, and that most of the components in a plant have at least some supporting value. Furthermore, certain types of processing seem to destroy the 'energy' of herbs — and this energy is not found in an isolated compound.

- Hypericin is also capable of reducing biological compounds in the brain (such as monoamine oxidase) that are implicated as possible causes of depression.[91]
- Some flavonoids (coloured pigments in plants) may also help brain chemistry. Other flavonoids may have antimicrobial activity, and the proanthocyanidins are antioxidants.[92] In general, flavonoids can have wide-ranging benefits, although the majority have a special affinity to blood vessel walls and connective tissue. Perhaps strengthening blood vessel walls may protect the brain from circulating toxins.
- Recent research indicates that a compound called hyperforin has antidepressant, relaxant and other nervous system effects.

St John's wort products

Tablets, capsules and liquid extracts are available in Australia.

A quality extract is said to have the appearance of claret wine — but not the taste, unfortunately.

Growing and making your own remedies

If you have access to the flowers, you can make an effective healing, anti-inflammatory and nourishing oil for the skin.

St John's Wort Skin Oil

100 g fresh St John's wort flowers (or 50 g dried)
200 ml almond oil (or sunflower, apricot kernel or olive oil)
6 capsules vitamin E (as an antioxidant)

1 Place the flowers in a clear glass jar, and pour the oil over. Cut the vitamin E capsules, and squeeze out the oil into the jar.
2 Leave to stand in the sunshine, with the lid on.
3 After six to eight weeks, the oil should be reddish in colour. Strain the liquid into a dark bottle or jar, pressing the flowers through a piece of fine cloth before discarding them.
4 The oil can be used immediately it is made. Date and label the jar, and seal before storing in a cool dry place. The dark glass should help prevent oxidation, but I recommend you mark the label to show that this oil should be used within three months.

Apply the oil undiluted on minor wounds and herpes; or gently massage it into areas of joint or nerve pain.

If you use it for household burns, wait until the heat has gone out of the injury first.

You could also use it for dry skin by mixing it into an aqueous cream. Generally, I use as much oil as the base can take, but it can stain your clothes and linen.

Dosages and duration of treatment

If you have a serious infection or depression, obtain standardised extracts, and take the dosage recommended by your health practitioner. You may need to take the remedy for two or more months, and subsequently at a lower dose or intermittently.

The usual dose is 2–4 g daily of the dried herb, or 2–4 ml of a liquid extract.

When indicated, use for children proportionately according to age (see pp. 4–5).

Summary

St John's wort is a proven remedy for depression, possesses antiviral activity, and may be an aid in a wide range of nervous and immune disorders. Externally, it is used for inflammation and nerve pain.

Withania
(*Withania somnifera*)

The Indian common name is *ashwagandha*. Some people refer to it as 'Indian ginseng'.

Background

Withania is native to India, Africa, the Mediterranean region and the Middle East. In the Ayurvedic system of Indian herbal medicine, it is used for impotence, for people who are thin and weak, to improve the skin, and for various symptoms of premature ageing. It is an important traditional tonic.

Although the Ayurvedic system is holistic, and herbal prescriptions relate to more than just a particular herb or a particular symptom, people with respiratory, digestive and joint disorders frequently receive herbal prescriptions containing withania. As a folk remedy it is used for a wide range of disorders in different countries.

The word *somnifera* relates to somniferous (that is, producing sleep). It may seem odd that a herb can be a tonic and a sedative at the same time, but modern scientific studies confirm that this herb has the capacity to energise, and to help with insomnia. Herbalists classify it as a nervine tonic.

The part used

The root.

Therapeutic use

Internal

Withania is highly recommended for anxiety and insomnia. Indian studies show that withania alone and in a formula (Geriforte) has a beneficial biochemical and psychological effect on people diagnosed with anxiety neurosis.[93]

I prescribe it as a general tonic, and part of the treatment for offsetting environmental and emotional stresses. It may be a useful treatment for athletes, and for people with low immune function, fatigue and weakness.

Herbalists prescribe it as part of the treatment for arthritis, cystitis, bronchitis and other inflammatory infections. Animal studies confirm its anti-inflammatory effects.

Withania helps protect the digestive tract from aspirin, and has some preventive action against gastric ulcers.

The adaptogenic effect of withania is similar to ginseng, which reinforces its antistress and adrenal supporting actions.[94]

In India a double-blind study using 2 g of withania in milk was successful as a tonic for thin, weak children; their body weight, blood haemoglobin and strength of their hand grip increased. Another controlled study in adults showed similar improvements, as well as a decrease in eryrocyte sedimentation rate (an indicator of inflammation reduction), a reduction in serum cholesterol, an improvement in hair and nail quality, as well as an enhancement in posture (indicating better energy).

Animal studies in India have shown that withania has an antitumour effect.[95] There are no controlled studies on human cancer patients, but in folklore withania has been used as a cancer treatment. Since cancer patients are invariably stressed and anxious, withania may be of assistance.

Cautions and adverse effects

- Withania is in the nightshade family, so you must follow the label doses if you are self-treating. The berries of the plant cause severe gastrointestinal upsets, especially in children.

- According to one author, withania may cause reduced urinary flow, prostate hypertrophy (swelling) and glaucoma, and therefore you should not use it if you have these problems.[96] (This reference was written by pharmacists, and is more an academic appraisal, largely based on the study of isolated components rather than clinical practice. Professional herbalists, whose experience is based on usage, do not give these warnings. Furthermore, animal studies indicate that very high doses can be taken in the short term without serious side effects.)

Known therapeutic components

- Alkaloids, notably isopelletierine and anaferine, are antihypertensive, and respiratory stimulators. These components also slow down the heartbeat, and produce sedative effects. In addition, they help relax the muscles that line the intestines, uterus, bronchial and arterial vessels.
- Steroidal compounds have antibacterial and anti-inflammatory effects.
- Two glycowithanolides were shown to modulate the immune and central nervous systems.[97]
- Rats' learning and memory were improved when they were fed with isolated compounds.

Withania products

Withania is available in tablets and as an extract.

Growing and making your own remedies

The withania plant is not available commercially in Australia.

Dosages and duration of treatment

I suggest an adult dose of 4 g withania daily, for up to three months, or 4 ml liquid extract.

Withania is an effective tonic for children; give proportionately according to age (see pp. 4–5).

Summary

Withania is a general and immune tonic that appears to balance the nervous system. It is the ideal remedy for people who are tired during the day, and have trouble sleeping at night.

Recommended reading

Bone, K. *Clinical Applications of Ayurvedic and Chinese Herbs: Monographs for the Western Herbal Practitioner.* Phytotherapy Press, Warwick, Qld, 1996.

In conclusion

The herbs I have chosen and the references cited represent a minuscule portion of the accumulated clinical and scientific evidence that now supports medicinal herbs. There are well over 100 000 published scientific papers validating herbal medicine.

I hope that you will be encouraged to take an active role in attaining abundant energy and good health and in preventing disease in the knowledge that herbal medicine is the oldest and safest medicine.

Four super culinary herbs

Fenugreek
Garlic
Ginger
Turmeric

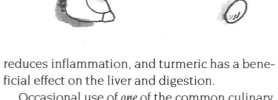

I chose these four herbs because they have the most scientific support. Many other culinary herbs have therapeutic benefits, especially those included in the lists at the end of this chapter.

Kitchen therapy — backed by science

Many of our ancient ancestors no doubt died from their basic experiments of tasting unknown plants. Through people's intuition, observation, tasting and superstition, many plants became known for their flavour and for their effects on wellbeing. Over time, people also noticed that certain herbs and spices seemed to offset some types of deterioration (oxidation) in foods and to improve digestion. Additionally, a connection was made between eating these plants and a reduction in illnesses, and this is how traditional remedies evolved.

It is surprising how many of these early observations are now backed by modern scientific tests and human trials. For instance, we now know that the intake of garlic can reduce cancer and cardiovascular risk, fenugreek has the capacity to lower blood sugar levels, ginger reduces inflammation, and turmeric has a beneficial effect on the liver and digestion.

Occasional use of *one* of the common culinary spices and herbs is unlikely to have significance for preventing and treating diseases, but there is increasing evidence that regular, normal culinary use of a variety of them is health enhancing. Sometimes you will notice immediate effects, such as reduction of intestinal pain and nausea from consuming even a few grams of ginger, but in most cases the effects of culinary herbs are long term and subtle.

The difference between living longer or dying longer

Taking ginger again as an example, its nutrient content is not important because you eat small quantities. However, some of ginger's other 400 or so components can produce a cascade of reactions that you may not be aware of:

- Its enzyme content can markedly improve your digestion. When your digestion improves, you obviously feel less abdominal discomfort, but in addition you will absorb nutrients from your foods more effectively — although the improved absorption may not produce any immediately noticeable reaction.

- The hot, spicy oleo-resins in ginger have many effects, including anti-inflammatory, so you could expect a range of effects throughout your body, including pain reduction.

- Twelve of ginger's components have antioxidant properties and, as explained in chapter 1, antioxidants help to counteract the effects of free radicals that are implicated in cardiovascular diseases, cancer and premature ageing.

- Constituents in ginger help reduce circulating fats and relax blood vessels, which means that blood flow is improved, there is less stress on blood vessel walls, and the cells of the body are better nourished and oxygenated.

Ginger as a culinary herb is not a miracle cure, but is one of 'nature's little helpers'. A combination of such little helpers incorporated in your diet on a regular basis may well provide a significant preventive, as well as a beneficial, treatment programme.

A few spices must be used sparingly, and occasionally, because they contain quite toxic components, even at moderate levels. Those in this category are nutmeg, and, to a lesser extent, cinnamon and cloves.

Generally, you can use most common culinary herbs quite generously in salads and in cooking. For instance, I often pick a handful a day of basil, chives, mint, nasturtium leaves and flowers, oregano, parsley, rocket and thyme, and chop them finely into any vegetable or savoury dish. Alternatively, I use about a teaspoon of mixed dried herbs.

Fenugreek
(*Trigonella foenum-graecum*)

Background

The plant is native to southern Europe and Asia, and is a type of legume. Ancient Egyptian, Indian, Arab and Chinese people used it. The seed of fenugreek is used as a medicine, for food and for its curry flavour. In traditional European herbal medicine fenugreek has long been recommended as a general and digestive tonic, and to treat excessive respiratory mucus. It also has the reputation of clearing toxic matter from the body through the skin, but I suspect what is actually eliminated is the aromatic components in the plant itself, because if you consume fenugreek regularly you — or someone else — will usually notice a curry-like body odour.

The part used

The seeds.

Specific health benefits

The most common use of fenugreek is for alleviating the symptoms of the common cold and coughs.

At high doses fenugreek is very helpful for lowering high cholesterol and high triglycerides. In a trial of sixty people over twenty-four weeks on 25 g powdered fenugreek seed per day, LDL cholesterol fell by 16 per cent and triglycerides by 15 per cent. A few participants in this trial reported temporary diarrhoea or flatulence early in the study.[1] Many people may not tolerate this quantity of fenugreek in the long term, but could use smaller quantities together with other remedies and as part of a prevention programme for heart, circulatory and blood sugar disorders.

In traditional herbal medicine fenugreek is classed as a digestive tonic that also soothes the intestinal wall and acts as a gentle bulk laxative.

Fenugreek has a long history of use for lowering blood sugar. A number of studies in India showed that non-insulin-dependent diabetics obtained a favourable outcome in reducing blood sugar levels when they took large quantities of fenugreek powder as part of their diet. However, those with the most successful outcomes used 100 g per day of a debittered and defatted fenugreek powder that is not available in Western countries — presumably because pharmaceuticals are used and therefore there is no demand. In Australia the law clearly states that only qualified medical practitioners may treat diabetes.

One study used 25 g fenugreek powder daily in two divided doses with food. This trial showed that blood glucose levels were significantly lower after the fifteen-day fenugreek diet.[2]

General health benefits

Herbs that contain bitter-tasting components act to stimulate digestion. When digestion is improved, nutrients are better absorbed, and you would expect some improvement in wellbeing. As fenugreek also reduces blood fats, the circulation would be improved, and this, too, enhances general health. Other components in fenugreek support its reputation as a tonic and convalescent aid.

Cautions and adverse effects

- People on diabetic medication should not use fenugreek as a food because this would lower their blood glucose levels too much. If you have *low* blood sugar, you would need to monitor the effect, although tablets and the small quantities used as flavouring are unlikely to affect your blood sugar level.
- Prolonged use of fenugreek often produces a curry-like body odour, although this is not usually rated as unpleasant.
- A toxicological study showed that there were no adverse effects in animals fed a diet that contained 20 per cent fenugreek for ninety days.[3]

Known therapeutic components

- Steroidal saponins, notably diosgenin, may be converted in a laboratory to various human hormones, but we are not certain of the hormonal effect of these plant saponins in the human body. I suspect that they are phyto-oestrogenic in some way. These saponins lower cholesterol and triglycerides, as well as improving intestinal health and absorption.
- The mucilage content has a soothing effect on the digestive tract, and acts as a gentle bulk swelling laxative.
- Lecithin is a fat emulsifier.
- Trigonelline, an alkaloid, has the capacity to lower blood sugar levels.
- The bitter components generally stimulate digestion.

Growing your own fenugreek

Fenugreek grows readily in warm temperate areas, but will tolerate a variety of climates and soils. In cold areas it would be a summer crop. Within about a month of flowering, each pod produces about ten to twenty seeds that are ready for harvesting.

I sometimes grow fenugreek as 'vegelets' — I sow the seeds in shallow containers of soil and organic compost, and harvest the greens when they are about 6–10 cm high.

How to use

You can grind fenugreek seeds into a powder to give a curry flavour in many dishes, or you can simply add the seeds to casseroles, curries and similar dishes. However, if you use too much, the food will have an unpleasantly bitter taste. My maximum taste tolerance is a dessertspoon per serve.

Many people buy fenugreek powder to make into a herbal tea, or to use as a culinary herb. Others simmer the seeds in water and use as a tea. The seeds are quite easy to sprout, and are quite pleasant added to salads or used as a thickening agent in cooked dishes.

Herbalists often prescribe fenugreek liquid extract, and you can buy tablets, usually in combination with vitamin C, garlic and horse-radish for sinus and respiratory infections.

In the old days fenugreek was used as a poultice on the chest to soothe an irritating cough, or to soften boils so that they burst gently. To prepare a poultice, mix the powder into boiling water to make a thick porridge-like consistency, cover with a lid and leave to cool somewhat so that it does not burn the skin. Wrap the mix in a washer or towel, and place over the affected area for about thirty minutes.

Suggested intake and duration of use

As a long-term preventive strategy, I recommend about 1–2 teaspoons of powder or seeds, every second day, added to food or as a herbal tea.

For coughs and colds, drink 2–3 cups fenugreek tea daily, or take fenugreek in tablet form, perhaps in combination with vitamin C, garlic, horseradish and other herbs. Take only the label dose. Although culinary herbs are recommended indefinitely, for infections use them in remedy form for the duration of the illness.

For more serious problems such as blood sugar problems, take a therapeutic dose of between 10–25 g powder daily, mixed into your food. Make sure you are monitored by a medical practitioner.

Children could be given an extract or powder in proportional dosages according to age (see pp. 4–5).

Summary

Fenugreek is a digestive and general tonic helpful for cold symptoms, reducing the levels of harmful blood fats and lowering blood sugar levels.

Garlic *(Allium sativum)*

Background

It is not known when people first began eating garlic, but we know it was culti-vated in various ancient civilisations of Europe and Asia, and that stone-age people used a wild form of the plant.

Garlic was appreciated more in warmer climates — perhaps because there was an in-stinctive feeling that the pungent odour was beneficial to offset the deterioration of food and to ward off the types of infectious illnesses prevalent at the time. Many different cultures have a long recorded history of the benefits of garlic as a food and a medicine.

Old herbal books give anecdotal accounts of their favourite garlic cures. For example, for ear-ache and toothache a German doctor recom-mended putting a fried garlic bulb on the upper arm so that the skin would redden, and the pain relieved through diversion; raw mashed garlic was wrapped onto the soles of the feet as a cure for bronchitis; and garlic cooked in milk was used to get rid of intestinal worms.

In 1858 Louis Pasteur verified the antiseptic

qualities of garlic — if you've ever travelled on the French Metro in peak hour, you will appreciate that it has remained very popular in France.

Detailed scientific research into garlic began in the middle of the last century when a German scientist discovered that under steam distillation crushed garlic produced an oil (allicin) that was composed solely of sulphur compounds. At present, allicin is favoured by researchers as garlic's most beneficial compound.

As there is so much information generally available on garlic, I will focus more on the scientific research.

The part used

The bulb.

Specific health benefits

At least forty studies have tested the effect of garlic on blood. Garlic has the capacity to suppress cholesterol and fatty acid synthesis in the liver. This is important because in the majority of cases, it is not dietary cholesterol that is the real culprit but the excessive cholesterol made by the liver.

Garlic helps to suppress the oxidation of LDL cholesterol (a harmful breakdown process). Most studies used garlic powder tablets in doses of 600–900 mg daily for four to sixteen weeks, and total cholesterol decreased between 9–12 per cent.[4] Triglyceride levels were lowered by 8–27 per cent.[5] A study using 7.2 g aged garlic extract daily for six months resulted in an average blood pressure reduction of 5.8 per cent.[6]

Garlic has anticlotting, antiplatelet and fibrinolytic actions — it gently thins the blood, and reduces the formation of clots and atherosclerotic deposits that form on the linings of blood vessels. Additionally, it helps relax the muscles in the linings of the arteries, so it can be helpful for a number of circulation disorders, including leg pain caused by restricted blood flow. One study showed that clot-busting activity increased by 70 per cent within a few

hours of eating raw garlic, and other trials confirm that an increase of at least 25 per cent can be expected.[7] Studies of large groups of people who eat garlic regularly back the experimental evidence that garlic helps keep the blood thin and flowing smoothly, as well improving the linings of the blood vessels.

A clinical trial of 432 cardiac patients showed that a garlic supplement reduced mortality by 50 per cent in the second year and by 66 per cent in the third year, compared to those heart patients who did not take the supplement.

In another study eight healthy men consumed one clove of garlic a day for sixteen weeks. There was a significant reduction in blood stickiness and level of cholesterol.[8] You don't have to buy garlic tablets because dietary garlic alone will provide these benefits.

Garlic is widely accepted as a preventive and treatment for colds, influenza, coughs and other respiratory illnesses. Asthmatic patients may be helped with garlic because, in addition to its immune enhancing effects, it has some anti-inflammatory or antihistamine activity. However, some asthmatics cannot tolerate garlic.

The antiparasitic effect on intestinal worms is well known, but scientific researchers say it may not be sufficiently effective by itself as a treatment. I recommend you use it as an adjunct to other treatment, and as a preventive for various intestinal infections.

Many population surveys indicate that high garlic consumption (raw and cooked) is associated with a low incidence of cancer. Garlic is likely to be preventive against colon cancer, and probably rectal, lung and breast cancers. Garlic can inactivate some cancer-forming substances, such as nitrosamines, and it has a number of antioxidant effects. Evidence from human surveys and animal studies shows that the allicin in garlic is not necessary to achieve significant cancer reduction. People who consistently eat cooked garlic have a low cancer risk, even though cooked garlic does not contain allicin.

Rats given garlic powder were able to offset the mutagenic effects of benzo(a) pyrene.[9] This chemical is strongly linked to cancer, and results from cigarette smoke and 'charred' meats.

The antioxidant effect of garlic protects blood vessels against the harmful effects of free radicals.

A laboratory trial showed that garlic suppressed Helicobacter pylori (the bacteria that causes peptic ulcers), and the researchers concluded that eating the equivalent of two small cloves of garlic (5 g) daily would achieve an effective level.[10] No information was given about the number of doses that would be required to kill this bacteria in the stomach of a human. Perhaps try one to three such doses weekly for a month, before meals (crushed, chopped or chewed, but not swallowed whole), as long as it does not aggravate your stomach. It is estimated that 35 per cent of Australians are infected with this bacterium, but only a very small percentage will develop peptic ulcers or stomach cancer. Another option is to crush the garlic into Manuka honey (which also has some antibacterial activity), and take 1 dessertspoon of this before a meal.

You can be infected with Helicobacter pylori without getting ulcers or digestive problems, but there is some evidence that this bacteria may lead to stomach cancer, another good reason why you should do all you can to treat it and prevent recurrences.

Garlic has antifungal effects, both internally and externally. If you want to try it as an external treatment for tinea (athlete's foot), make a garlic tea, let it cool, and then add it to tepid water in a footbath. An alternative is to sprinkle a little plain garlic powder over the affected areas, but always do a tiny test patch first in case it irritates your skin.

A number of studies show that garlic can reduce blood glucose levels so, with the guidance of a medical practitioner, it could be one of a number of preventive or early measures for non-insulin-dependent diabetes. One study, using a stabilised product at 800 mg a day for four weeks, produced a 16 per cent decrease in blood sugar levels.

Garlic can also increase thiamine (vitamin

B1) absorption, reduce the liver-damaging effects of some toxic substances, increase bile flow and protect the intestines. It may act as a buffer against heavy metal toxicities, such as lead, cadmium and mercury — although if you have these problems you must seek advice from a medical practitioner. An animal study showed that garlic reduced formaldehyde-induced arthritis, and that this effect was increased by boron supplementation. (Boron is a trace element that is used in dosages of about 3 mg daily to treat some forms of arthritis.)

General health benefits

Population studies frequently link garlic with improvements in wellbeing, longevity and effective immune functioning. In mice, garlic was shown to beneficially affect central nervous system changes related to ageing; the researchers thought this was due to the antioxidant and immune enhancing effects of garlic.[11]

Laboratory studies confirm that garlic is effective against many common bacteria.[12] It has repeatedly been demonstrated that bacteria never develop resistance to garlic.

Garlic can increase phagocyte, natural killer cell, lymphocyte and other immune related activity — all of which mean an improved ability to fight infections and cancer, as well as assisting with wound healing and health restoration.

Some of the therapeutic effects of garlic have been verified only with very high doses of cooked garlic, powdered capsules or aged extract. However, literally millions of people can't be wrong, and garlic in almost any form as an internal remedy is likely to provide a wide spectrum of health benefits.

Cautions and adverse effects

- Garlic, and related plants such as onions and chives, are common allergens.
- Internally, garlic can be irritating to people with sensitive gastrointestinal tracts — bloating, colicky pains and diarrhoea are

common signs. Some people can tolerate a little supplemental odourless garlic, but, as a rule, if you are allergic or sensitive to anything it is best avoided.

- Garlic oil products seem to cause more adverse reactions.
- Fresh garlic on an empty stomach can be irritating and painful for some people, especially those with gastric ulcers. People with ulcers should consult a health practitioner.
- It may not be advisable to swallow whole cloves, as there has been a case of this causing a blockage in the intestines that required surgery.
- Skin burns and rashes have occurred with external application of garlic.
- Inhaled garlic powder irritates the bronchioles, especially in asthmatics.
- As garlic has blood-thinning capacity, people on blood-thinning medication, including aspirin, should not take garlic without medical approval.
- People with porphyria should not take garlic, because the sulphur-containing compounds worsen the disease.
- Garlic gets into breast milk, which may cause colic in some babies, but may also help their immune system. It is said that mothers who love garlic produce garlic-loving children.
- Garlic may slightly elevate the 'good' cholesterol (HDL), which is why people treated for high cholesterol need to have the types of their cholesterol checked.

Normal levels of cholesterol (mmol/L)	
Total cholesterol	3.9–5.5
HDL cholesterol	
female	0.9–2.1
male	0.8–1.8
LDL cholesterol (the 'bad' one)	0–3.5

Known therapeutic components

- Garlic contains thirty-nine compounds containing sulphur (thiosulphinates, notably

allicin) that are responsible for most of its immune enhancing activities. Sulphur compounds have antibacterial, antifungal and antiparasitic activity.

The allicin content is now considered to be responsible for most of the antioxidant, antimicrobial, antithrombotic and anti-platelet effects, and lowering the levels of blood lipids and blood glucose. Many commercial products show the allicin content on the label, but 'no garlic product contains allicin until active alliinase is released' according to Drs Koch and Lawson.[13] This means that products should actually give the allicin potential on the label. If you chew or cut fresh garlic, this too releases the allicin.

- Ajoene is a component that reduces blood stickiness, and laboratory studies show that it reduces the uptake of fats.
- Scordinin is a plant hormone in garlic that can reduce blood pressure and cholesterol, and tone muscles, so perhaps the ancient Egyptian slaves were right when they demanded their daily serving of garlic to give them strength.
- Saponins in general tend to promote healthy fat metabolism, and those in garlic also have blood-thinning, antimicrobial and anti-candida activity. Saponins are also beneficial to the intestines, and improve nutrient absorption.
- Triterpenoids, flavonoids, fructans and other compounds in garlic give further support for the varied, traditional reputation of garlic.
- Nutrients are not an important factor in garlic, because only small quantities are consumed; however, it is a good source of selenium and boron — two valuable trace elements.

For more scientific data on the components and processing of garlic, read the book by Koch and Lawson (see **Recommended reading**).

Growing your own garlic

Garlic is quite easy to grow, but it will rot in the ground if you overwater it, and it takes a long time to mature into a full bulb. Some nurseries sell 'society' garlic, which grows quite well in a tub; harvest the leaves to give a mild garlic flavour in cooking or salads.

How to use

Garlic is sold as a fresh whole plant, crushed, pickled, or as a vegetable oil macerate for culinary use.

Garlic is also sold as a medicine in aged, odour-reduced or odourless powdered tablets and capsules, as steam-distilled oil, and so on. These products have somewhat different effects because the various manufacturing processes reduce, increase or alter the therapeutic components in the plant.

Removing the odour or potential odour of garlic reduces some of the medicinal principles.

In general, you will notice that odourless actually means odour-reduced. I suspect that a completely odourless product may have only minimal therapeutic activity.

At present I favour dried capsules of odour-reduced garlic, with a stated allicin potential, for cardiovascular problems. Aged, odourless garlic may be preferable as a cancer preventive.

Buy well-known brands, otherwise you cannot be certain that the manufacturing process has preserved the main therapeutic components. Alternatively, use raw, crushed or chopped garlic if you can tolerate it. Try chewing a few caraway seeds afterwards to reduce the odour. Cooking destroys an enzyme that is important for converting one of the most beneficial components.

Traditionally, some Asian people make their own pickled garlic, using vinegar or wine.

Aged, odour-reduced garlic (my recipe)

500 g garlic cloves
1 tablespoon caraway seeds
apple cider vinegar (to cover)

1 Peel garlic cloves, and chop into small pieces.
2 Pack the garlic lightly into a glass jar, sprinkling with caraway seeds.
3 Fill the jar with apple cider vinegar.

4 Seal with a firm lid, label and date, and store in a cool, dark place for two years!

This aged garlic vinegar will lose some of the therapeutic components, but it is less reactive for sensitive people, and may even have more anticancer properties.

It is excellent as a marinade for grilled meats or in salads.

The caraway is added to (hopefully) reduce the garlic odour!

Suggested intake

I recommend you eat one clove of fresh garlic daily, if tolerated, otherwise cook it first. No authority has set a specific level, but a clove would be between 2–4 g, depending on its size, water content, growing conditions, and so on.

As products have different strengths, be guided by the manufacturer's dosages.

Young children and frail elderly people do not tolerate strong-smelling garlic products, although a little cooked garlic is acceptable. Use odour-reduced forms for the elderly, and for children those special products labelled for children's use.

Summary

Garlic has the capacity to reduce cholesterol, triglycerides and high blood pressure, to decrease the stickiness of blood, improve blood flow and dilate blood-vessel walls. These benefits to the cardiovascular system have been confirmed by the majority of medical reports from many different countries.[14]

This plant also has anticancer, antifungal, antibacterial, antiviral and antimicrobial activity.

Recommended reading

Goldberg, I. (ed.). *Functional Foods: Designer Foods, Pharmafoods, Nutraceuticals.* Chapman & Hall, New York, 1994.
Koch, H. P. & Lawson, L. D. *Garlic: The Science and Therapeutic Application of Allium sativum and Related Species.* 2nd edn. Williams & Wilkins, Baltimore, 1996 (2240 references).

Other plants in the garlic family

Plants in the same family include chives, leeks and onions.

Onions

A regular intake of onions in the diet is linked to a reduction in some degenerative diseases. A large group of Finnish adults was studied for twenty-five years, onions and apples being their main source of flavonoids. Those who had the highest intakes proved to have about half the risk of heart disease.

Onions have been used therapeutically in various ways.

How to use

Remedy for hayfever, coughs and colds

2 medium onions
4 dessertspoons honey

1 Peel and finely chop the onions.
2 Put the onions into a jar, add the honey, and stir.
3 Leave to stand, with the lid on, for at least 2 hours.
4 Label and date before storing; use within two weeks.

Take 1 dessertspoon, 3–4 times daily.

General tonic — an old French recipe

300 g grated or finely chopped onion
100 g honey
500 ml white wine

1 Combine all the ingredients in a large jar, and leave to stand for at least two days.
2 Shake the jar frequently.
3 Strain.
4 Label and date before storing. Although it will last indefinitely in the fridge, I recommend using it within three months.

Take up to 40 ml daily.

Other treatments

URINARY TRACT PROBLEMS

Wrap raw grated onion in a tea towel, and place it on your lower abdomen for 30 minutes a day for one week.

ARTHRITIS

Use in the same way as the poultice above, but apply over the affected joint.

CHILBLAINS

Bandage grated onion over the affected areas and change daily for at least a week.

BOILS

To bring boils to a head, and ease the pain, apply baked mashed onion *warm* over the boil as a poultice. Leave on for 15–30 minutes. Reapply a fresh poultice if required.

EARACHE AND TINNITUS (RINGING OR BUZZING IN THE EARS) — AN OLD TREATMENT

Soak a cotton ball in onion juice and gently pack this into your ear. Leave in place for two hours, and repeat daily, if required, over a period of one week.

Of course, if you have an ear problem have it checked out by a medical practitioner before doing any self-treatment.

Ginger (*Zingiber officinale*)

Background

Ginger probably originated in India, but it has been used widely throughout Asia and Africa for thousands of years. It was well known to the ancient Greeks and Arabs, and by the Middle Ages it was well established in Europe.

Ayurvedic (traditional Indian doctors) pre-scribe ginger for colds, respiratory infections, fevers and arthritis. In traditional Chinese herbalism both fresh and dried ginger have been prescribed for centuries, mainly for respiratory and digestive ailments.

The part used

The rhizome; although most people refer to this part of the plant as the root, the rhizome is actually the underground swollen portion of the stem, and the roots are the finer string-like parts that spread out into the soil.

Specific health benefits

For centuries ginger has been recommended for stomach and intestinal complaints, including colic and dyspepsia. Ginger, in common with other spices, enhances digestion by increasing the activity of lipase and other digestive enzymes.

The spicy, hot compounds in ginger (gingerols) are responsible for ginger's action in stimulating bile flow.[15]

Components in ginger (gingerol and zingiberene) have antiulcer effects, as they protect the stomach lining from damage.[16] A Japanese study indicated that ginger tea should work better for gastric ulcers caused by high acid output, whereas alcoholic ginger extracts should be more effective for treating pepsin-induced gastric ulcers.[17] Many people with ulcers cannot tolerate any hot spices, and large doses of fresh ginger in particular might not be tolerated.

A number of controlled scientific trials have shown that ginger is useful for treating travel sickness, and reducing the tendency to vomiting and cold sweats.[18]

For nausea of pregnancy capsules containing ginger as powdered root (250 mg, four times daily) gives significant relief.[19] The medical researcher also considered that this dosage of ginger was safe during early pregnancy. In a hospital trial ginger was given to women after gynaecological surgery, and it reduced nausea more than the tested pharmaceutical; the need for antivomiting treatment was much lower in the ginger-treated group.[20]

Studies in animals show that ginger can reduce vomiting caused by cancer chemotherapy drugs.[21]

Aside from the historical use of ginger for treating arthritis, medical studies confirm that it can give pain relief to sufferers of osteoarthritis, rheumatoid arthritis and muscular discomfort. The anti-inflammatory and antirheumatic properties of ginger have been confirmed by a number of studies.[22]

Animal trials demonstrate that gingerol helps prevent contraction of blood vessels and therefore improves circulation, and could be considered as part of the therapy for treating hypertension.[23] Earlier studies showed that ginger had beneficial effects on the blood vessels and circulation, although for high blood pressure the tablet form of ginger would be better because the hot taste can produce a short-term stimulatory effect on blood vessels. To get a good therapeutic effect, you would need to use a guaranteed potency tablet.

Using carbon tetrachloride as the toxin, a series of animal studies showed that the oleoresins in ginger were able to reduce the toxic damage to liver cells.[24] Laboratory studies show that ginger has some antibacterial action and can reduce aflatoxin — a dangerous liver toxin that can be present in peanuts, stored grains and various other foods.

Ginger is helpful for the common cold because it has mild antirhinoviral properties.[25]

Essential oils in ginger have potential anticancer activity.[26]

Ginger has the capacity to reduce the amount of cholesterol produced by the liver, and to improve glucose tolerance. Given that we do not eat large quantities of ginger, it should be regarded as a 'helper' rather than as the main therapy.

Many herbalists use ginger to help regulate menstruation, for feverish conditions, pain and muscle spasms, and to prevent the spread of intestinal parasites. In my clinic I found ginger reduced migraines in some difficult cases where all else has failed, and this is probably a consequence of ginger's anti-inflammatory and relaxant effects on blood vessels.

General health benefits

I frequently add ginger to herbal formulas because it has so many useful properties. Studies of isolated components show multiple benefits, including uterine relaxing, warming, immune tonic, antibacterial, antifungal, antihistamine and antimicrobial effects, and tonifying the heart and dilating blood vessels. It acts as a mild circulatory and general tonic.

The antioxidant components in ginger extend the shelf-life of meat, reduce harmful fat oxidation in the body, and help to protect human blood cells. Ginger acts as a gentle blood thinner by reducing the side effects of dietary fats.

A number of studies show that the active components in ginger have anti-inflammatory and liver protecting effects.[27]

Cautions and adverse effects

- Some people are allergic to ginger, and should not take it.
- I recommend that low doses (2 g daily) be used for morning sickness and during pregnancy, and that, apart from minor use as a flavouring in food, it not be used otherwise by pregnant women, unless prescribed by a medical practitioner.

There are no risks associated with ginger, and the majority of major reference texts and trials show no adverse effects. Studies show that ginger has no cancer causing effects.[28] One of the gingerols is mutagenic according to a laboratory study, but further studies showed that another constituent, zingerone, suppresses this potentially harmful activity.

Based on animal studies, it has been estimated that a hazardous dose of ginger would be about 6 kg of dried ginger taken at one time, so it is generally regarded as safe.

Special note: A few studies show that ginger has anticlotting effects, while others do not. My assessment is that it probably has very mild activity, and therefore if you are taking anticoagulant (anticlotting) medication, including aspirin, do not use it as a medication without your doctor's approval — although the occasional use of ginger as a culinary herb should not be a problem.

The studies that have been done could all be criticised on some grounds, such as testing people who have normal rather than excessive blood-clotting ability. In some cases herbs exert effects only when there are abnormal levels. Furthermore, no controlled studies have been done on patients taking ginger and anticoagulant medication.

Known therapeutic components

Over 450 different components have been identified in ginger.

- The pungency (hotness) gives most of the medicinal value of ginger, and the constituents that are responsible for these effects are called gingerols. These gingerols are classed as oleo-resins; when the ginger is dried or heated, the gingerols are partly converted to shogaols.

   The degree of pungency depends on where the ginger was grown, and how it is processed. A product that can guarantee the level of gingerols is obviously going to be more expensive than another, which may or may not be very therapeutic. The gingerols are largely responsible for the anti-inflammatory, antinausea and antioxidant effects.

- Essential oils provide the distinctive odour and pleasantly sweet-lemonish aroma. The most flavoursome of these oils is considered to be zingiberene, and the aromatic oils in general are helpful for digestion and flatulence. The essential oils also contain the antiviral activity, which means that for treating the common cold fresh ginger is more effective than dried. The essential oils also contain the anticancer activity. If you make a tea from the fresh ginger, keep the lid on while the tea is brewing.

Essential oils extracted from plants are extremely strong, and you should not take them internally without the supervision of a qualified health professional.

The best way to obtain these oils is by eating the fresh plant; grate about 1 teaspoon ginger into your food after cooking.

- Another important component in ginger is zingibain, a powerful protein-digesting enzyme.

How to use

Ginger as a remedy		
Fresh ginger	**Dried ginger**	**Standardised tablets (gingerols)**
Common cold and influenza	Non-mucousy coughs	Arthritis
Cancer preventive	Antivomiting; vertigo; nausea of pregnancy	Serious circulatory problems

Ginger juice

A traditional Chinese doctor has written:

During my more than 20 years of practice, I have used fresh ginger in treating 400–500 cases of burns without a single failure. Method: Fresh ginger root is mashed to release juice that is soaked up in a ball of cotton and applied to burned area. Pain will be immediately relieved. Blisters and inflammation will subside. There will be no irritation even when blisters are broken. Due to ginger's antibiotic activities, no wound ulceration will occur. In light cases, a single application suffices. In severe cases, keeping the cotton moist periodically with fresh ginger juice for 36 hours accomplishes the desired effect.[29]

I would not recommend that anyone self-treat serious burns, and suggest that for household burns you firstly cool the burnt area with water; if you then want to try ginger as a treatment, simply drop some ginger juice onto your burnt skin.

Fresh ginger juice can also be rubbed into sore muscles, but it would be too strong over a large area. Another option is to dilute about 10 drops of ginger oil in some plain oil for this purpose. Always do a skin test patch first when using anything new on your skin.

As an internal remedy for upper respiratory infections, influenza and coughs, dilute a teaspoon of ginger juice in water and lemon juice. Take this twice daily until the infection clears.

Fresh ginger

Grated fresh ginger is excellent in a marinade to tenderise and flavour meat. In laboratory studies ginger and its isolated oleo-resins can kill various types of flukes, nematodes and worms, and this may be an added reason for marinating fish and meat with grated fresh ginger, or simply using it freely as a culinary herb.

In any dish a little grated fresh ginger could be added after cooking to help digestion. (Remember, cooking destroys enzymes and aromatic oils).

Ginger tea

1–2 teaspoons grated fresh ginger
2 cups water
1 teaspoon herbal tea

1 Combine the ginger and the water in a small saucepan and bring to the boil.
2 Simmer for a few minutes, then turn the heat off.
3 Add 1 teaspoon herbal tea, and leave to stand, with the lid on, for several minutes.
4 Strain, and serve with a slice of lemon.

If you are fond of ginger, or have a therapeutic need for it, you can have ginger tea daily.

Chamomile combines well with ginger.

Drink plain ginger tea hot or cold, for nausea. I find it a pleasant cold drink mixed with fruit or vegetable juice.

For sore muscles or bruises use a stronger tea as a hot compress. Strain the mix onto a washer — as you will have to wring the washer with your hands, it will have cooled down sufficiently to prevent burning of your skin. Apply as a poultice to the affected area.

Ginger powder

Ginger powder mixed into cooked savoury dishes is the simplest way to use ginger. I add it to biscuit recipes.

Start with about I dessertspoon per batch, and increase the quantity according to your taste.

Crystallised ginger

If I use crystallised ginger, I wash off the excess sugar, and store the ginger in the fridge.

Ginger tablets

Tablets of ginger are available in varying strengths.

Growing your own ginger

Ginger grows best in rich, loamy soils that are well drained. In hot, moist climates grow ginger in conditions that give some shade.

Suggested intake and duration of use

As a general preventive and flavouring I recommend you use ginger regularly in cooking, either fresh or powdered, at a dose of about ½ teaspoon (2 g), every second day or so.

For therapeutic purposes, such as for arthritis, use 3–7 g powder daily (or twice that quantity of the fresh herb). If you need this high dose, another option is to buy a guaranteed

potency product. Take this amount for three months (if it has not helped your condition within that time, then it probably never will). About 2–4 g daily could be used as a maintenance dose for an indefinite period.

A number of tablet products are available for travel sickness, and these are obviously more convenient. Weaker forms of ginger tablets rather than guaranteed potency products are more appropriate for pregnant women and children. Children could be given a portion of a tablet according to age (see pp. 4–5), but I do not recommend ginger or any hot spices for toddlers or babies.

Summary

Due to its beneficial effects on digestion and circulation, ginger has the capacity to produce a wide range of improvements in health and well-being. It is useful as an antioxidant, and is antiviral and anti-inflammatory.

Recommended reading

Schulick, P. *Ginger: Common Spice and Wonder Drug.* 3rd edn. Herbal Free Press Ltd, Brattleboro, Vermont, 1994 (356 references).

Turmeric *(Curcuma longa)*

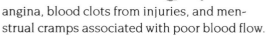

Background

In traditional Asian herbal medicine turmeric is prescribed as part of a formula to fit each individual's needs, and has been used for angina, blood clots from injuries, and menstrual cramps associated with poor blood flow.

The Ayurvedic (Indian) system uses turmeric as a digestive, liver, gallbladder and rheumatic remedy, as well as for various inflammatory disorders. It is also the yellow spice used in Indian curry dishes.

Tumeric is also an external folk remedy for sprains, swellings, sores, and as a general wound healer.

The part used

The dried rhizome, ground to a powder.

Specific health benefits

A number of studies show that components in turmeric can increase bile production and bile flow, and stimulate the muscles of the gallbladder, reinforcing its reputation as a gallbladder tonic. In general, if you eat bitter-tasting plants the reaction in your mouth from the bitterness stimulates your digestive organs.

A study on rats showed that curcumin (the main therapeutic compound in turmeric) reduced the effects of iron-induced liver damage. Lipid peroxide levels were lowered by 27 per cent, and some liver enzymes were also reduced by about one-third; both effects confirming turmeric's potential to offset toxic damage.[30] Other animal studies confirm that turmeric has significant liver-protectant effects.[31]

Another animal study supported the use of turmeric as an antiulcer agent. Turmeric increased the protective mucus secreted by the stomach wall, and gave a measure of defence from damage caused by pharmaceutical drugs and surgery.[32]

Turmeric's cholesterol and triglyceride-lowering effects have been observed in a number of animal trials. Although turmeric by itself may not be sufficient to rectify high cholesterol, it is one of the 'herbal helpers', and probably works on fat metabolism via the liver.

Both curcumin and turmeric have mild blood-thinning action and antioxidant activity, supporting the observation that there is a low incidence of cardiovascular disease in regions where spices such as turmeric are consumed regularly.[33]

Studies with animals support turmeric's traditional use for arthritis, as it can reduce joint swelling and inflammation in mice.[34]

Turmeric powder sprinkled over external wounds accelerates healing time. This may be due to mild antibacterial and antifungal activity, as these effects have been observed in laboratory studies.

General health benefits

Turmeric is a digestive aid that may help reduce flatulence and protect intestinal linings.

Antitumour and cancer preventing effects have been confirmed by many laboratory studies.[35] A three-month study on fifty-eight people with a precancerous condition of the mouth showed that turmeric capsules were helpful in markedly reducing the number of damaged cells. There were also improvements in the protective white blood cells.[36] This result supports a number of trials showing that turmeric circulates in the body, and has a measurable preventive effect for a number of different cancers, including those caused by known irritants such as smoking and alcohol.

The antioxidant effects of curcumin have not been fully evaluated, but it is known from animal studies that it can act to prevent cataract formation.[37]

Cautions and adverse effects

- Turmeric stains clothing, and will temporarily discolour your teeth and tongue.
- When rats were fed a diet that was 10 per cent turmeric, some hair loss occurred. This is a massive dose, and I am not sure how the rats were able to eat that quantity because in large doses turmeric is unpleasantly bitter.
- A few early reports suggested that turmeric had an antifertility effect in male animals, but more recent studies showed that turmeric gave no significant signs of toxicity, including spermatotoxicity. In fact, turmeric-fed mice

showed some signs of increased male hormone activity.[38]

- One laboratory study showed chromosomal breakage and other aberrations; however, when animals were fed turmeric there were no significant changes in bone marrow cells.[39] This research is interesting because a medical journal reported that turmeric caused chromosomal damage but failed to mention that this happened *only* in a test tube.

Turmeric is generally regarded as safe. Doses given to animals in the range of 1–3 g per kilo of bodyweight gave no signs of toxicity or change in organ weights. This converts to more than 12 teaspoons daily for an adult human, far above the maximum recommended dose.

Known therapeutic components

- So far ninety-four different compounds have been identified in turmeric, curcumin currently being assessed as the most therapeutic.
- Yellow-coloured phenolic compounds curcumins I and III inhibit carcinogenesis, lending support for turmeric's anticancer effects.[40]
- Curcuminoids are antioxidants that protect DNA and harmful fat breakdown. They also destroy harmful free radicals and block nitric oxide.[41]
- The oleo-resins, components that are gumlike and generally pungent to the taste, are both cancer protective and antiinflammatory. Some types of inflammatory activity are linked to cancer.
- The essential oils in turmeric also have antiinflammatory effects, and may help preserve connective tissue.[42] Turmeric essential oils also have cancer preventive properties.

An animal study showed that the isolated curcumin may protect against breast cancer and cataract formation, probably due to its antioxidant effect. It is worth repeating that the connection between an isolated component given to animals and turmeric powder consumed by humans is weak, but at least it may dispel the myth that 'Worry, hurry and curry are killers' —

at least as far as curry is concerned. A sensible way of looking at studies on isolated components is to consider that the effect of the total plant is obviously weaker. An isolated component that is harmful is likely to be offset by numerous beneficial components. An isolated component that is beneficial needs to be supported by other evidence before the whole plant can be recommended as a therapeutic aid.

There is considerable evidence that culinary spices actually afford protection to those who regularly consume them.

Growing your own turmeric

The turmeric plant grows best in tropical regions, but you can cultivate it in temperate climates such as Sydney. I recommend that you buy the powder, as it is not easy to dry and powder the root; or use a little grated fresh root.

How to use

I recommend you use the powdered herb, as it has a wide range of benefits and few adverse effects. Add the powder to dishes such as curries, casseroles and stir-fries, or use it in a herbal vinegar; see the following recipes.

A few brands of tablets contain turmeric in their formula. Professional herbalists can prescribe liquid extracts.

The isolated compound, curcumin, is available in a few countries as a remedy, but it is more likely to cause adverse effects.

Curry powder recipe

All ingredients are dried and powdered.

2 teaspoons each turmeric, ginger, chilli, fenugreek, coriander

1 teaspoon each cumin, cardamom, garlic, pepper, bay leaf

1 teaspoon bouillon powder or sea salt

1 Put all the ingredients together in a jar, seal, and shake thoroughly to combine.

2 Label and date. Use, according to taste, within three to six months.

I like my food very hot and spicy, so I add about ½ teaspoon per cup of food.

Suggested intake and duration of use

Take turmeric tablets according to the label instructions. Liquid extracts are usually prescribed in doses of 2–3 ml, three times daily.

As a flavouring agent, and for wellbeing and preventive purposes, add ¼–½ teaspoon powder or a teaspoon grated fresh root to your food every second day or so.

For self-treatment therapeutic purposes take about 1 teaspoon powder daily for a maximum of two to three months, and then about ¼–½ teaspoon every second day in the long term.

Give children proportionately less according to age as a culinary flavouring herb (see pp. 4–5). Note: Turmeric should be stored in dark glass away from sunlight, as the main therapeutic component, curcumin, decomposes on exposure to light.

Summary

Turmeric is a spice that helps the digestive system, liver and blood, as well as having anti-inflammatory and antioxidant effects. It is likely to produce a wide range of health benefits.

Culinary herbs and spices

Advantages and benefits

The main use of herbs and spices is to flavour other foods and partially replace unhealthy flavourings such as excessive salt and fats. However, culinary herbs have another common advantage — they all function as a digestive aid. They also have other therapeutic benefits, and the main ones are listed below.

Antioxidant

Rosemary and sage are considered to have the most potent antioxidant effect.

Others in this category include:

allspice	clove	nutmeg
aniseed	coriander	oregano
basil	cumin	pepper
bay	ginger	savory
cardamom	mace	thyme
chilli (hot)	marjoram	turmeric
cinnamon	mints	

Cancer preventive

allspice	cumin	oregano
cardamom	coriander	parsley
chilli (hot)	garlic	rosemary
cinnamon	ginger	sage
clove	mustard	turmeric

Anti-ulcer

chilli (hot)	garlic	pepper (black)
cinnamon	ginger	poppyseed
clove	mustard	turmeric
cumin	oregano	

Antimicrobial

These prevent food deterioration and multiplication of harmful micro-organisms.

allspice	garlic	oregano
bay	ginger	pepper
caraway	mace	rosemary
cinnamon	marjoram	sage
clove	mustard	thyme
coriander	nutmeg	

Most common culinary herbs have at least some inhibitory activity against harmful bacteria and other micro-organisms. Coriander, for instance, contains twelve antiviral components, and twenty antibacterial compounds.

A number of herbs are repeated in each

category — plants contain many different components, and therefore each has a variety of effects.

By using normal flavouring quantities of culinary herbs on a regular basis, you may well prevent ulcers because, for example, it is known that garlic cinnamon and thyme can kill *Helicobacter pylori* (the bacteria largely responsible for causing stomach ulcers). No one knows what causes these particular bacteria to multiply in the first place.

Many other common culinary herbs have some antimicrobial action, and the aromatic oil components play an important part in this activity, as well as being helpful for digestion generally.

James A. Duke, a world-renowned economic botanist, wrote:

> Given the choice of a natural and a synthetic drug, of equal efficacies (and toxicities), I prefer the natural, because, during evolution, my genes and immune system have already been exposed to numerous natural toxins, in many cases evolving strategies for dealing with them. My genes and immune system cannot yet have been exposed to tomorrow's new synthetics.[43]

Herbal vinegars

Using herbal vinegars is a practical way to increase your intake of culinary herbs.

In spite of all the claims that you may have read or heard, I could not find even one independent scientific research study verifying the therapeutic effects of apple cider or any other vinegar. However, because of its acidity (acetic acid), vinegar is undoubtedly a digestive aid because you need

acid to digest foods. Vinegar is an effective preservative, and it draws out some of the therapeutic components in plants. You can judge this for yourself from the taste and colour of the vinegar.

Another advantage of vinegar is that a small quantity added to food is tangy, and can be a salt replacement, so this might help reduce weight and excess fluid in the body. Adding appropriate herbs to the vinegar is an additional boost to the digestive process.

How to use

Add 2–4 teaspoons herbal vinegar daily to your salads, cooked vegetables, potatoes, rice dishes or similar foods. If you use herbal vinegars with a teaspoon or two of salt-reduced tamari or shoyu, plus other herbs and flavourings, you will have less desire for oils and salt, and, consequently your weight and health problems will be reduced.

You can make your own therapeutic and flavouring vinegars, and I give a few of my recipes below as a guide.

Digestive herbal vinegar

2 teaspoons turmeric powder
2 teaspoons ginger powder
1–2 crushed caraway or cumin seeds
½ teaspoon hot chilli powder
contents of 1 chamomile teabag
475 ml apple cider vinegar
a large handful of chopped fresh herbs (such as fennel, mints, oregano, tarragon)

1 Completely fill a bottle or large jar with the herbs and vinegar.
2 Seal, label and date, and store on its side for at least a few days before use.

After a time, the herbs will settle to the bottom. Shake the mix before use, or add the vinegar only to your foods.

Immune system herbal vinegar

1 whole garlic, peeled and finely chopped
2 teaspoons liquorice powder
1–2 teaspoons crushed aniseeds
1 teaspoon mustard powder
a selection of fresh herbs (such as angelica, aniseed, sweet or holy basil,* rosemary, thyme)
475 ml rice or balsamic vinegar

1   Completely fill a bottle or large jar with the herbs and vinegar.
2   Seal, label and date, and store on its side for at least a few days before use.

After a time, the herbs will settle to the bottom. Shake the mix before use, or add the vinegar only to your foods.

Arthritis herbal vinegar

2 teaspoons ginger
1 teaspoon turmeric
contents of 2 teabags of dried willow tea (or other herbal arthritis tea)
1 teaspoon celery or parsley seeds
a selection of fresh herbs (including feverfew leaves, gotu kola, rosemary, lemon verbena, mints)
475 ml apple cider vinegar

1   Completely fill a bottle or large jar with the herbs and vinegar.
2   Seal, label and date, and store on its side for at least a few days before use.

After a time, the herbs will settle to the bottom. Shake before use, or add the vinegar only to foods.

Notes

- You can add all dried herbs if fresh ones are not available, but they swell considerably in the vinegar, so restrict the dried herbs to less than 8 teaspoons in total.

---

* You can grow holy basil in the ground or in a pot. It is ornamental and therapeutic, and grows all year round in temperate to hot climates.

- Herbal teas can be used in vinegars.
- If you add too many crushed seeds, the oil in them will form into a white clump in the vinegar. This is not harmful, but as it doesn't look 'inviting' I usually remove it.
- Herbal vinegars could be used simply as salt substitutes. If you want to use them for a specific therapeutic purpose, my book on natural therapies will guide you regarding the herbs to include in your vinegar.
- I usually date and label the jar that the herbal vinegar should be used within six months, although it should last much longer.
- Vinegar contains weak acetic acid, which may be upsetting for people with heartburn, hiatis hernias and gastric ulcers.

Recommended reading

Beckham, N. *The Australian Family Guide to Natural Therapies*. Viking/Penguin, Melbourne, 1996.

In conclusion

A large proportion of culinary herbs are flavoursome, and gently boost digestion, circulation and the immune system. These effects are supported by centuries of observation, as well as by recent scientific evidence.

CHAPTER 5

Four super oils

Evening primrose oil
Fish oil
Olive oil
Tea tree oil

I chose these four oils because evening primrose and fish oil have specific health-enhancing properties that have been proved in human trials, virgin olive oil is the most highly recommended dietary oil, and tea tree oil is a remarkable external remedy.

Restricting dietary fats and oils is now accepted as a wise strategy for wellbeing and disease prevention. In nature there are no isolated edible oils or fats, and as a naturopath I am convinced that we would be far healthier if we ate foods in their natural state, getting our oils and fats from foods such as fish, lean game meats, nuts, seeds, olives, avocados, whole grains and legumes.

Oils and fats are tempting to the smell and taste buds, as well as satisfying to our stomachs. They are also satisfying to that part of our brain that tells us we have eaten enough (the satiety centre in the hypothalamus, which may be malfunctioning in some of us).

Little things weigh a lot

Oils and fatty foods are very high in kilojoules, and often they are added to the diet as extras, for example:

- 1 medium-sized potato baked in its jacket gives 290 kilojoules. If you flavour the baked potato with herbs and 2 teaspoons low-fat yoghurt, you add 60 kilojoules, or with 2 teaspoons butter another 290 kilojoules.
- 100 g small-cut French fries gives 1130 kilojoules. The oils used for the fries have been repeatedly reheated so they have lost their antioxidant effect and have become loaded

with toxic oxidants and harmful trans fatty acids. Over time these oils damage our cells — the oils are not only unhealthy, they are also fattening.

- salad or vegetable flavourings: 20 g mayonnaise could add as much as 597 kilojoules; 20 g soy sauce and herbal vinegar dressing add only about 57 kilojoules.

Essential fatty acids — the 'good oils'

Fats and oils in foods, and as separated ingredients, contain essential fatty acids. All humans need at least small quantities of these to keep the body and brain functioning, and they have to be in the diet because the body cannot make them. Many people, notably fad dieters, are likely to be physically and mentally unwell because they are not getting a reasonable quantity of essential fatty acids in their diet. Others get them in their foods, but cannot utilise them in the body because of digestive problems or enzyme malfunctioning. That is why some special types of supplemental oil, such as evening primrose, are therapeutically useful for some people.

Explanatory note on evening primrose and fish oils

Some studies mentioned in this chapter refer to evening primrose by itself, some to fish oil, while others relate to combinations. For instance, as far as I know fish oil has not been tested in a controlled scientific study as a treatment for PMS, but evening primrose oil has. Evening primrose is recommended as support therapy for diabetes, but not fish oil. Fish oil has been studied and helps some cases of inflammatory intestinal diseases.

Interestingly, when evening primrose is given alone it does not help calcium metabolism, whereas fish oil does, but when they are given together there is an even greater improvement, which suggests that evening primrose oil acts as a helper in this instance. However, there is no scientific evidence that the combination works more effectively for *everything*. As far as I can judge in my clinic, the combination generally gives good results.

I prefer to use an oil supplement that contains vitamin E because oils oxidise and that vitamin is an antioxidant.

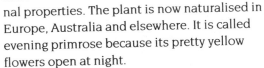

Evening primrose oil

This oil is derived from the seeds of *Oenothera* species.

Background

Evening primrose grows in the wild in North America, and the whole plant was widely used by the American Indians for its medicinal properties. The plant is now naturalised in Europe, Australia and elsewhere. It is called evening primrose because its pretty yellow flowers open at night.

Thirty years ago scientists discovered that the oil from the seeds of evening primrose were a rich source of gamma-linolenic acid (GLA) — a special type of lipid (oil) previously thought to be unique to breast milk. Evening primrose oil contains about 10 per cent GLA. Basically GLA has the major advantage of being in a form that the body can use — it does not have to be transformed by enzymes.

Ten years of research were required to breed a suitable plant for cultivation so that the seeds could be commercially harvested on a large scale to produce the evening primrose oil that is now on the market.

Specific health benefits

Women with mastalgia (painful breasts) and fibrocystic breast disease (lumpy breasts) have had good results and few adverse effects.[1]

In laboratory and animal studies the types of oils found in evening primrose have the capacity to suppress some types of cancer cell growth. More specifically, evening primrose and fish oil were found to reduce cell growth in breast cancer.[2] I recommend a combination of these fish and evening primrose oils to women at risk of breast cancer and for all women on hormone replacement therapy.

Evening primrose oil is one of the most successful general remedies for premenstrual syndrome (PMS). Trials show that around 90 per cent of women get relief from PMS symptoms in two to three months, after which time a low maintenance dose may be required.[3]

Although not a cure, evening primrose can relieve some of the painful menstrual problems associated with endometriosis.

The most biologically active component in evening primrose oil, gamma-linolenic acid, can lower triglycerides, LDL cholesterol and total cholesterol, as well as reduce blood clotting and blood stickiness. It is also helpful for treating hypertension, especially when taken in combination with fish oil. Another therapeutically active oil compound has also been successful for treating pregnant women with high blood pressure.[4] If you are pregnant, always discuss any supplementation with your medical practitioner.

If you reduce your consumption of animal fats and processed oils, and increase the biologically active essential fatty acids, this is one factor that will reduce your risk of cardiovascular disease.

Evening primrose oil has been used successfully in controlled studies for eczema, dermatitis, psoriasis and dry skin. My clinical experience is that evening primrose oil works better in combination with fish oil and vitamin E. These oils can also be used externally by pricking open a capsule and applying the oil, undiluted, directly on affected areas.

If dermatitis is caused by nervous or allergy problems, then a remedy is unlikely to be successful unless the cause is also treated. Natural remedies don't work for everyone because they help the body to restore itself rather than overriding biological processes, so it is worth trying to establish the cause of your health problems.

A controlled study of patients with post-viral fatigue syndrome showed that evening primrose oil (80 per cent) combined with fish oil (20 per cent) improved symptoms, as well as normalising red blood cell walls.[5]

For rheumatoid arthritis (a disease that is very hard to treat) the results of controlled trials have been mixed, but many people report that evening primrose gives a reduction in stiffness and pain after they have used it for at least six months. My recommendation is to use a combination of evening primrose and fish oil, as well as diet, appropriate exercise and supplementation.

For diabetic neuropathy (the nerve damage that affects diabetics) evening primrose oil is highly recommended, as it may prevent deterioration and in some cases reverse the condition.[6] In England it is a government-approved remedy for diabetic neuropathy. It may also decrease total cholesterol level and blood stickiness in diabetics, therefore reducing the heart and circulatory problems associated with this disease.

Fish oil is known to beneficially affect calcium metabolism, and evening primrose oil makes this effect more efficient. I recommend a combination as part of the treatment for osteoporosis, recurring kidney stones, and other problems relating to calcium deposition that is inadequate in bones, excessive in kidneys and joints, as well as excessive calcium secretion in urine.

Elderly people with dementia and Alzheimer's

disease have shown improvements in some aspects of brain function when taking evening primrose oil. Attention deficit hyperactivity disorder (ADHD), expressed as lack of concentration, impulsive and unmanageable behaviour, may be linked to disordered essential fatty acid metabolism in some cases,[7] and a combination of evening primrose and fish oil is likely to be helpful. A number of studies have shown that children who are awkward or unco-ordinated may be helped by this therapy as well.

Evening primrose oil may reduce the severity of migraine, but it has to be taken for at least three months, supplemented by other natural therapies such as feverfew, ginkgo, ginger and magnesium. Sjögren's syndrome (an auto-immune disorder that causes extremely dry eyes and mouth) may be relieved by taking evening primrose oil as an internal remedy.

General health benefits

Evening primrose is one of the few plants known to contain gamma-linolenic acid (GLA); others are blackcurrant and borage. GLA can be made in the body from linoleic acid (a fatty acid). However, it is becoming apparent that the conversion from linoleic acid is inadequate in a number of people because:

- some people, such as fad dieters, may not be getting adequate essential fatty acids to make the conversion to the beneficial byproducts
- most margarines and processed oils contain a high proportion of trans fatty acids and other fats that cannot be converted by the body to the necessary and healthy fats
- enzyme defects or insulin inadequacies restrict the beneficial conversions in the body.

GLA is necessary for the production of hormone-like compounds called prostaglandins. Prostaglandins are important regulators with wide-ranging effects on blood flow, organs, skin, hormones and the immune system. Obviously, if you are short of these prostaglandins, your health will be impaired.

Cautions and adverse effects

- Researchers list headaches and mild nausea as adverse effects, although most of these cases relate to very high doses (a high dose is above 5000 mg a day).
- People taking 2000 mg per day of gamma-linoleic acid show increased arachidonate levels. Over a year or more a build-up of arachidonate might lead to inflammation, thrombosis and immunosuppression.

  Note that 1000 mg evening primrose oil contains no more than 100 mg gamma-linoleic acid. In other words, to get 2000 mg GLA a day you would have to take 20 000 mg evening primrose oil (twenty or more capsules, depending on the strength of each capsule)!

  Read the small print on labels, and buy a product that includes some vitamin E to prevent oxidation of the oil.
- Do not take evening primrose oil if you are an epileptic, as there is a possibility that it may interfere with your medication.
- If you are taking phenothiazine and related antipsychotic drugs, do not take evening primrose oil.
- Although it may help some types of schizophrenia, if you have this condition you must consult your medical practitioner before adding any remedies to your medical treatment.

In a relatively short time evening primrose has become the most overprescribed natural therapy. Many people I see in my clinic are using it — when I ask them why, many do not have a sensible reason for taking it. Indeed, an article in a British medical journal suggested that 'it is used in many conditions with little justification'.[8]

It is unlikely to be harmful at the label dosages, but for a number of people the expense may not be warranted. They might get more benefit from dietary improvements or some other treatment.

Known therapeutic components

Essential fatty acids, about 65 per cent being linoleic acid and 8–10 per cent GLA: these essential fatty acids are important for the structure and function of cell walls and the body's membranes (linings). In addition, they have a intermediary role in reducing inflammation and blood stickiness.

Growing your own evening primrose oil

It is not practical for you to grow and produce your own products because the flowers produce relatively few seeds.

Supplements

Evening primrose oil is available in capsules, commonly in strengths of 500 mg and 1000 mg.

Suggested intake and duration of use

As a general guideline for self-treatment of PMS and skin problems, I suggest a maximum dose of around 2000 mg evening primrose oil, twice daily, for three months, together with 100 IU vitamin E, twice daily; then once daily as a maintenance dose.

For rheumatoid arthritis, high cholesterol, high blood pressure and diabetes a somewhat higher dose may be more therapeutic, but I recommend that you get advice from a health practitioner because other additional remedies may give a better result, and the treatment is long term, often years.

For osteoporosis I prescribe about 1000 mg,

twice daily, in combination with fish oil, calcium and other supplements. The total programme must be taken for one year before the bone mineral density is rechecked. Serious diseases should always be monitored by a qualified health practitioner.

When children's dosage is not given on the label, give proportionately according to age (see pp. 4–5). For young children, prick open the capsule and give the oil in juice or food. Swallow the leftover oil yourself.

Summary

Evening primrose oil is a useful treatment for premenstrual syndrome, eczema and other dry skin conditions, as well as for diabetic neuropathy, and as part of the prevention and treatment of a wide variety of health problems. Basically it compensates for dietary inadequacies or failure of the body chemistry to make effective use of essential fatty acids.

Fish oil

The therapeutic oils found in fish are known as omega-3 fatty acids.

Background

Long before anyone had heard of omega-3 fatty acids, a common old wives' tale was that fish was good for the brain. Scientists now confirm that these types of oils are indeed an important structural component in the brain, and may even help attention deficit hyperactivity disorder (ADHD).

By 1970 it was noted that Eskimos had low rates of heart disease, in spite of having a high-fat diet; subsequent investigation revealed that fish oil protects the heart.

Specific health benefits

A number of studies on rheumatoid arthritics show that fish oil can reduce the number of tender joints, the duration of morning stiffness and, importantly, how patients feel.[9]

Psoriasis and eczema are often markedly improved by fish oil, although I find that this oil works better in combination with evening primrose oil and vitamin E. This combination is often helpful used externally as well.

Fish oil has been used in over thirty controlled trials, at an average dose of 4.8 g daily, and found to be effective at lowering high blood pressure.[10] You should also consider your lifestyle, exercise and diet if you need to lower your blood pressure.

Bypass surgery patients who took fish oil in addition to either aspirin or warfarin had less graft blockage compared to those who took only aspirin or warfarin.[11] Fish oils prevent blood stickiness and lower the level of proteins involved in atherosclerosis. Additionally, they help prevent blood clotting. The overall effect is that fish oils keep the blood flowing more smoothly and the arteries more open.

It is thought that the oils in fish and fish oil products not only reduce the development of atherosclerosis but also prevent ventricular fibrillation (rapid, irregular heartbeat) and sudden death of cardiovascular patients.[12] This is also supported by most surveys of people who have a high fish diet. Most studies have shown that triglycerides are reduced by fish oil supplements. High triglycerides are one of the risk factors linked to cardiovascular disease.

Preliminary tests show that fish oil injections can reduce muscle constriction and inflammation and enhance the immune system after surgery.[13] More studies are needed to find out optimal dosages, but in the meantime surgery patients could discuss with their surgeon the internal benefits of fish oil supplements.

A survey of over 450 Australian children revealed that children who ate fresh oily fish were found to have one-fourth the risk of asthma compared to children who did not eat oily fish.[14]

Canned fish, non-oily fish and total fish intake were *not* protective against asthma, wheezing or breathing difficulty. Researchers have concluded from studies that fish *oil* may alleviate minor asthmatic symptoms, and decrease the severity of more serious attacks.

One study of adolescents suffering from period pain showed that 1.8 g fish oil daily, for two months, was helpful.[15]

DHA (one of the omega-3 fatty acids) is particularly important in infant brain development, and breast milk is a good source of this fatty acid. One study revealed that children who had consumed breast milk in the early weeks of life had a significantly higher IQ than those who received none.[16] Some children with attention deficit hyperactivity disorder (ADHD) benefit from fish oil.

Small trials on ulcerative colitis and Crohn's disease patients indicate that fish oil is useful in treating these inflammatory intestinal diseases. One study showed that less than one-third of Crohn's disease patients who took 2.7 g omega-3 fatty acids daily had a relapse in one year, compared to over two-thirds of those who did not take the supplement.[17]

A small German trial showed that fish oil capsules contributed to biochemical and intestinal changes that are considered to be protective against colon cancer.[18]

Patients with IgA nephropathy (a kidney disorder), glomerular disease and kidney transplants can benefit from omega-3 fatty acids in doses from 2.7 to 7.7 g daily.[19]

People with recurring kidney stones have fewer recurrences if they take fish oil; less calcium is excreted in the urine and more calcium stays in the bones. My experience is that, along with other nutrients, fish oil can be a useful adjunct in treating osteoporosis. This has been verified by bone mineral density scans.

General health benefits

Omega-3 fatty acids (oils) generally normalise cell walls; they are necessary for brain and retina (eye) membranes; they reduce the risk of heart disease and lower inflammation, especially that associated with arthritis, asthma and some skin diseases.

Some people have gone to extremes when following a low-fat diet, and can end up with skin, cardiovascular and other health problems. A small quantity of fish oil as a supplement can offset some of the adverse effects of an extremely low-fat diet.[20]

Cautions and adverse effects

- There are a few studies showing that long-term, high doses of fish oil may increase oxidative damage, which might even promote atherosclerotic plaques (harmful deposits on arterial walls).[21]

  To offset this, I always prescribe fish-oil supplements combined with vitamin E, as at this stage no one has clearly established which type of antioxidant best counteracts this potential adverse oxidation effect. If you take more than 2 g fish oil daily, take it with your meals, which should include natural antioxidants such as fruit and vegetables. Alternatively, take the supplement with some fruit juice.
- A study of people with moderately high cholesterol found that 12 g (12 000 mg) fish oil daily (a very high dose) actually increased the LDL cholesterol levels. This was offset by taking garlic at a daily dosage of 900 mg.[22]
- There is some debate about fish oil increasing blood glucose levels. If diabetics need

fish oil for other health problems, then they should take it with about 500 IU vitamin E and about 900 mg garlic daily, as well as doing regular exercise.[23] Better still, they should eat the fish recommended below. All diabetics should discuss dietary changes with their medical practitioner.
- To avoid burping or reflux from fish oils, buy enteric-coated capsules, as these do not break down in the stomach; the contents are released in the intestines, where absorption takes place.

Suggested intake and duration of use

I generally prescribe a combination of 2000 mg fish oil, 2000 mg evening primrose and 400 IU vitamin E, in two divided doses daily, for three months, and then I make another evaluation. Half this quantity is recommended on a long-term basis (e.g. for one year).

I suggest that this is the maximum dosage for self-treatment. As always, all serious diseases should be monitored by a health practitioner.

If you cannot find specific formulations for children or the dosages are not provided on the label, you will need to estimate a proportion of the capsule's contents in accordance with the recommended dosage and depending on the child's age (see pp. 4–5). Prick open the capsule, and squeeze the oil into juice or honey. Swallow the balance of the remedy yourself.

Fish as a source of beneficial oils

Modern research indicates that omega-3 fatty acids should be in a ratio of 1:5 with omega-6 fatty acids — similar to the ratio found in breast milk. The typical Australian diet now has a ratio of about 1:15. To correct this you need one meal per day of oily fresh fish. Fish in this category include Atlantic salmon, blue grenadier, blue warehou, luderick, rainbow trout, sea mullet, tailor, trevally silver, and yellowtail kingfish, and, to a lesser extent, blue eye, blue mackerel, golden perch, pilchards, redfish, silver warehou, tarwhine and yellowfin bream.

Fish consumption may reduce the incidence of strokes.[24]

Summary

Fish oil supplements and fresh oily fish have a wide range of benefits for the cardiovascular system, the brain, kidneys and other organs of the body. Potential adverse effects of high-dose supplementation can be avoided by adding antioxidants and garlic.

Cod liver oil

This oil is different from the fish oil I have described, because it also contains vitamins A and D. Many people find that one cod liver oil capsule daily is helpful for preventing colds, and even helps arthritis.

To my knowledge, no controlled scientific trials have been done to see if cod liver oil is useful for treating osteoporosis and other serious problems.

If you take this oil, do not take more than the label dose, as you can get vitamin A and vitamin D toxicity from an overdose.

Olive oil

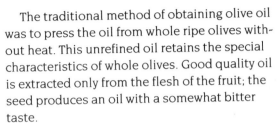

This oil is obtained from *Olea europaea*.

Background

The olive tree originated in the Eastern Mediterranean region, where it has been cultivated for thousands of years. Olives contain about 20 per cent oil.

The traditional method of obtaining olive oil was to press the oil from whole ripe olives without heat. This unrefined oil retains the special characteristics of whole olives. Good quality oil is extracted only from the flesh of the fruit; the seed produces an oil with a somewhat bitter taste.

Any processed olive oil not marked 'virgin' has been subjected to very high temperatures, solvents, refining, bleaching, deodorising or other processes that not only cause nutrient losses but also have the potential to damage our health because the molecular structure of the oil has been altered. Some non-virgin olive oils are made from the seeds only, which means that they are limited therapeutically, even without processing.

Specific health benefits

The health advantages are related to virgin or extra virgin olive oil, and not to processed oils. Extra virgin olive oil is a higher quality, and only the best olives are used to produce it.

For patients with peripheral artery disease (blood vessel and blood flow problems in the legs), a switch from refined corn oil to virgin olive oil significantly lowered LDL cholesterol and increased the 'good' cholesterol.

It was shown that virgin olive oil reduced the production of cholesterol gallstones compared to refined corn oil. Bile secretion also improved, which means that breakdown products from the liver were more readily eliminated, and fat digestion was enhanced.

Researchers in Spain have noted that the incidence of breast cancer has risen 100 per cent since 1960, particularly among women in the 35–64 age group. A likely connection is the decreased consumption of all types of complex carbohydrates (bread, rice, vegetables, legumes and pasta) and increased consumption of saturated fatty acids (particularly from beef) and a tendency to consume oils other than olive oil. The Canary Islands, where there is a high consumption of sunflower oil, registered Spain's highest incidence of breast cancer.[25]

General health benefits

It has been demonstrated that virgin olive oil helps keep the body's membranes healthy. A study of Israeli Jews found that they have high rates of heart disease, diabetes and cancer, and this was linked to a high intake of polyunsaturated oils compared to non-Jewish Israelis who consume olive oil.[26]

A number of population surveys link olive oil to the relatively good health of Mediterranean people.

Cautions and adverse effects

If beneficial oils are heated to a brown colour, their chemistry has changed, and they have lost their health enhancing properties.

Known therapeutic components

Olive oil contains around 10 per cent essential fatty acids and 85 per cent non-essential monounsaturated and saturated fats, which theoretically may seem to increase cardiovascular risk. However, population studies do not show this. The benefits of the oil may relate to other so-called minor factors, such as the following:

- phytosterols — hormone-like substances, notably beta-sitosterol, that have cholesterol lowering properties
- caffeic and gallic acids — bile flow stimulators
- triterpenes and polyphenols — antioxidants and digestive enzyme stimulators
- one polyphenol (oleoeuropein) that lowers blood pressure
- important antioxidant nutrients, such as vitamin E and beta-carotene, lecithin and squalene.

Processed olive oil does not contain many of these therapeutic components.

Growing your own olives

Olive trees will grow in areas of Australia with high summer heat and some winter chill. Your local nursery will advise you which species are suitable for your area.

Without an expensive press, it is not practicable for you to express the oil from the olives, but you can harvest and preserve the fruit.

How to use

The healthiest way of using oils is to cook the food first, and then add a little oil for flavouring before serving.

Salad dressing (Serves 2–4)

1 tablespoon lemon or orange juice, or herbal or
   plain vinegar
1 dessertspoon salt-reduced tamari or shoyu (quality
   soya sauces)
1 teaspoon mustard powder
1 tablespoon olive oil
1 tablespoon finely chopped fresh basil, chives,
   thyme, oregano (or 1 teaspoon dried herbs)

OPTIONAL EXTRAS
1 tablespoon tomato juice
1 clove crushed garlic
pinch of hot chilli powder

1   Mix the dry ingredients to a paste with the lemon juice in a glass jar.
2   Add the olive oil and herbs.
3   Put the lid on, and shake the jar until the ingredients are thoroughly mixed.
4   Store in the fridge, and use the same day — fresh plant matter and oils can provide an environment for the growth of harmful bacteria.

Suggested intake and duration of use

I recommend small quantities of extra virgin olive oil. As all oils are high in kilojoules, use only 1–2 teaspoons daily, life long.

Use proportionately less for children according to age (see pp. 4–5).

Summary

Virgin olive oil is one of the factors that confer good health on Mediterranean people. Many experts consider it to be the most health-enhancing dietary oil.

Recommended reading

Erasmus, U. *Fats that Heal, Fats that Kill.* Alive Books, Burnaby, Canada, 1995.

Tea tree oil

Tea tree oil is obtained from *Melaleuca alternifolia*, which is native to northern coastal New South Wales. Its desired medicinal characteristics occur because of the soil and climate of that region.

Background

Captain Cook's journal states that on his voyage to Australia in 1770 he brewed a tea from a type of tea tree and that he found it 'spicy and refreshing'. Captain Cook was remarkably ahead of his time in regard to the health of his crew. In a later voyage he experimented with tea tree, and found it improved a type of beer they had made.

It is said that Aboriginal people used the crushed leaves of the tea tree to treat wounds and infections, and the water of a particular lagoon where tea trees had fallen was considered to have healing properties.

Some early white settlers may have used the leaves for external medicinal purposes, and as a tea, although most Europeans considered the tree to be a pest and tried to eradicate it. The upper part of the tree can be cut back extensively and within a year the tree will completely regrow. This must have been quite frustrating to the settlers, and possibly retarded the research into this plant because it was an obstacle to farming.

The real discovery of tea tree oil as a therapeutic agent occurred in 1925, when Arthur Penfold, a government scientist, completed a three-year period of testing and concluded that the aromatic oil from this species of tea tree was both antiseptic and antibacterial. In 1930 the *Medical Journal of Australia* published an article on tea tree's medicinal use.

Australian soldiers in World War II were supplied with tea tree oil in their first-aid kits.

In 1962 an American medical journal reported that aqueous solutions dissolve pus and leave the surfaces of infected wounds clean and deodorised, without apparent irritation to the tissues. The presence of organic matter reduces the efficiency of ordinary antiseptics; contrariwise, the pus solvent and tissue cleansing actions of *Melaleuca alternifolia* oil increase the antiseptic coefficient considerably.[27]

The medical specialist had used strong dilutions of tea tree oil successfully for infections such as trichomonal vaginitis, Candida, cervicitis and chronic endocervicitis. He stated that at no time did patients have to remove the packing or discontinue the douches because of irritation, burning or other complaints. Patients commented favourably on its pleasant odour and its cooling, soothing effect. They were especially pleased with the effect of the oil, when used as a douche, in removing obnoxious vaginal odours.

The *Australian Journal of Dentistry* published an article in 1930, pointing out that tea tree oil was a strong, non-toxic antiseptic that did not damage healthy tissue.

With the widespread use of antibiotics, which are effective against bacterial infections, the use of tea tree oil faded into the background. However, it is now recognised that antibiotics can have serious adverse effects and some bacteria are becoming resistant to these drugs. Tea tree oil is once again being considered an option in the treatment of a number of external infections.

Tests have found that the aromatic oil components of trees of this species vary considerably. The Australian Tea Tree Industry Association Inc. now offers certification for oil that contains more than 30 per cent of terpinen-4-ol (the healing components) and less than 15 per cent cineole (which can be irritating).

Specific health benefits

Acne and pimples occur when sebum is trapped in the glands below the surface of the skin. Subsequently these glands becomes infected and form pimples. Tea tree oil can penetrate through the skin's surface and helps treat the infection.[28]

There are different types of acne and different causes, and it is a difficult condition to cure. If you are treating a very small area of the skin, try tea tree oil undiluted, otherwise start with about one part oil to ten parts water. As a guideline, you will need to apply the oil twice daily for one month. If no improvement occurs within that time then you should try something else, or get the advice of a health practitioner because you may need help in treating the cause of the problem rather than the external manifestation of it.

For more serious infections, such as boils, drop undiluted tea tree oil onto the infected area, although I recommend you seek advice from your health practitioner, as an appropriate poultice may be required to bring the boil to a head to reduce the pain and the possibility of recurrence. Strict hygiene must be observed when treating boils as they have a tendency to spread to other parts of the body, and I recommend tea tree oil as part of your external cleansing programme.

Tea tree oil can be effective for treating vaginal candida (thrush) and trichomonas, but as a wash or douche the tea tree oil must be diluted to 1–20 parts oil to 100 parts commercial saline solution. Always start with the lower dose as vaginal tissue can be extremely sensitive. In addition, use a tampon saturated with tea tree oil solution at this strength. Your health practitioner, pharmacy or health food store could also supply you with an appropriate product. Vaginal pessaries may be useful for treating anaerobic vaginosis.[29]

Fungal nail infections (*Paronychia*) can be treated successfully with the undiluted oil.[30] Tinea (athlete's foot) is also helped by the full-strength oil. However, for young children and where there is inflamed or broken skin, the oil must be diluted in saline solution at a strength of 20–50 per cent initially. Some medical trials have not shown good results, but the oil was used at strengths of between 1 and 10 per cent.

One drop of tea tree oil on your toothpaste is an effective mouth freshener and plaque remover, and promotes healthy gums. For mouth ulcers use 3–6 drops of oil to ¼ cup tepid water as a mouth rinse, or put a few drops directly onto the ulcer. This strength could also be used as a mouth wash for oral thrush (Candida). For preventing dental caries, gingivitis and periodontitis (inflammatory gum diseases that are linked to plaque build-up) try a daily mouthwash with a few drops of tea tree oil, as well as cleaning your teeth in accordance with your dentist's instructions.

The oil added to water, or preferably saline solution, can be used to clean wounds and injuries. Apply the oil undiluted to minor cuts and wounds, once they have been cleaned. If you treat all minor injuries properly, this often prevents them developing into serious infections.

For minor household burns, once you have cooled the area with cold water, drop undiluted tea tree oil onto the burnt area if it is small.

As an insect repellent, tea tree oil can be mixed into a plain cream or oil, and applied over the body. Insect bites and stings are best treated with full-strength oil. It is said that leeches will fall off immediately if you drop undiluted tea tree oil on them.

As a treatment for head lice, use tea tree shampoo boosted with ten drops of the oil, and leave on for 10 minutes, covered with a shower cap or cling wrap. This method may also help some cases of dandruff. As a treatment for cradle cap mix 5 drops of tea tree oil into a few teaspoons of olive oil, and rub this gently into the baby's scalp. After 5 minutes, wash the baby's hair with tea tree shampoo, being especially careful that none gets into the baby's eyes.

For sinus and excess nasal mucus add about 6 drops of the oil to a vaporiser, or use it as an inhalation in a cup of hot water. When you use an inhalation, put only your nose under the towel, not your whole head. About 10 drops of oil on a tissue under your pillow at night will help to keep your nostrils clear.

For coughs, rub about 10 drops of oil into the chest and back, or use in a vaporiser. As a gargle for sore throats, add 3–6 drops of water to ½ cup tepid water.

General health benefits

The NSW Department of Agriculture's pamphlet, *Agfacts* 184, says

> Tea tree oil is a valuable germicide in a wide variety of septic conditions. It has the unique property of penetrating deeply into infected tissue and pus, mixing with it and causing the infected tissue to slough off, leaving a healthy surface, while at the same time showing a negligible toxicity to the host. Consequently it is of special value in surgical and dental work and is most effective against boils, carbuncles and even intractable infections of *Staphylococcus* sp. Its usefulness extends to the treatment of skin, mouth, throat and vaginal infections. It is not only a germicide, but also a fungicide and can be used to treat such conditions as ringworm and tinea.

A medical investigation team considered the potential for tea tree oil in hygienic hand disinfection, and concluded that

> Tea tree oil has demonstrated potentially useful antimicrobial activity in vitro and its potential as an active ingredient in handwashing preparations warrants further examination. In addition to its antibacterial activity, the antifungal and antiviral activity of tea tree oil also requires investigation.[31]

An advantage of tea tree oil is that it penetrates the outer layers of the skin and may enhance its activity by means of a residual effect. Furthermore, constant handwashing with products containing tea tree oil does not lead to the skin problems associated with some current hand-care preparations.

In my practice I make up various types of external creams and gargles, and, wherever there is a possibility of secondary infections, I add a small quantity of tea tree oil as a germicide.

I also use tea tree oil as a household disinfectant in my bathroom and kitchen.

Cautions and adverse effects

- Unless specifically directed by your health practitioner, do not take tea tree (or any other aromatic oil) as an internal remedy.
- In common with all external treatments, always do a tiny skin test first in case you are one of the rare people who react to tea tree.

If you have a sensitive skin, dilute the oil in water, or buy a product that is not full strength.
- Do not use vaginal tea tree oil products on children, or during pregnancy.
- Do not apply tea tree oil in or around the eyes.
- Keep all tea tree oil products out of the reach of children.

Studies to date show that tea tree oil only temporarily suppresses the natural bacterial balance, which means that there is no long-lasting disturbance to the body's good bacteria. There is no evidence that bacteria are becoming resistant to tea tree oil, as happens with some antibiotic pharmaceuticals.

Known therapeutic components

- The aromatic oil is made up of at least forty-eight different compounds.
- In general, the terpene-like components are more therapeutic, although no single compound is especially effective by itself.
- The cineole content might irritate sensitive skins.

Growing your own tea tree

The essential or aromatic oil is extracted by a steam distillation process. Unless you have specialised equipment, and access to the right species of tea tree, it is not feasible to try to produce your own oil.

How to use

A wide range of tea tree oil products is now available for external use:

oil in varying strengths and sizes
creams
acne lotion
lip salve
hair shampoo
hair conditioner
soaps
deodorants
lozenges
toothpaste
pessaries
douche gel
foot sprays and foot powder
insect repellent
anti-itch pet shampoos

For more serious infections, use the oil or specific products, such as vaginal pessaries. However, if a good result is not achieved in, say, two weeks, then consult a health practitioner.

Suggested intake and duration of use

Labels of tea tree products will have the methods of use on the labels. Various ways of using tea tree oil have been covered under **Specific health benefits** and **General health benefits**, and the following is a general overview of the guidelines.

If a small area of skin is involved, such as a few pimples, dab a little full-strength tea tree oil on each pimple with your finger or a cotton bud. You may need to do this three to four times daily initially, and then less frequently.

If a large area is involved, dilute the oil in commercial saline solution or water, or use a tea tree oil product. As a general guide, I start with about 10 per cent of the oil as an external skin wash for serious infections (although I use a weaker solution, initially, when treating the vagina). Put this on a gauze pad, and place over a wound. Commercial products are often less than 1 per cent strength, which is unlikely to irritate but may not be strong enough.

Tea tree oil can be used long term, as it does not damage the skin.

Summary

Tea tree oil is the best aromatic oil for treating a wide range of skin infections. It is antiseptic, antifungal and antibacterial, and is rarely irritating to the skin.

Recommended reading

Drury, S. *Tea Tree Oil: A Medicine Kit in a Bottle*. C. W. Daniel, Saffron Walden (UK), 1992.

In conclusion

Your wellbeing is likely to improve if you use unheated virgin olive oil in your diet, evening primrose oil for therapeutic purposes, plus two or three servings a week of cold-water oily fish.

Keep tea tree oil in your first-aid kit to use on minor injuries.

CHAPTER 6

Three super supplements

Grapeseed extract
Green tea
Vitamin E

I chose these three supplements because they represent the diversity of useful supplements now available. You will see how a seed extract, a traditional tea and a common vitamin are valuable therapeutically, and have the support of modern scientific research.

Don't we get everything we need from food?

In a word, 'No'. However, a number of prominent scientific nutritionists state that supplements are completely unnecessary, even harmful, and that all we need is a balanced diet and moderation in everything.

A balanced diet (protein, carbohydrates, fats, fruit and vegetables) may prevent deficiency diseases, but whether it is health enhancing depends on what types of these foods you eat, the quantities of each of them, and the many other things you eat and drink. Some people eat generous servings of sausages, sugary processed cereals, takeaway foods, cakes and fatty foods, plus a few small servings of vegetables and the occasional piece of fruit. Their idea of 'moderation in everything' might include a daily packet of salty snacks, confectionery, six cups of

coffee, soft drinks and 'a few' beers. One of my patients thinks that six schooners a day is 'a few beers', and was quite shocked to hear that my idea of moderation is one small glass!

Another patient showed me the weight-reduction diet given to her by a hospital dietitian with a PhD in nutrition. The diet was low in kilojoules, but included foods such as crumpets, Sao biscuits, jams, salami, corned beef and 'as much as you like' of tea, coffee, diet soft drinks and cordials. Generally, the diet sheets she was given were full of processed, refined foods. Two pieces of fruit a day were allowed

and most vegetables, but these were not emphasised. The main objection is this: if you are going to restrict the intake of foods, it is even more important to eat those things that are going to supply you with maximal beneficial nutrients, antioxidants and other plant components. Even this 70-year-old lady, who had never taken any interest in health matters until she began to put on a little extra weight, judged that this was not good nourishment. If I hadn't seen this 'scientific dietary advice' with my own eyes I would not have believed it!

A few people do maintain seemingly good health on their version of a balanced diet and moderation in everything, but others become very ill. Of course, food is not the only thing that keeps us well or makes us sick, although it has an important influence.

Our food supply is generally adulterated with literally hundreds of food additives, contaminants and agricultural chemicals. Many of the nutrients have been processed out of our foods. Refined wheat, for instance, is depleted in seven B vitamins, vitamin E and five minerals, and in some cases only 10–30 per cent of these nutrients remain in the products we eat. As you will have seen in chapter 5, the way many fats and oils are processed results in unhealthy changes in their chemical structure. Additionally, much of our food has been harvested weeks, months, even years before we eat it. This further reduces vitamin C and other nutrients. Unless you grow all your own food, quality is often beyond your control.

Extra nutrients and antioxidants are required to counteract:
- harmful chemicals deliberately or accidentally added to our foods
- the nutrients and phytochemicals that are destroyed during processing and storage
- environmental toxins
- stress
- vigorous exercise
- dieting, and digestion and absorption problems.

Despite thousands of scientific studies showing the benefits of natural supplements, some dietitians and medical practitioners still maintain that we get everything we need from our food, and that supplements are nonsensical or dangerous. The majority of people eat a balanced diet according to standard nutritional recommendations, but you can observe for yourself that the majority are not brimming with energy, nor are they disease free.

However, the misleading view of some people is gradually changing. For instance, a registered dietitian, B. Levin, has written: 'More toxicities have occurred through ingestion of products manufactured by the American Dietetic Association corporate sponsorship than by all nutritional supplementation in the history of mankind'.[1]

Aspartame (NutraSweet) is a good example of a widely used food additive promoted by some scientifically trained dietitians. It is now reported to cause over fifty-five different adverse reactions, including severe neurological impairment and thyroid problems. Perhaps this is one explanation for the current 'epidemic' of severe behavioural problems in children. Aspartame accounts for more than 75 per cent of all the adverse reactions reported to the US Government Adverse Reaction Monitoring System.[2]

Many people drink large quantities of diet drinks that contain caffeine.

These few examples are the 'tip of the iceberg', and no doubt many common reactions such as diarrhoea and headaches go unreported, as people may not link these to a food additive that they eat every day in supposedly healthy foods, soft drinks, dieters' snacks, and so on.

Another problem with the 'balanced diet and moderation in everything approach' is that you can have a balanced diet but eat the same things every day. Without variety, you will not be getting all the valuable phytochemicals that have disease preventing potential.

Unfortunately, in my clinical experience some people do not thrive even on a good diet. There may be many causes for this, including hereditary and environmental factors, but there is enough good scientific evidence to show that diet is an important factor.

For those who get ill for whatever reason, pharmaceutical drugs and other medical strategies have their place. Pharmaceutical remedies take over a particular aspect of the body or replace something, such as antibiotics replacing the work of your immune system. Natural remedies tend to work by giving your body the capacity to do the restoration; for example, grapeseed extract provides special components that increase the strength of blood vessels.

There is nothing as valuable as a varied whole-food diet of uncontaminated food, but how many get it? In real life many people are suffering and fatigued, and a surprising number benefit from appropriate supplementation. The majority of people know when they 'feel better', and that is why supplements are becoming increasingly popular.

Scientific surveys show that supplement users, especially those who take beta-carotene and vitamins C and E, have a reduced risk of diseases such as cataracts and heart disease.

Cautions and adverse effects

- Natural supplements tend to work slowly, and must be taken at the appropriate medicinal dose.
- Very large doses of single nutrients, particularly minerals, may interfere with other nutrients. Consult a health practitioner before you take isolated mineral products.
- In my clinic I occasionally see people who are taking more than twenty different remedies, and, when I ask them what the pills are for, the reasons are often unsound. Sometimes you read an article on a topic and think, 'Yes, that sounds just what I need'. Depending on how much you read, it is quite

possible to end up taking a heap of pills. If you fall into this category, I suggest that you consult a health practitioner.

- An overzealous attempt at self-treatment is not only expensive but might be harmful, and there may be more beneficial ways of spending your health budget, such as buying organically-grown wholesome foods.

Grapeseed extract
(*Vitis vinifera*)

Background

Grape seeds have been found in prehistoric sites in various parts of Europe, and it is well known that grapes were cultivated and made into wine in biblical times. Grape cures and red wine have been considered medicinal foods for centuries. Dr E. A. Maury has even written a book, *Wine Is the Best Medicine* (Corgi, London, 1978). However, research now indicates that alcohol itself is unlikely to be healthy, but there are other components in some drinks that are beneficial. Most researchers now agree that health benefits come from the flavonoids in wine. Three generations of mice that are susceptible to tumours were fed modest quantities of red wine with the alcohol removed. Compared to the mice that didn't get the de-alcoholised wine, these mice had delayed tumour onset.[3] Of course, we have no way of knowing if the mice lived happily and died peacefully.

In 1534 French explorers in Canada were trapped by ice, and forced to live on salted meat and biscuits. They soon showed signs of vitamin C deficiency (scurvy). An Indian told them to make a tea from pine needles, and this offset the deficiency.

Over 400 years later Professor Jack Masquelier of the University of Bordeaux, France, read the story about this expedition, and became curious about the components in pine needles that produce this vitamin C-like effect. He subsequently confirmed that pine needles, grape seeds and a variety of plants contain special components that were collectively given the name pycnogenols. These are now known as proanthocyanidins, oligomeric proanthocyanidin complexes (OPCs) and procyanidolic oligomers (PCOs). Professor Masquelier did the pioneering work, and devised a particular method of extracting these components from plants. Grape seeds are now considered to be the best source of these therapeutically active compounds.

Specific health benefits

French doctors prescribe grapeseed extract as part of the treatment for varicose veins and haemorrhoids, because it strengthens the walls of blood vessels. A number of clinical trials have confirmed the circulatory benefits. Patients with leg circulation problems, for example, have reduced leg pain, cramps, fluid retention, and pins and needles following treatment with this supplement.

Grapeseed extract may also help lower LDL cholesterol levels, and be useful as a general heart and circulatory remedy.

I have used it successfully as an internal remedy to treat mild lymphoedema (fluid retention following surgery) and for various wounds that are slow to heal. A few trials have shown that grapeseed extract is able to reduce inflammation and increase healing before and after surgery — although I usually recommend it in conjunction with bilberry, ginkgo and vitamin E.

There is some evidence that grapeseed extract can help eye problems such as diabetic retinopathy and myopia (nearsightedness).

Grapeseed extract can also reduce eye stress caused by glare.[4] Computer workers take note!

The anti-inflammatory effect may help some cases of hayfever and eye allergies.

Research shows that grapeseed extract has the capacity to reduce inflammation in various parts of the body, and can improve connective tissue, which explains its therapeutic benefit for arthritis and sports injuries.

One trial showed that 200 mg daily of grapeseed extract markedly improved premenstrual swelling and headaches, although up to four months' treatment was needed in some cases. It may also help relieve the urinary symptoms of non-cancerous prostate enlargement.

In animal studies OPCs markedly reduced dental caries. Keep your eyes open for the OPC chewing gums that will soon be on the market. The chewing gum should be effective, as it will be in the mouth for a much longer period of time than the toothpaste.

General health benefits

A study on the antioxidant effects of grapeseed proanthocyanidins showed that these compounds are markedly more effective as antioxidants than vitamins C and E.[5]

A remedy that can improve blood and lymph vessel strength and elasticity will have wide-ranging benefits because every cell in the body benefits from a good circulatory system. If the connective tissue of the body is strengthened, this also confers a wide range of benefits, not only to joints and blood vessels but also to strengthen the gums, the linings of the digestive tract, the blood flow to organs, and so on.

Animal studies using Pycnogenol (the original patented form of grapeseed extract) showed that in AIDS-infected and alcohol-fed mice, this supplement improved natural killer cells and other immune cells. Therefore, it may be a valuable addition for the treatment of people with low immune functioning.[6]

Compounds in grape seed are known to help

connective tissue. Connective tissue becomes weaker with age and, to some extent, grapeseed extract might be considered an antiageing remedy. No doubt cosmetic manufacturers will soon be using grapeseed components because the skin is another form of connective tissue.

Theoretically, grapeseed extract should be a useful addition for treating a variety of disorders, including weak, bleeding or receding gums, high blood pressure, and liver and kidney diseases.

The compounds in grape seed help sustain and protect vitamin C in the body, so that indirectly it has the advantages of vitamin C.

Could the components in grape seeds be an explanation for the 'French paradox' — why French people who drink red wine have a 35 per cent lower risk of heart disease than those who drink beer or spirits, in spite of both groups having a high-fat diet? The question is: Would wine drinkers live even longer if they took grapeseed extract or consumed organic black grapes instead of alcoholic drinks? But, also would they be happier?

During the process of making red wine the whole grapes are crushed, and the flesh, skins and seeds are left together for two to three weeks. The skin and seeds contain the OPCs. White wine and champagne are usually made from the juice only, the skins and seeds being discarded, and only a tiny residual quantity of OPCs is left behind. The skins are usually discarded because they cause a strong tannin taste in wine.

As a horticulturist I was shocked at the quantity of pesticides and fungicides used in the vineyards I visited. In government tests Australian grapes may contain residues of eight different agricultural chemicals.[7]

In addition, most Australian wines contain sulphur dioxide to preserve the colour and flavour of wine, and this must be shown on the label. Additive Nos 220–8 are the various forms of this preservative; this is useful to know, because sulphur dioxide is a common allergen. Although I suggest that you buy only organic wines a few wineries produce wine without preservatives, and this is marked on the label as a selling feature; however, I could not find any organic wines that did not contain sulphur dioxide.

Resveratrol is a component in grapes — and wine — that has antioxidant and anticancer properties.[8]

Binge drinking tends to cause a rebound effect on the stickiness of blood, which means that, say, a glass a day is probably beneficial but six glasses one day a week is not; white wine causes more of a rebound effect.

Cautions and side effects

- In sensitive people grapeseed extract may cause digestive upsets or diarrhoea, in which case stop the supplement or lower the dose.
- Grapes and grape seeds contain chemical residues because grapes are customarily sprayed repeatedly with fungicides and pesticides. However, grapeseed extract is used as a medicine, not a food, so the quantity of harmful residues consumed in remedies would be minute.

Known therapeutic components

- Catechins and oligomeric procyanidins are special categories of flavonoids or polyphenols. They are colourless, but the oligomeric procyanidins can be transformed into the red pigments known as cyanidins. Nature provides these valuable antioxidants to protect the oil in the plant's seeds.
- Oligomeric procyanidins are small molecules, and they have a favourable effect on collagen. They also protect vitamin C in the body.[9]

Products

According to Professor Masquelier, the oligomeric procyanidins (OPCs) must be extracted in a specific way so that there is minimal solvent residue and the maximum possible therapeutic activity. The product marketed in Australia as Pycnogenol, showing a picture of Professor Masquelier on the packet, has been independently tested by ESA Laboratories in the USA, and shown to be more effective as an antioxidant compared to ten other grapeseed products.

The therapeutic effect is enhanced by taking grapeseed extract together with some vitamin C.

Growing and making your own remedies

It is not possible for you to make your own grapeseed extract because laboratory testing and equipment is required to test each batch of seeds. Grapeseed extract is not simply crushed grape seeds, but specific components are concentrated in the end product.

Grapes, however, are a highly recommended food, particularly if you can buy them organically grown.

Suggested intake and duration of treatment

For serious conditions I usually prescribe up to 200 mg grapeseed extract daily, for three months, and then reduce this to about 50 mg daily, long term.

As an antioxidant and preventive, I recommend 50 mg daily, together with about 250 mg vitamin C.

Grapeseed is usually prescribed for adult health problems. However, if warranted, there is no reason why children could not be given this supplement in proportionately lower doses according to age (see pp. 4–5).

Summary

Grapeseed extract is a potent antioxidant, has anti-inflammatory action, strengthens blood and lymph vessels, as well as connective tissue generally, so it can exert a wide range of healing and protective effects in the body.

Recommended reading

Schwitters, B., in collaboration with Professor Jack Masquelier. OPC *in Practice*. Alfa Omega Editrice, Rome, 1995.

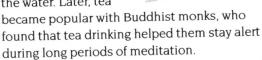

Green tea
(*Camellia sinensis* or *Thea sinensis*)

Background

It is said that tea drinking began 5000 years ago in China when a few tea leaves accidentally fell into some hot water. It was noted that this enhanced the taste of the water. Later, tea became popular with Buddhist monks, who found that tea drinking helped them stay alert during long periods of meditation.

By the seventeenth century tea drinking had spread to Europe, and within a century had become very fashionable. The Boston Tea Party and the tea ration given to Australian convicts are testimony to the demand for this drink.

Black tea is made by processing and drying green tea leaves. Green tea is less processed, and has five times more polyphenols than black tea.[10] Polyphenols are the compounds with the powerful antioxidant effects.

Some Chinese believe that red tea is more therapeutic, and has some anticancer activity, thought to be due to the micro-organisms that are used in the special fermentation process of making this type of tea.

An old saying was, 'A daily dose of tea will

save a doctor's fee', and scientists are now confirming that tea is indeed a therapeutic drink.

Specific health benefits

A population survey related a reduced risk of stomach cancer to drinking ten or more cups of green tea each day.[11]

In animal experiments green tea inhibited lung cancer. Researchers also report a reduction in rectal and pancreatic cancers.[12] In laboratory experiments some of the components in green tea were shown to curtail an enzyme implicated in prostate cancer.

It has been observed that, when people drink green tea, they tend to have a reduction in dental caries. This effect has been verified by animal studies.

General health benefits

Both green and black teas have powerful antioxidant activity, although the antioxidant effect of green tea is six times greater than black tea.[13] *Note:* The addition of milk totally inhibits the antioxidant effect of both teas.

People who drank 4.7 cups of black tea a day had 69 per cent lower risk of stroke compared with those drinking less than 2.6 cups.[14] Substituting at least some green tea and black tea (both without milk) for other drinks is likely to be beneficial. In summer make iced tea by adding crushed ice, slices of lemon and mint leaves to make the tea more attractive and palatable.

Cautions and adverse effects

- Teas contain various types of tannins and other components, some of which are beneficial and some potentially harmful. Tannins, for example, can strengthen tissues, but can also irritate the gastrointestinal tract — especially if you drink strong black tea without milk. However, green tea without milk

does not seem to produce intestinal irritation, insomnia or other problems linked to caffeine and excess tannins.
- Do not drink extremely hot tea because the heat can damage the linings of your mouth, throat and upper digestive tract.

Known therapeutic components

- Catechins and phenolic compounds in green tea inhibit a number of different types of tumours in experimental studies, and it is thought that this anticancer effect is due to the antioxidant activity.[15] In a laboratory study, polyphenols were shown to inhibit the formation of harmful DNA activity in cells exposed to oxidants — DNA directs cell growth.[16]
- Tea also contains caffeine, but not in the same quantity as coffee.

Products

Both green and black teas are available as teabags and as loose tea. Tablet forms of green tea extract are also becoming available.

Growing your own tea

This tree does not tolerate frosts and droughts. Make tea from the soft, young, pale-green tips. Dry the tips, and store them in an airtight container.

How to use

For therapeutic purposes drink green tea or weak black tea, without milk.

Suggested intake and duration of use

No one has yet defined a therapeutic quantity of green or black tea, but I suggest that 2–4 cups a day is a reasonable intake, given that antioxidants will be also obtained from various foods.

Tea is not appropriate for infants, but there is

no reason why children could not be given small quantities of weak tea.

Summary

Green and black teas are a good source of antioxidants, which provide anticancer and other health benefits.

Vitamin E

Background

The use of vitamin E as a supplement began in the 1940s, mainly as a result of the work of Dr E. Shute, who formed the Vitamin E Society in Canada and the Cardiac Society in the USA.

During the following years many cardiac specialists tried to get supplemental vitamin E banned, and medical journals published scornful articles with titles such as 'Vitamin E — a vitamin in search of a cure'.

Dr Shute treated serious heart and circulatory disorders with vitamin E internally, and also used it externally in powder form. Ignoring criticism from many of his medical colleagues he kept on prescribing and recommending this supplement. I can remember going to one of his lectures about twenty years ago, and seeing slides of the severe circulatory cases he had treated successfully. He always warned that a trial would not be successful unless the dose was adequate, and that there may not be much benefit in treatment of less than six months.

People all over the world started taking vitamin E as a supplement, despite mainstream medical opinion that it was useless. There were

a few medical reports that it caused fatigue and infections, but millions of people were convinced that vitamin E was a beneficial therapy.

Many foods are now used for the purpose of obtaining this vitamin, and natural vitamin E is becoming somewhat difficult to obtain. It has gone from a so-called waste byproduct of the food-oil industry to a valuable remedy.

Recently an American medical journal contained an article on the 'Potential health economic benefits of vitamin supplementation', and concluded that coronary artery disease could be reduced by 38 per cent if everyone over fifty years of age took a daily vitamin E supplement of at least 100 IU.[17] In the USA this supplementation would represent a reduction of about $7 billion dollars a year in hospital charges. The researchers recommended a healthful diet, but from the scientific studies they examined they concluded that 'it was not possible through diet alone to attain the levels of nutrients demonstrated to be beneficial'. So now, after fifty years, there is finally *some* medical recognition that vitamin E is a beneficial supplement.

Specific health benefits

As there are more than 25 000 published scientific studies on vitamin E, the examples given below are a small representative sample.

A survey of over 11 000 elderly people verified that users of vitamin E supplements had a significantly reduced risk of death from cardiovascular diseases and all other causes.[18]

Vitamin E can reduce the number of angina attacks, including among people taking pharmaceutical calcium channel-blocker drugs.[19]

A dose of 400–800 IU vitamin E was given for one to two years to 1035 patients with proven atherosclerosis, and compared to a similar group who took a placebo. Those on the vitamin E had a 43 per cent decrease in heart attacks or cardiovascular death.[20] Other studies confirm that vitamin E decreases the risk of major heart and circulatory diseases, and the results may be even better over a period of many years.

A small group of men undergoing surgical repair of an abdominal aortic aneurysm were given 600 IU of vitamin E every day for eight days before surgery, and then compared with those on a placebo. This showed that vitamin E was effective in reducing the oxidative damage that occurs during periods of oxygen deficit and the return of blood flow. Vitamin E is also likely to be helpful before and after angioplasty.

Vitamins A, C and E and beta-carotene were shown to be useful in treating suspected acute heart attacks if given within a few hours of the onset of the symptoms. I doubt whether any hospitals in Australia administer these nutrients to their patients. Patients with congestive heart failure are known to have relatively high levels of harmful oxidants in the body, and vitamin E at doses of around 400 IU can reduce these levels.[21] The evidence supports the likelihood that various types of heart patients would benefit from antioxidant supplementation.

People with low vitamin E concentrations in the stomach and duodenum tend to have higher levels of Helicobacter pylori (the bacteria associated with gastric ulcers and a higher incidence of stomach cancer).[22] It is likely that vitamin E protects the linings of the digestive tract through its antioxidant activity. Healthy mucosal linings are less prone to disease and infection.

A study of elderly people showed that vitamin E can boost the immune system. For this purpose a relatively low dose of 200 IU was more successful than 800 IU.

Another controlled study with vitamin E supplementation indicated that it may help reduce the secondary side effects of diabetes, including eye, heart, circulation and neurological complications.[23] Vitamin E supplementation gave a significant reduction in LDL (the harmful fats) oxidation in diabetic patients. A number of studies confirm the usefulness of vitamin E supplementation, especially to elderly insulin-resistant patients with heart disease.

Fish oil tends to increase blood sugar levels, but taking vitamin E counteracts this.[24] I suggest that anyone taking fish oil supplements also take added vitamin E if this vitamin is not incorporated into the supplement.

Prolonged physical activity leads to higher-than-normal oxidation levels and DNA damage, which can be offset by vitamin E supplementation.[25] Athletes and anyone working to the point of physical exhaustion should take vitamin E in dosages of about 800 IU daily.

Used both internally and externally, vitamin E protects against sun damage and skin tumours, reduces scar tissue, promotes wound healing and decreases the harmful skin effects of radiation treatments. Most people find that vitamin E is an effective skin moisturiser, and it is part of many cosmetics. If your skin is very dry, prick open a capsule, and apply the oil undiluted.

An animal study indicated that vitamin E reduced brain cell death brought on by the accumulation of a particular protein (amyloid) that accumulates in Alzheimer's disease.[26] A controlled trial showed that compared to those given the placebo, fewer people on vitamin E had to be institutionalised, and more were able to carry out normal day-to-day activities.[27]

Aside from my own clinical observations that high-dose supplementation (around 1000 IU vitamin E) seems to alleviate menopausal symptoms, there is some evidence that antioxidant nutrients support the body's production of hormones. Scientific data also suggests vitamin E as a useful adjunct in treating cystic fibrosis, pancreatitis, Parkinson's and various diseases that cause neurological (nerve) damage.

It may help relieve the symptoms of transient ischaemic attacks and various other problems that relate to restrictions of blood flow. Some breastfeeding mothers have found that vitamin E supplementation helps stimulate the flow of breast milk.

Vitamin E supplementation may help prevent cataracts, kidney damage, asthma, osteoporosis and hypertension. A number of studies have shown that vitamin E might be useful in preventing lung tumours, and perhaps breast cancer. One group of researchers concluded that supplementation 'in excess of dietary requirements may reduce a woman's risk of developing breast cancer'.[28]

Antioxidants have cancer preventive properties, and animal studies have shown that vitamin E can inhibit some types of abnormal cells.

General health benefits

Anything that can help combat the biological consequences of free radical and oxidative damage is likely to reduce diseases in general, and to increase life span and improve the quality of life. The majority of studies confirm that even low doses of vitamin E protect LDL from oxidation.[29] In other words it helps prevent the damaging breakdown of the harmful fats in the body.

Vitamin E deficiency has been shown to influence the ratio of specific cells involved in disordered immune reactions in early stages of AIDS. Animal studies show that high-dose vitamin E helps restore immune cells and spleen function.[30] This means that a number of serious diseases related to immune function and sensitivity reactions might be helped by vitamin E at high doses.

Cautions and adverse effects

- Vitamin E is highly recommended for preventing and treating many health problems, but not as the sole treatment for serious diseases, which all require professional monitoring.
- There are some adverse reports of the use of vitamin E, but in twenty years of prescribing this supplement I have not noted any, except one patient thought it caused insomnia if she took it late in the day.

Vitamin E will always have its critics, but the overwhelming evidence from human trials and surveys is that it is generally valuable to human health as a supplement.

Vitamin E in foods

The vitamin E content in foods is another possible reason why Mediterranean people have a lower incidence of heart disease compared to other European countries.[31]

Vitamin E content (IU/100 g)	
Wheat germ oil	216.0
Sunflower seeds	90.0
Safflower oil	72.0*
Almonds	48.0**
Wheat germ	22.0
Butter	3.6
Spinach	3.2
Oatmeal	3.0
Bran	3.0
Asparagus	2.9
Salmon	2.5
Brown rice	2.5

* Most oils are a reasonable source of vitamin E, although only small quantities of these are consumed. Processed oils, however, are an unreliable source, as vitamin E may be removed from them and replaced by a synthetic antioxidant.
** Nuts and seeds are good sources.

Deer and other game meats have reasonably good levels of vitamin E, but domesticated meats do not.[32]

A survey of 3000 postmenopausal women found that those with the highest levels of vitamin E intake from foods had less than half the risk of coronary artery disease compared to women with the lowest intakes.[33]

Generally, what is called a low-fat diet is a diet low in vitamin E. The increased consumption of processed polyunsaturated oils and the decreased intake of vitamin E are likely to have harmful long-term consequences, in spite of the promotional information of the manufacturers of margarine and processed oils.[34]

Products

I recommend natural vitamin E in capsule form. Eight compounds (tocopherols and tocotrienols) found in nature have vitamin E activity, the most potent being d-alpha-tocopherol and its activity (1.49 IU/mg) sets the standard for all forms of this vitamin. Natural and synthetic forms of vitamin E are *not* equivalent.

One study showed that the more expensive water-miscible forms of vitamin E do not have better absorption unless people have gall-bladder problems or fat malabsorption.[35]

You can buy commercial external vitamin E creams, but these may contain very little vitamin E. Depending on the area of the body requiring treatment, you could instead prick open a capsule and apply it undiluted on your skin.

Suggested intake and duration of use

At present there is no standard dose. A medicinal dose of vitamin E varies from 100 IU up to 1000 IU or more a day. My general recommendation is for a daily dose of around 400 IU in the long term.

I suggest that doses of more than 1000 IU per day should be taken only on the advice of your health practitioner.

I mentioned in chapter 1 that antioxidants might be likened to players in an orchestra, as they all have their special roles. For this reason I recommend that you take high doses of vitamin E (over 800 IU) with a fruit juice so that the vitamin E does not crowd out other antioxidants.

Summary

Vitamin E has so many benefits that I have been recommending it for ten years as the most useful of all the supplements, especially for people over forty.

The advantages of a multinutrient supplement

I have not included a combined multivitamin and mineral in the main part of this chapter, but it is an important general health-enhancing strategy for the majority of people; it compensates for the nutritional losses in modern foods; and it helps counteract some of the bad effects of additives, chemicals, environmental toxins and stress. A useful multisupplement contains about eighteen vitamins and eleven minerals, and this also gives reasonable antioxidant activity.

The following are a few examples of studies that justify this type of supplementation.

In a study of over 3000 Chinese people those who received a combined multivitamin and mineral supplement had slightly reduced death rates compared to those who received a placebo. The researchers concluded that the additional vitamins and minerals may have reduced the prevalence of high blood pressure and death from stroke, particularly among men.[36]

People who had abnormal (precancerous) cells in the oesophagus and stomach were given a broad-spectrum supplement containing antioxidants and nutrients, and this resulted in a return to normal cells in 32 per cent of people after 30 months, with abnormal cell growth being 14 per cent lower in the supplemented group as a whole compared to those on the placebo.[37]

A study on ninety-six elderly people showed that the group given supplements over a twelve-month period had a lower frequency of illness, with shorter duration of each infection and a quicker response to antibiotics, than the group on the placebo.[38]

Final comment on super foods and remedies

The foods and herbs recommended in this book have stood the test of time because people have experienced their benefits, and modern scientific studies have confirmed their value to human health.

When your energy levels are low or you are unwell, wholesome foods and no-harm remedies are suggested as the best first option.

If we all lived in a stress-free, close-to-nature lifestyle, eating a variety of fresh organic foods, and getting the right mix of work, rest and play, we might not need supplemental help.

Finally, I think it is important for your general wellbeing to enjoy your meals. If you have visited Mediterranean countries you will have seen the uncomplicated joy that people get from taking their time over a good meal. Don't become fanatical or so rigid in your eating patterns that you eat without pleasure, or cannot enjoy an exotic meal out or a few treats. The recipes and suggestions given in this book can be adapted to suit your tastes and, as suggested in the Introduction, it is better to make dietary changes slowly.

The wild yam scam — the *non*-super remedy

In this book, and in articles and talks, I recommend a wide range of natural therapies; however, I must warn when something is wrong.

Wild yam *cream* is the silliest remedy that has hit the market in over 2000 years of recorded natural therapies. Wild yam (D*ioscorea villosa*) is a traditional *internal* herbal remedy for colic. I find it helpful for treating digestive disorders, and scientists have shown that it promotes healthy fat metabolism. Based on animal studies, wild yam is likely to have some oestrogenic effect, and recent research shows more benefits of it as an internal remedy.

A component in wild yam (diosgenin) can be used *in a laboratory* to make pharmaceutical cortisone, progesterone, oestrogen, testosterone and an adrenal hormone. However, the human body cannot make these conversions, and this has been confirmed by laboratory tests.

Diosgenin is chemically similar to cholesterol. To say that wild yam is a precursor hormone in the human body, and that less than a teaspoon of an external cream will correct hormonal disturbances, is as rational as saying that putting a little butter on your skin acts as a hormone balancer!

The manufacturers of wild yam cream promote it in conjunction with information on natural progesterone implying that they are the same thing. A herb is not a hormone.

Anyone promoting new uses for traditional remedies must provide good evidence of purported new benefits.

Glossary

acute In medicine, this relates to an illness or reaction that is sudden, severe and of short duration. Sometimes, a chronic illness, such as arthritis, has acute episodes.

adaptogen This is a natural non-toxic remedy, capable of helping the body cope with a range of physical, mental, chemical and biological stresses, and helpful for normalising the body's functioning.

alkaloids These are plant components that are sometimes medicinal and sometimes poisonous. They usually represent around 1 per cent of a plant's weight, and occur in many common foods, such as potato. When consumed as part of an edible food or herb, they are rarely hazardous, but when taken in an isolated form, as in a drug, they tend to produce adverse effects. However, plants such as deadly nightshade are dangerous poisons because of their alkaloid content.

amino acids Protein is formed from amino acids. The human body needs twenty-two amino acids to assemble protein, and nine of these must be eaten in foods because the body cannot manufacture them. If your diet contains these nine, then the body can make the other thirteen. The essential amino acids are histidine, isoleucine, leucine, lysine, methionine, phenylalanine, threonine, tryptophan and valine. Some researchers say that arginine is also essential in the diet.

anthocyanosides Found primarily in blue-black berries, these compounds destroy free radicals, have blood-thinning activity, stabilise collagen, and have wide-ranging benefits, notably for eyes and circulation.

antioxidants These substances counteract excess oxidation in the body. Oxidation is a natural process in the body resulting from energy production, cell building and other processes. Undesirable oxidation also occurs naturally from infections, inappropriate fat metabolism, environmental toxins, pesticides, and so on.

Glutathione and other antioxidants occur naturally in the body; some antioxidants are nutrients such as vitamin C and E, others are plant components, notably flavonoids; and there are also synthetic antioxidants. Specific antioxidants have different roles in protecting the body.

antispasmodic see **spasmolytic**

arteriosclerosis This is commonly referred to as hardening of the arteries — the blood vessels that carry oxygenated blood. What happens with ageing and lack of exercise is that the smooth muscles in the artery walls lose their elasticity. This lack of stretch leads to restriction of blood flow and pressure on the walls of the blood vessels (hyperten-

sion). If the blood does not flow smoothly, this can create damage to the blood vessel walls, and consequently free radical activity and deposits.

atherosclerosis There are many causes of this problem, but basically it is a condition where there is a build-up of plaque on the walls of the heart's main arteries. Plaque deposits form because of injury to the arterial walls, poor blood flow, oxidised cholesterol, and the presence of calcium and other material in the bloodstream. The end result is that there is a narrowing of the space in the arteries, and so the arteries are stressed and the flow of oxygenated blood is restricted.

beta-carotene Beta-carotene is the commonest carotenoid occurring in plants, and it has various forms. It is an antioxidant, and scientific opinion is divided regarding its usefulness as a supplement for preventing cancer and other degenerative diseases. My assessment is that *synthetic* beta-carotene is probably *not* useful therapeutically. Small amounts of natural beta-carotene in a supplement are likely to be beneficial, but almost everyone agrees that the best forms of beta-carotene and other beneficial carotenoids are in fruits and vegetables.

bioflavonoids Natural antioxidants found in vegetables and fruits that help maintain blood vessel walls and connective tissue, and protect cells from lipid peroxidation (a damaging oxidation process that can increase the risk of clogged arteries and other cardiovascular problems).

carcinogen see **mutagen**

carotenoids Naturally occurring compounds found in various fruits, the cabbage family in particular, as well as in all yellow and dark-green vegetables. There are over 500 of these, the most common being beta-carotene.

cholesterol This category of fat is found in animal foods, but not in plants. Excess cholesterol in the body is linked to cardiovascular disease, but cholesterol also has necessary functions; for example, it is the starting material for the body's production of reproductive hormones.

Cholesterol is divided into two types: HDL (healthy) and LDL(harmful). There is also VLDL (very harmful).

HDL stands for high density lipoprotein, and you could think of it as a tiny ball with a relatively high ratio of protein to fat. This ball is one of the 'carriers' that transport cholesterol and other fats in the bloodstream. When cholesterol is 'packaged' in this ratio, it gets back to the liver, the liver converts it to bile acids, and these get into the intestines via the gallbladder, where they aid fat digestion and then get excreted. (The liver has an important role in cholesterol metabolism, and that is why you can have high cholesterol, even though you are on a low-fat diet.)

LDL stands for low density lipoprotein. This is another tiny ball of fat, but when 'packaged' in a low ratio of protein to fat it is more likely to get deposited in the walls of blood vessels, and cause blockages or clots.

Normal levels	
Total cholesterol	3.9–5.5 mmol/L
HDL cholesterol	
female	0.9–2.1
male	0.8–1.8
LDL cholesterol (the nasty one)	0–3.5

chronic Medically, chronic is a term for long-lasting illnesses and symptoms. These problems can be minor, severe or changeable.

connective tissue A fibrous non-cellular collagen tissue forms the structural part of the body. It supports and connects internal organs, forms bone structure and the walls of blood vessels, attaches muscles to bones (tendons), attaches bones to bones (ligaments), and provides a cushion between joints (cartilage). It is part of our outer skin and internal linings, and also replaces injured tissue as scars.

controlled studies Most medical scientists believe that these are the only valid way of testing whether or not a compound is therapeutically effective. The standard is a double-blind, placebo-controlled study.

Example: 100 people are randomly (by chance) divided into two even groups. The participants have no choice; fifty are given the remedy and fifty a placebo. The placebo is either a sugar-coated inert pill or some other camouflaged non-active substance. The people in the trial do not know what they are getting, and those handing out the treatment do not know either. The substances are coded.

Both groups are monitored by blood or other tests and/or questionnaires, and the results are assessed at the end of the trial period when the codes are made known.

Sometimes there is a crossover trial period, and the groups are switched.

This system is obviously better than anecdotal evidence or manufacturers' promotional material, but it is not perfect. For instance, if a pharmaceutical drug is being tested, most people would notice a distinct change in the body, since pharmaceuticals are very potent. Controlled trials are difficult and expensive to carry out over long periods of time. Many people do not feel comfortable giving a sick person a placebo.

Natural therapists endeavour to treat the whole person, and encourage a healthy diet and lifestyle, together with individually prescribed remedies used with the aim of supporting the body's own functioning. This approach does not lend itself to the standard double-blind medical trials, which commonly test one tiny component for a specific therapeutic effect over a short period of time.

decoction A decoction is usually made with dried herbs that are simmered in water for about ten minutes, and then strained. This is suggested when making a tea is not sufficient to bring out the components in the plant. Do not use aluminium saucepans when making herbal remedies.

designer foods One of the terms being used to describe foods with specific health properties beyond essential nutrients. An extension of this is the manipulation or processing of foods — presumably to make them 'healthier'. Some scientists envisage that we will be able to offer children broccoli with a chocolate flavour. Perhaps the ultimate designer food will be a bite-size product that contains known beneficial compounds from many different plants.

DNA Deoxyribonucleic acid is the genetic or hereditary part of a cell, and it directs production of protein and how cells divide and grow. Anything that disturbs DNA will have major consequences in the body.

enzymes A type of protein in the body that starts and accelerates reactions. Enzymes are numerous and tiny, each type having a specific function, such as breaking down or absorbing a particular nutrient or compound. Most are essential for life processes, while others can be damaging if they are malfunctioning or in excess.

essential fatty acids Essential fatty acids are alpha-linolenic acid and linoleic acid, and these must be obtained from the diet because the body cannot make them. Good sources of essential fatty acids are unprocessed and unheated linseed; virgin olive oil; soya beans; walnuts; pumpkin; safflower, sunflower and sesame seeds; and dark-green leaves. It is now recommended that these fatty acids should represent about one-third of the total fats that we eat.

essential nutrients 'Essential' has a special meaning in nutrition. It is used only for those specified nutrients, including essential fatty acids, vitamins, minerals and amino acids, that must be obtained from the diet because they are necessary for human life, but the body cannot manufacture them. Non-essential nutrients, such as cholesterol and vitamin K, are needed for good health, but they can be produced in the body.

extract A concentrated liquid product made from the dried, powdered plant material according to specific manufacturing standards that are somewhat different for each herb. Specialised equipment is required, and the product is preserved in varying strengths of alcohol and water. Extracts preserved with glycerine are also becoming available.

fibre Insoluble dietary fibres are cellulose, lignin and some hemicelluloses. Cellulose is the most common fibre in plants, and it forms the outer walls. Lignin is also found in the outer part of plants. Generally, humans are not able to digest and absorb insoluble fibres, which absorb water, swell, and therefore put 'bulk' in the intestines.

Soluble dietary fibres include hemicellulose, pectin, gums, mucilages and algal polysaccharides. These are not fibrousy or woody, but gel-like. They also absorb water in the intestines, but their gelatinous nature makes them a more soothing type of laxative. Soluble fibre have other benefits. For instance, pectin, which is found in citrus fruits, apples and other plants, absorbs toxins in the intestines, enhances intestinal function, helps treat diarrhoea, lowers cholesterol, and has some antioxidant activity.

flavonoids Over 4000 chemically unique flavonoids have been identified in plants. Authoritative textbooks group them into categories such as anthocyanins, biflavonoids, flavans and isoflavonoids (there are differences in how some of them are spelt). They have the capacity to affect human enzymes, hormones and the immune system, and provide anticancer, anti-inflammatory, antioxidant, antitoxic, antiviral and liver protective effects.

free radicals Free radicals originate from body processes, and also result from environmental and agricultural chemicals, including solar and ionising radiation, cigarette smoke, air pollutants, heavy metals, ozone, organic solvents, pesticides and food additives. They are molecules that have an odd number of electrons, which means that they have a tendency to react with other stable molecules. Once formed, free radicals react in several ways, such as damaging cell walls and DNA, so that a chain reaction of disturbances can occur and, as a consequence, cells do not function properly. Antioxidants help destroy these damaging molecules.

Free radicals could be likened to nasty gossips who don't have enough to occupy themselves so they circulate around, busily searching for someone to latch onto. If someone picks up the gossip and extends it, then that can lead to long-term problems in innocent victims.

guaranteed potency A term used in herbal medicine to describe a remedy that contains a specific level of a particular component or group of components. Obviously these components have been established as therapeutically paramount, as is the case with herbs such as ginkgo, milk thistle and St John's wort. Other herbs, for example, echinacea, are not manufactured with guaranteed potency because the therapeutic value is related to a range of different components or the plant as a whole.

heavy metals These occur naturally, and result from industry and various human activities. Heavy metals such as lead, mercury and cadmium occur naturally in small quantities. Excess heavy metals in the body cause numerous adverse physical and mental reactions, as well as being outright poisons.

histamine An enzyme that is released as a result of bacterial infection, heat, chemicals, injury or allergies. It dilates blood vessels, and causes swelling and inflammation. Excess histamine causes headaches and typical allergic reactions, but it also has useful functions in the body such as stimulating gastric juice.

hypertensive The action of something to increase blood pressure. Blood pressure readings are taken based on the movement of mercury in a column (sphygmomanometer) or by equipment that gives the pressure in figures (digital). When you have your blood pressure taken, this gives a reading of the amount of pressure that the blood is exerting on your artery walls. The pressure depends on the force of the heartbeat and the condition of artery walls. In Australia you are judged to have hypertension if your reading exceeds 140/90. The 140 relates to the pressure on your arteries when the heart is pumping (systolic), and the 90 relates to the pressure when your heart is resting (diastolic). When you are excited your blood pressure rises, but this is normal as long as you are not in a constant excited state.

There are many causes of hypertension, including hardened or blocked arteries, malfunctioning kidneys and hormonal disorders; sometimes no specific cause can be found.

hypotensive The action of a substance to lower blood pressure, so it is used to treat hypertension.

A person with low blood pressure is said to have hypotension. Having excessively low blood pressure can cause health problems such as dizziness, headaches and weakness. It can be caused by weak heart function, anaemia, malnutrition, dehydration and shock; sometimes the cause cannot be identified.

interferon This is a particular type of protein that the body produces. In the body it has antiviral activity, but it also generally acts to overcome infections in the body by blocking some specific types of viruses, as well as bacteria and some other micro-organisms. Some anticancer activity also occurs.

The body produces extremely tiny quantities of interferon and, although there are some interferon pharmaceuticals now available, it is difficult to make them, they are very expensive, and are used only for severe chronic infections and a few forms of cancer. The pharmaceuticals are very complex, and have a long list of potential adverse effects.

intracellular This means within a cell or cells.

isoflavonoid, isoflavone These two words are used interchangeably. In nature there are about 200 different isoflavonoids, some of which are classed as isoflavonic phyto-oestrogens. See also **phyto-oestrogen**.

leaky gut The inside of your intestines is selectively permeable and acts like a fine sieve, allowing nutrients and other tiny-sized beneficial compounds through the intestinal wall to the blood circulation, which then transports them to various cells in the body. When the intestinal wall is irritated or malfunctioning, its filtering function becomes inefficient, and larger fragments from foods or toxic material of various kinds escape through the intestinal wall. The end result may be 'leaky gut syndrome', which manifests as a variety of health problems, including allergic reactions, reactive arthritis, autoimmune joint diseases, and possibly a number of other illnesses. Natural therapists have always maintained that intestinal health is a prerequisite for general good health.

lignans Components in plants that ultimately form the hard outer layer known as lignin tissue. A

number of lignans in edible plants are known to be beneficial; the common sources are seeds, nuts and whole grains, and all plant foods to a lesser extent. If you eat refined foods you are not getting lignans in the diet. Linseed meal is currently the most famous lignan-containing plant.

lipids Fats and oils are classed as lipids, as are phospholipids and steroids.

macrophage These are white blood cells that are part of your immune system. Their main function is to 'clean up' the debris of damaged and abnormal cells.

malignant Technically this term applies to any disease that is potentially life-threatening, for instance, malignant hypertension. However, in common usage, it is a cancerous tumour.

Mediterranean paradox Scientific dietary surveys always show that people living in Mediterranean regions have less cardiovascular disease when compared with people living in, say, Scotland, even though both groups are eating the same level of fat. Some researchers put this down to the fact that most Mediterranean people eat more vegetables and fruit, olive oil and garlic, and drink red wine.

membranes In your body, membranes are basically internal skin. They are the linings of cells, organs and the brain. Their main function is to keep structures in the right shape and to act as a filter, so that nutrients and oxygen get through, while toxins are screened out.

mutagen A mutagen changes the information stored in the hereditary blueprint (DNA) of a cell. This occurs slowly and infrequently in nature. When the change (mutation) is rapid, as happens when certain chemicals, oxidants or excess radiation get into cells, the changed DNA messages may cause new cells to be malignant (cancerous). A substance that causes this type of change in cells is known as a carcinogen.

natural killer cells A special type of white blood cell with sentry-like activity against viruses and tumour cells. Natural killer cells are less active at times of severe stress, which may explain why people tend to get infections following emotional trauma.

oxidation In the body this is a reaction that is necessary for providing energy for cell functioning. Free radical formation is a byproduct of this natural process. Excess oxidation is a factor in a number of degenerative diseases and premature death, which is why antioxidants are becoming popular.

phytic acid (phytates) A component of plants that is highest in the fibre part of grains. Although phytic acid reduces the absorption of minerals, whole grains have a higher mineral content to begin with compared to refined grains. Recent research shows that phytates have antioxidant and immune enhancing effects, and laboratory studies indicate some cancer preventive potential. This may be another reason why a high-fibre diet is linked to a reduction in cancer.

phytochemical 'Phyto' means plant. Aside from nutrients, it is now known that many chemicals in plants have favourable effects in the body. In common usage, a phytochemical usually relates to a beneficial component.

phyto-oestrogen A number of different compounds in plants have oestrogen-like structures that can act like a weak oestrogen, and the most important of these are considered to be isoflavonoids. Other types of phytooestrogens, such as **lignans**, are converted to oestrogen-like compounds in human intestines, and are able to exert mild oestrogenic or anti-oestrogenic activity, depending on the oestrogen status of the individual.

In the body these weak plant oestrogens can compete for absorption with stronger oestrogens, thereby reducing the effect of stronger human hormones. However, when the body's natural oestrogens are low, they can be absorbed and have some oestrogenic effects, which explains why foods such as soya and whole grains can be helpful for menopause symptoms.

Recent studies indicate that a diet rich in phyto-oestrogens is likely to be protective against cancer and cardiovascular-problems.

phytosterols There are about fifty-seven of these hormone-like substances in plants. The most common are sitosterol and stigmasterol. They are found in plant oils, nuts, seeds, legumes, whole grains and vegetables. In general they are cholesterol-lowering and some are currently being studied for their potential, beneficial hormonal effects.

significant In controlled scientific trials this word means that the results are clearly better than for a placebo. When something is non-significant it means that the result is probably not due to the remedy being tested, and therefore the result should be ignored.

spasmolytic (antispasmodic) A substance that prevents or reduces muscle spasms, cramps, contractions, restrictions or muscle twitching. These substances also affect the smooth muscles that line the digestive tract, the respiratory system and blood vessels. Natural spasmolytic substances include magnesium, herbs and some aromatic oils.

systemic pesticide A chemical that penetrates and circulates within a plant. This type of pesticide is used to kill insects that 'suck' to feed, or inject their eggs into the plant. A common systemic pesticide is Rogor (dimethoate) and the label gives a withholding time of seven days, which means that you should not harvest fruits and vegetables within seven days of spraying. Surveys of Australian foods often reveal dimethoate residues.

T cells These cells are preprocessed by the thymus gland, and form a major part of your body's immune system because they help combat viruses, fungi and bacteria that cause chronic infections. They are also active against malignant cells.

tincture A tincture requires a particular maceration (soaking) process, and more alcohol is used than with an extract. Some are made from the fresh plant, but usually dried, finely powdered herbs are used.

trans fatty acids The word trans in this context relates to the chemical construction of oils. Trans fatty acids are found in nature, but only in tiny amounts. When oils are extracted from plants and turned into commercial polyunsaturated oils and margarine, the processing involves bleaching, heating, filtering and, in the case of margarine, solidifying. This processing changes the natural chemistry that exists in the plant oils, and the resultant products contain a high proportion of trans fatty acids. Scientific evidence is accumulating that these trans fatty acids have a wide range of detrimental effects on body functions, such as interfering with the functions of the fats that we require to be healthy.

triglycerides The storage form of fats in the body's tissues. Triglycerides provide useful functions in the body, such as protecting us from the cold, and are used for energy. While they are circulating in the blood, the levels can be checked by a blood test; a normal (healthy) level is considered to be less than 2.0 mmol/L. If you are above this level, you have an increased risk of heart and circulatory diseases.

Notes

Introduction

1 *Townsend Letter for Doctors and Patients*, April 1997: 77.
2 *The Cost of Diet-related Disease in Australia: A Discussion Paper*, Australian Institute of Health and Welfare, September 1992.
3 *Planta Medica*, 1991, 57: 299–304.

1 Nine super vegetable and fruit groups

1 *Lancet*, 1996, 348; 898–9.
2 *British Medical Journal*, 1996, 313: 775–9.
3 *Angiology*, 1996, 47: 43–9.
4 *Journal of the National Cancer Institute*, 1996, 88: 340–8.
5 *Preventive Medicine*, 1995, 24: 646–55.
6 *International Journal of Cancer*, 1995, 63: 85–9.
7 *Epidemiology*, 1996, 7: 465–71.
8 *Cancer*, 1997, 80: 858–64.

Antioxidant-rich foods

9 *American Journal of Clinical Nutrition*, 1995, 61: 1228–33.
10 *Free Radicals, Biology and Medicine*, 1996, 20: 793–800.
11 B. Frei (ed.), *Natural Antioxidants in Human Health and Disease*, Academic Press, San Diego, 1994.
12 *Veris Research Summary*, November 1996, 1–13.
13 *Townsend Letter for Doctors and Patients*, May 1997, 112–14.
14 *Mutation Research*, 1996, 351: 199–203.
15 *Proceedings of the Nutritional Society*, 1996, 55: 1A, 33a.
16 *Annals of Rheumatic Diseases*, 1997, 56: 323–5.
17 *American Journal of Clinical Nutrition*, 1992, 56: 684–90.

The bilberry, and other berries

18 *Planta medica*, 1996, 62: 212–16.
19 *Pharmacology Research*, 1995, 31: 183–7.
20 *Fitoterapia*, 1996, 67: 3–29 (a major review paper containing 119 references).
21 *Annals of Medicine*, 1997, 29: 95–120.

Other berries

22 *New England Journal of Medicine*, 1991, 324: 1599.
23 *Professional Nurse*, 1996, 11: 525–6.
24 *Cancer Letters*, 1997, 114: 191–2.

The cabbage family

25 *Nutrition and Cancer*, 1992; 18: 237–44.
26 *Carcinogenesis*, 1996; 17: 793–9.
27 *Clinical Cancer Research*, 1995; 1: 1153–63.
28 *BNF Nutrition Bulletin*, 1996; 21: 26–33.
29 *Carcinogenesis*, 1995; 16: 969–70.
30 *Cancer Research*, 1992; 52: 2719S–22S.
31 *Proceedings of the National Academy of Sciences*, 1997; 94: 10367–72.
32 N. Beckham, *Menopause: A Positive Approach Using Natural Therapies*, Viking, Melbourne, 1995.

The carrot family

33 *Lung Cancer*, 1996; 14: S85–91.
34 *Journal of the American Dietetic Association*, 1996; 96: 1027–39.
35 *British Journal of Dermatology*, 1996; 134: 101–6.
36 *Health*, 1988; 20: 17.

Citrus fruits

37 *Planta Medica*, 1996; 62: 222–6.
38 *International Journal of Cancer*, 1996; 65: 308–13.
39 *Nutrition and Cancer*, 1996; 26: 167–81.
40 *Farmaco*, 1996; 51: 219–21.
41 *International Journal of Vitamin and Nutrition Research*, 1996; 66: 113–18.
42 *Annals of Epidemiology*, 1996; 6: 41–6.
43 *Nutrition Research*, 1997: 17: 415–25.
44 *Planta Medica*, 1996; 62: 222–6.
45 *Clinical Cardiology*, 1988; 11: 589–94.

Carotenoids

46 *Journal of the American Dietetic Association*, 1993; 93: 284–96.
47 *International Journal of Cancer*, 1996; 63: 67–73.
48 *Nutrition and Cancer*, 1996; 25: 281–96.
49 *Contemporary Internal Medicine*, 1995; 7: 9–14.
50 *Journal of the American Medical Association*, 1994; 272: 1413–20.
51 *American Journal of Clinical Nutrition*, 1996; 64: 772–7.
52 *European Journal of Dermatology*, 1996; 6: 200–5.
53 *Nutrition Research*, 1996; 16: 1881–90.
54 *American Journal of Clinical Nutrition*, 1996; 64: 87–93.
55 *International Journal of Alternative and Complementary Medicine*, May 1996: 11–12.
56 *Journal of the National Cancer Institute*, 1996; 88: 1560–70.
57 *American Journal of Clinical Nutrition*, 1996; 63: 729–34.

Flavonoids

58 *Gastroenterology*, 1996; 110: 12–20.
59 *Cancer Letters*, 1997; 112: 127–33.
60 *Lancet*, 1997; 349: 699.

Reishi

61 *Phytotherapy Research*, 1995; 9: 533–5.
62 *International Journal of Alternative and Complementary Medicine*, July 1992; 15–16.
63 ibid.
64 *Quarterly Review of Natural Medicine*, 1997; Summer: 99–100.
65 *Journal of Ethnopharmacology*, 1995; 47: 33–41.
66 *Biological and Pharmaceutical Bulletin*, 1997; 20: 417–20.

Shitake

67 *Review of Natural Products*, monograph, May 1997.
68 *Chemistry and Pharmaceutical Bulletin*, 1987; 6: 2459–66.
69 *12th International Gastroenterology and Endoscopy Congress*, Lisbon, September 1984.

[70] *Review of Natural Products*, monograph, May 1997 (44 references).

Other medicinal mushrooms
[71] *Nutrition Research*, 1996; 16: 1953–7.
[72] *Townsend Letter for Doctors and Patients*, July 1997; 86–8.

The potato family
[73] *Journal of Bioscience*, 1987; 12: 143–52.
[74] *Japanese Journal of Pharmacology*, 1991; 55: 147–55.
[75] *Food Technology*, 1992; 46: 65–8.

Sea vegetables
[76] *Microbial Ecology in Health and Disease*, 1995; 8: 259–65.
[77] *Nutrition and Cancer*, 1997; 27: 74–9.
[78] *Journal of Nutrition*, 1995; 125: 2511–15.
[79] *International Journal of Food Sciences and Nutrition*, 1993, 44: S23–5.

In conclusion
[80] *Journal of the American Dietetic Association*, 1996; 96: 1027–39.

2 Six super grains, legumes and seeds

[1] *Journal of Nutrition*, 1996; 126: 871–7.
[2] G. H. Bourne (ed.), *Nutritional Value of Cereal Products, Beans and Starches*, Karger, Basel, 1989.
[3] *Townsend Letter for Doctors and Patients*, April 1997; 900.
[4] *Nutrition and Cancer*, 1997; 27: 14–21.
[5] F. Moore-Lappe, *Diet for a Small Planet*, Ballantine Books, New York, 1982.

Buckwheat
[6] *European Journal of Clinical Pharmacology*, 1995; 50: 443–7.
[7] *Nutrition Research*, 1995; 15: 691–8.
[8] *Planta Medica*, 1996; 62: 106–10.
[9] ibid.

Lentils
[10] N. Beckham, *Menopause: A Positive Approach Using Natural Therapies*, Viking, Melbourne, 1995, p. 81.
[11] D. K. Salunkhe & S. S. Kadam (eds), CRC *Handbook of World Food Legumes: Processing Technology and Utilisation*, vol. 2, CRC Press Inc., Boca Raton, Florida, 1989.

Linseed
[12] *European Journal of Clinical Nutrition*, 1995; 49: 169–78.
[13] *Carcinogenesis*, 1996; 17: 1373–6.
[14] *Environmental Health Perspectives*, 1995; 103 (Supplement 7): 103–12.

Other plants containing beneficial plant lignans
[15] *Annals of Medicine*, 1997; 29: 95–120.

Millet
[16] A. H. Ensminger et al., *Foods & Nutrition Encyclopedia*, 2nd edn, vol. 2, CRC Press Inc., Boca Raton, Florida, 1994.

Rice
[17] *American Journal of Clinical Nutrition*, 1996; 63: 22–31.
[18] *Annals of Nutritional Metabolism*, 1994; 38: 249–56.
[19] *Journal of the American College of Nutrition*, 1991; 10: 593–601.

Soya beans
[20] N. Beckham, *Menopause: A Positive Approach Using Natural Therapies*, Viking, Melbourne, 1995.
[21] *New England Journal of Medicine*, 1995; 333: 276–82.
[22] *Proceedings of the Society for Experimental Biology and Medicine*, 1995; 208: 124–30.
[23] M. Messina, V. Messina & K. Setchell, *The Simple Soybean and Your Health*, Avery Publishing, New York, 1994.
[24] *Nutrition and Cancer*, 1994; 21: 113–31.
[25] *Journal of Nutrition*, 1995; 125: 757S–70S.
[26] *The Soy Connection*, 1997; 5: 1.
[27] *American Journal of Clinical Nutrition*, 1994; 59: 1203S–12S.
[28] *Medical Journal of Australia*, 1996; 164: 575.
[29] J. A. Duke, *A Handbook of Phytochemical Constituents of Gras Herbs and Other Economic Plants*, CRC Press Inc., Boca Raton, Florida, 1992.
[30] *Food Technology*, 1992; 46: 65–8.
[31] *Townsend Letter for Doctors and Patients*, April 1997; 90.
[32] *American Journal of Clinical Nutrition*, 1994; 60: 333–40.
[33] *Clinical Chemistry*, 1996; 42: 955–64.

3 Fourteen super medicinal herbs

Aloe
[1] *Phytomedicine*, 1996; 2: 247–51.
[2] *Tropical Medicine and International Health*, 1996; 1: 505–9.
[3] *Journal of the American Academy of Dermatology*, 1988, 19 (Part 1): 82.
[4] *Planta Medica*, 1989; 55: 509–12.
[5] J. E. Pizzorno & M. T. Murray, *A Textbook of Natural Medicine*, John Bastyr College Publications, Seattle, 1992.
[6] M. B. Skousen, *Quotations from Medical Journals on Aloe Research*, Aloe Vera Research Institute, Cypress, Calif., n.d. (81 references).

Cat's claw
[7] N. Maxwell, *Witch-Doctor's Apprentice: Hunting for Medicinal Plants in the Amazon*, Citadel Press, New York, 1990.
[8] *Journal of Natural Products*, 1991; 54: 453–9.
[9] *Information for Physicians and Dispensing Chemists*, 3rd

rev. edn, Immodal Pharmaka GmbH, Volders, Austria, September 1995.

10 *Journal of Ethnopharmacology*, 1993; 38: 63–77.

Chamomile

11 *International Journal of Alternative and Complementary Medicine*, September 1994; 12.

12 *Journal of Natural Products*, 1983; 46: 626–32.

13 *British Journal of Medical Psychology*, 1992; 65: 197–9.

14 *HerbalGram*, 1994; 28: 30–1.

15 *HerbalGram*, 1997; 39: 65.

16 *HerbalGram*, 1991; 24: 44–5 (63 references).
Echinacea

17 *Kings American Dispensatory*, 18th edn, 1898; reprinted by Eclectic Medical Publications, Portland, Oregon, 1983.

18 H. W. Felter MD, *The Eclectic Materia Medica, Pharmacology and Therapeutics*, vol. 1, 1922; Eclectic Medical Publications, Portland, Oregon, 1983.

19 *HerbalGram*, 1997; 39: 63.

20 *Townsend Letter for Doctors*, January 1995; 134–5.

21 *Immunopharmacology*, 1997; 35: 229–35.

22 R. F. Weiss MD, *Herbal Medicine*, Beaconsfield Publishers, UK, 1988.

23 N. Beckham, *The Australian Family Guide to Natural Therapies*, Viking, Melbourne, 1995.

Ginkgo

24 *Nutrition Research*, 1996; 16: 1913–23.

25 *Quarterly Review of Natural Medicine*, 1997, Summer: 91–6.

26 *Pharmacopsychiatry*, 1996; 29: 47–56.

27 *Angiology*, 1994; 45: 413–17.

28 *HerbalGram*, 1997; 39: 63.

Asian ginseng

29 *British Journal of Phytotherapy*, 1991; 2: 3–14 (151 references).

30 *Phytotherapy Research*, 1996; 10: 49–53.

31 *La Semana Medica*, 1989; 9: 148–54.

32 *Postgraduate Medical Journal*, 1988; 64: 841–6.

33 *Diabetes Care*, 1995; 18: 1373–5.

34 *Chemistry and Pharmaceutical Bulletin*, 1993; 41: 549–52.

35 *HerbalGram*, 1991; 25: 18.

36 *British Herbal Compendium*, vol. 1, British Herbal Medicine Association, Bournemouth, 1992.

Siberian ginseng

37 N. Beckham, *Menopause: A Positive Approach Using Natural Therapies*, Viking, Melbourne, 1995.

38 *British Journal of Phytotherapy*, 1991; 2: 61–71 (49 references).

Gotu kola

39 J. E. Pizzorno & M. T. Murray, *Textbook of Natural Therapies*, John Bastyr College of Natural Therapies, Seattle, 1989.

40 *Fitoterapia*, 1992; 63: 232–7.

41 *Planta Medica*, 1994; 60: 133–5.

Hawthorn

42 F. Ellingwood MD, *American Materia Medica, Therapeutics and Pharmacognosy*, Eclectic Medical Publications, Portland, Oregon, 1983.

43 *Journal of the American College of Toxicology*, 1994; 13: 103–11.

44 *Quarterly Review of Natural Therapies*, Autumn 1997: 201–9.

45 *Townsend Letter for Doctors and Patients*, January 1996: 140–1.

46 *Quarterly Review of Natural Medicine*, Summer 1995, 107–17.

47 I. Goldberg (ed.), *Functional Foods: Designer Foods, Pharmafoods, Nutraceuticals*, Chapman & Hall, New York, 1994.

48 *Journal of the American College of Toxicology*, 1994; 13: 103–11.

Kava

49 *Quarterly Journal of Studies on Alcohol*, 1967; 28: 328–41.

50 *Pharmacopsychiatry*, 1997; 30: 1–5.

51 *British Journal of Phytotherapy*, 1993/94; 3: 147–53.

52 *Fortschritte der Medizin*, 1990; 108: 49–54.

53 *Fortschritte der Medizin*, 1991; 109: 119–22.

54 *European Journal of Pharmacology*, 1992; 215: 265–9.

55 *Clinical Experiments in Pharmacology and Physiology*, 1990; 17: 495–507.

56 *Clinical Experiments in Pharmacology and Physiology*, 1991; 18: 571–8.

57 *Journal of Pharmaceutical Sciences*, 1988; 77: 1003–6.

Liquorice

58 *Townsend Letter for Doctors and Patients*, August/September 1996: 156–7.

59 *Chemistry and Pharmaceutical Bulletin*, 1986; 34: 897–901.

60 *Quarterly Review of Natural Medicine*, 1977, Summer, 103–8.

61 *Japanese Journal of Cancer Research*, 1986; 77: 33–8.

62 *Phytotherapy Research*, 1994; 7: 335–47.

63 *Immunology and Cell Biology*, 1993; 71: 181–9.

64 *Journal of Ethnopharmacology*, 1996; 53: 1–4.

65 *Lancet*, 1990; 335: 1060–3.

66 *Environmental Health Perspectives*, 1994; 102: 65–8.

67 *Planta Medica*, 1994; 60: 136–9.

68 J. E. Pizzorno & M. T. Murray, *A Textbook of Natural Medicine*, John Bastyr College Publications, Seattle, 1985.

Milk thistle

69 *Acta Physiologica Hungarica*, 1992; 80: 363–7.

[70] *European Bulletin of Drug Research*, 1992; 1: 131.
[71] *Quarterly Review of Natural Medicine*, 1997; Summer: 103–8.
[72] *Quarterly Review of Natural Medicine*, 1995; Spring: 9–10.
[73] *Current Therapeutic Research*, 1994; 55: 537–45.
[74] *Zeitschrift für Phytotherapie*, 1991; 12: 162.
[75] *Quarterly Review of Natural Therapies*, 1996, Summer: 103–12.
[76] *Fitoterapia*, 1996; 67: 166–71.
[77] *Journal of Hepatology*, 1989; 9: 105.
[78] *Planta Medica*, 1995; 61: 116–19.
[79] *Current Therapeutic Research*, 1993; 53: 533–45.
[80] *European Journal of Cancer*, 1996; 32A: 877–82.
[81] *Review of Natural Products*, monograph, January 1997; 9.
[82] *Arzneim–Forsch Drug Research*, 1995; 45: 61–4.

Pau d'arco
[83] *Planta Medica*, 1990; 56; 669–70.
[84] H. Wagner et al., *Economic and Medicinal Plant Research*, Academic Press, London, 1985.
[85] J. E. Pizzorno & M. T. Murray, A *Textbook of Natural Medicine*, John Bastyr College Publications, Seattle, 1987 (57 references).
[86] T. Willard, *The Wild Rose Scientific Herbal*, Wild Rose College of Natural Healing, Alberta, 1991 (53 references).

St John's wort
[87] *Zeitschrift für Phytotherapie*, 1993; 14: 255–64.
[88] *Phytomedicine*, 1995; 2: 67–71.
[89] *British Journal of Phytotherapy*, 1991/92; 2: 181–2.
[90] *HerbalGram* 1992; 32: 10.
[91] 'St John's Wort', *Review of Natural Products*, monograph, November 1997.
[92] *Fitoterapia*, 1995; 66: 43–68.

Withania
[93] M. R. Werbach & M. T. Murray, *Botanical Influences on Illness: A Sourcebook of Clinical Research*, Third Line Press, Tarzana, California, 1994.
[94] *Journal of Ethnopharmacology*, 1994; 44: 131.
[95] *Indian Journal of Experimental Biology*, 1992; 30: 169–72.
[96] C. Newall et al., *Herbal Medicines: A Guide for Healthcare Professionals*, Australian Pharmaceutical Publishing Co., Hawthorn, Vic., 1997.
[97] *Phytotherapy Research*, 1989; 3: 201–6.

4 *Four super culinary herbs*

Fenugreek
[1] *Phytotherapy Research*, 1996; 10: 332–4.
[2] *Phytotherapy Research*, 1994; 8: 83–6.
[3] *Nutrition Research*, 1996; 16: 1495–505.

Garlic
[4] *Annals of Internal Medicine*, 1993; 119: 599–605.
[5] *Journal of the Royal College of Physicians*, 1994; 28: 39–45.
[6] *American Journal of Clinical Nutrition*, 1996; 64: 866–70.
[7] S. Brewer, *Beating Heart Disease the Natural Way*, Galen Publishing, Catsfield, UK, 1995.
[8] *Prostaglandins, Leukotrienes and Essential Fatty Acids*, 1995; 53: 211–12.
[9] *Cancer Letters*, 1997; 114: 185–6.
[10] *Nutrition and Cancer*, 1997; 27: 118–21.
[11] *Experimental Gerontology*, 1997; 32: 149–60.
[12] *Fitoterapia*, 1996; 67: 374.
[13] H. P. Koch & L. D. Lawson, *Garlic: The Science and Therapeutic Application of* Allium sativum *and Related Species*, 2nd edn, Williams & Wilkins, Baltimore, 1996 (2240 references).
[14] *European Journal of Clinical Research*, 1996; 8: 15–36.

Ginger
[15] *Journal of Ethnopharmacology*, 1985; 13: 217–25.
[16] *Journal of Ethnopharmacology*, 1988; 23: 299–304.
[17] *Chemistry and Pharmaceutical Bulletin*, 1989; 37: 215–17.
[18] *Planta Medica*, 1994; 60: 17–20.
[19] *Current Opinion in Obstetrics and Gynecology*, 1992; 4: 43–7.
[20] *Anaesthesia*, 1990; 45: 669–71.
[21] *Journal of Ethnopharmacology*, 1989; 27: 353–5.
[22] *Pharmacology*, 1994; 49: 314–18.
[23] *Japanese Journal of Pharmacology*, 1989; 50: 253–61.
[24] *Journal of Ethnopharmacology*, 1985; 14: 31–9.
[25] *Journal of Natural Products*, 1994; 57: 658–62.
[26] *Nutrition and Cancer*, 1994; 21: 169–75.
[27] *Chemistry and Pharmaceutical Bulletin*, 1992; 40: 387–91.
[28] *Journal of Ecotoxicology and Environmental Monitoring*, 1992; 1: 81–90.
[29] Translated by Dr A. Leung from *Journal of New Chinese Medicine*, 1984; 2: 22.

Turmeric
[30] *Toxicology*, 1996; 107: 39–45.
[31] *American Journal of Chinese Medicine*, 1995; 23: 243–54.
[32] *Journal of Ethnopharmacology*, 1990; 29: 25–34 (74 references).
[33] *British Journal of Phytotherapy*, 1991; 2: 51–60.
[34] *Planta Medica*, 1991; 57: 1–7 (59 references).
[35] *British Journal of Phytotherapy*, 1991; 51–60 (74 references).
[36] *Cancer Letters*, 1997; 116: 265–9.
[37] *American Journal of Clinical Nutrition*, 1996; 64: 761–4.
[38] *Planta Medica*, 1992; 58: 124–7.
[39] *Mutation Research*, 1984; 136: 85–8.
[40] *Journal of the American College of Nutrition*, 1992; 11: 192–8.

41 *Journal of Pharmacy and Pharmacology*, 1997; 49: 105–7.
42 *Planta Medica*, 1991; 57: 1–7.

Culinary herbs and spices
43 G. Charalambous, *Spices, Herbs and Edible Fungi*, Elsevier Science, New York, 1994, p. 225.

5 Four super oils

Evening primrose oil
1 *Journal of the Royal Society of Medicine*, 1992; 83: 12.
2 *British Journal of Surgery*, 1989; 76: 1069.
3 D. F. Horrobin (ed.), *Omega–6 Essential Fatty Acids, Pathophysiology and Roles in Clinical Medicine*, Alan R. Liss, New York, 1990.
4 ibid.
5 *Acta Neurologica Scandinavica*, 1990; 82: 209.
6 *Quarterly Review of Natural Medicine*, Summer 1995: 129–33.
7 *American Journal of Clinical Nutrition*, 1996; 62: 761–8.
8 *British Medical Journal*, 1994; 309: 824–5.

Fish oil
9 *Arthritis and Rheumatism*, 1996; 38: 1107–14.
10 *Circulation*, 1993; 88: 523–33.
11 *American Journal of Cardiology*, 1996; 77: 31–6.
12 *American Journal of Clinical Nutrition*, 1997; 66: 188–9.
13 *Metabolism*, 1996; 45: 1208–13.
14 *Medical Journal of Australia*, 1996; 164: 137–40.
15 *American Journal of Obstetrics and Gynecology*, 1996; 174: 1335–8.
16 *Lancet*, 1992; 339: 261–4.
17 *New England Journal of Medicine*, 1996; 334: 1557–60.
18 *Nutrition and Cancer*, 1996; 25: 71–8.
19 *The Supplement*, 1996; 4: 4.
20 *European Journal of Clinical Nutrition*, 1996; 50: 617–24.
21 *American Journal of Clinical Nutrition*, 1996; 64: 297–304.
22 *American Journal of Clinical Nutrition*, 1997; 65: 445–50.
23 *Diabetes Care*, 1997; 20: 913–21.
24 *Archives of Internal Medicine*, 1996; 42: 537–42.

Olive oil
25 *European Journal of Epidemiology*, 1996; 12: 141–8.
26 *Israeli Journal of Medical Science*, 1996; 32: 1134–43.

Tea tree oil
27 *Obstetrics and Gynecology*, 1962; 19: 684.
28 *Medical Journal of Australia*, 1990; 153: 455–8.
29 *Lancet*, 1991: 337: 300.
30 *Journal of Family Practice*, 1994; 38: 601–5.
31 *American Journal of Infection Control*, 1996; 24: 186–9.

6 Three super supplements

1 *Quarterly Review of Natural Medicine*, Spring 1996: 44.
2 *Journal of Applied Nutrition*, 1988; 40: 85–94.

Grapeseed extract
3 *American Journal of Clinical Nutrition*, 1996; 64: 748–56.
4 *Fitoterapia*, 1995; 66: 291–317.
5 *Research Communications in Molecular Pathology and Pharmacology*, 1997, 95: 179–89.
6 *Life Sciences*, 1996; 58: 87–96.
7 Australia New Zealand Food Authority, *The 1994 Australian Market Basket Survey*, ANZFA, AGPS, Canberra, 1996.
8 *Science*, 1997; 275: 218–20.
9 *Townsend Letter for Doctors and Patients*, 1996; 46–7.

Green tea
10 *European Journal of Clinical Nutrition*, 1996; 50: 28–32.
11 *Japanese Journal of Cancer Research*, 1988; 79: 1067–74.
12 *International Journal of Cancer*, 1997; 70: 255–8.
13 *European Journal of Clinical Nutrition*, 1996; 50: 28–32.
14 *Archives of Internal Medicine*, 1996; 154: 637–42.
15 *Carcinogenesis*, 1989; 10: 1003–6.
16 *Free Radical Biology and Medicine*, 1997; 23: 235–42.

Vitamin E
17 *Western Journal of Medicine*, 1997; 166: 306–12.
18 *American Journal of Clinical Nutrition*, 1996; 64: 190–6.
19 *Circulation*, 1996; 94: 14–18.
20 *Lancet*, 1996; 347: 781–6.
21 ibid.
22 *Gut*, 1996; 39: 31–5.
23 *Journal of the American College of Nutrition*, 1996; 15: 458–61.
24 *Nutrition Research*, 1995; 15: 953–68.
25 *Mutation Research Letters*, 1995; 346: 195–202.
26 *Biochemical and Biophysical Research Communications*, 1992; 2: 944–50.
27 *New England Journal of Medicine*, 1997; 336: 1216–22.
28 *Nutrition and Cancer*, 1997; 27: 109–17.
29 *Arteriosclerosis, Thrombosis and Vascular Biology*, 1995; 15: 325–33.
30 *Immunopharmacology*, 1995; 29: 225–33.
31 *European Journal of Clinical Nutrition*, 1994; 48: 822–31.
32 *Journal of Internal Medicine*, 1995; 237: 49–54.
33 *New England Journal of Medicine*, 1996; 334: 1156–62.
34 N. Beckham, *The Australian Family Guide to Natural Therapies*, Viking, Melbourne, 1994, p. 120.
35 *American Journal of Clinical Nutrition*, 1996; 64: 329–35.

The advantages of a multinutrient supplement
36 *American Journal of Epidemiology*, 1996; 143: 658–64.
37 *American Journal of Clinical Nutrition*, 1995; 62 (Supplement): 1420S–3S.
38 *Nutrition Reviews*, 1995; 53: S80–5.

Index

This index focuses on the therapeutic benefits of the recommended foods, herbs and supplements.